T0136420

Network Performance
Modeling and Simulation

Network Performance Modeling and Simulation

Edited by

Jean Walrand

University of California at Berkeley

Kallol Bagchi

Florida Atlantic University at Boca Raton

and

George W. Zobrist

University of Missouri at Rolla

Gordon and Breach Science Publishers

Australia Canada China France Germany India Japan Luxembourg
Malaysia The Netherlands Russia Singapore Switzerland Thailand

Amsteldijk 166
1st Floor
1079 LH Amsterdam
The Netherlands

British Library Cataloguing in Publication Data

Network performance modeling and simulation
    1. Computer networks – Computer simulation 2. Computer
    networks – Evaluation
    I. Walrand, Jean II. Bagchi, Kallol III. Zobrist, George W.
    (George Winston), 1934 –
    003.3

ISBN   90-5699-596-0

This book is dedicated to
all the people
who helped make it a success

CONTENTS

EDITORS' PREFACE

Performance modeling and simulation have been used extensively in computer and communication system design for some time. This book makes the argument that this topic has become a central issue in computer science and engineering research and should be considered seriously. Its object is to lead researchers, practitioners and students involved in this discipline. Distinctive in many ways, it provides tutorials and surveys on important topics, relates new research results that should be of interest to all working in the field and covers a broad area in the process. Each chapter presents background, describes and analyzes important work in the field and provides direction to the reader on future work and further readings. The volume can be used as a reference book by all associated with computer and communications systems. Our hope is that this set of carefully selected papers will be of interest to computer and communication scientists and engineers.

This book deals primarily with theory, tools and techniques as related to communications systems. Topics range from traffic models for ATM networks (chapters 4 and 5), simulation environments (chapters 2, 3, 8 and 10), analytical methods (chapters 6, 7 and 11) and interprocessor communications (chapter 1) to an evaluation of process architectures (chapter 9). A soon-to-be published accompanying volume deals with network models and simulators.

Chapter 1 is a tutorial on inter-processor communications in a multiprocessor architecture; it reviews network topologies and routing algorithms. Chapter 2 describes a communication network simulation environment designed for reusability. The third chapter is a tutorial on reduction methods for generalized stochastic petrinets and for stochastic well-formed nets. These reduction methods, we are told, result in a lumped Markov chain by eliminating immediate transitions in GSPNs and also by simplifying the color structure in SWNs.

In chapter 4 Carey Williamson describes traffic models for MPEG video, Ethernet traffic and WWW traffic. The fifth chapter is a tutorial on a number of traffic models, their correlation characteristics, and their implications on the multiplexing of sources. Chapter 6 derives bounds on the moments of the delay in networks.

Marco Combé and Onno Boxma show how a Markov modulated queuing system can be used to model systems with dependence between interarrival and service times (chapter 7). A hierarchical modeling approach that replaces submodels by single queues is explained in chapter 8.

Chapter 9 details an approach for evaluating task-based and message-based process architectures. An environment for specifying and executing protocols is introduced in chapter 10.

The final chapter by Gerardo Rubino is a tutorial on the reliability theory based on stochastic graphs.

If readers find these articles useful and of substantial benefit, we will consider our efforts successful.

ACKNOWLEDGMENTS

Dr. Carey Williamson of the University of Saskatchewan in Canada and Prof. Jason Lin of National Chiao Tung University in Taiwan deserve special mention for providing help with LaTeX-generated scripts that many contributors used in preparing the final versions of their chapters. Many other authors provided feedback for improving the structure of the book. Thanks are due to all of them. We are grateful to the reviewers, editorial board members and all the contributors—who deserve a great deal more than thanks. Without their help, patience and cooperation, this book would not have been possible.

Jean Walrand

CONTRIBUTORS

Ian F. Akyldiz, School of Electrical Engineering, Georgia Tech, Atlanta, Georgia 30332 USA email: ian@armani.mirc.gatech.edu

Onno J. Boxma, CWI, P.O. Box 94079, 1090 GB Amsterdam, The Netherlands email: onno@cwi.nl

Atika Cohen, Universite Libre de Bruxelles, Service Phoneematique et Communication, CP 230, Bd du Triomphe, 1050 Brussels, Belgium email: cohen@helios.iihe.rtt.be

Marco B. Combé, N.V. Bank Nederlandse, Gemeenten, Koninginnegracht 2, 2514 AA Den Haag, The Netherlands

Marco Conti, CNR – Istituto CNUCE, Via Santa Maria 36, 56126 Pisa, Italy email: M.Conti@cnuce.cnr.it

Wlodek Dobosiewicz, Department of Computer Science, Monmouth University, West Long Branch, New Jersey 07764-1898 USA email: dobo@moncol.monmouth.edu

Susanna Donatelli, Dipartimento di Informatics, Universita' di Torino, C.so Svizzera 185, 10149 Torino, Italy email: susi@di.unito.it

Giuliana Franceschinis, Dipartimento di Informatica, Universita' di Torino, C.so Svizzera 185, 10149 Torino, Italy email: giuliana@di.unito.it

Pawel Gburzynski, Department of Computing Science, University of Alberta Edmonton, Alberta, Canada T6G 2H1 email: pawel@cs.ualberta.ca, http:/web.cs.ualberta.ca/ ~ pawel

Yen-Wen Lu, 826 University Avenue, Los Altos, California 94024 USA email: yenwen@nova.stanford.edu

Marco Ajmone Marsan, Dipartimento di Elettronica, Politecnico di Torino, C.so Duca degli Abruzzi 24, 10129 Torino, Italy email: marson@di.unito.it

Raffaela Mirandola, Laboratory of Computer Science, Dip. di Informatica, Sistemi e Produzione, Universita' degli Studi di Roma "Tor Vergata," Via della Ricerca Scientifica, 00133 Roma, Italy email: mira@di.unipi.it

Radouane Mrabet, Universite Libra de Bruxelles, Service Phoneematique et Communication, CP 230, Bd du Triomphe, 1050 Brussels, Belgium

Fabio Neri, Dipartimento di Elettronica, Politecnico di Torino, C.so Duca degli Abruzzi 24, 10129 Torino, Italy email: neri@polito.it

Ioanis Nikolaidis, European Computer Industry Research Centre GmbH, Arabellastrasse 17, D-81925, Munich, Germany email: Yannis.Nikolaidis @ecrc.de

Gerardo Rubino, IRISA, Campus Universitaire de Beaulieu, 35042 Rennes Cedex, France email: Gerardo.Rubino@irisa.fr

Douglas C. Schmidt, Jolley Hall, Room 536, Department of Computer Science, Washington University, Campus Box 1045, One Brookings Drive, St. Louis, Missouri 63130-4899 USA email: schmidt@cs.wustl.edu

Sridhar Seshadri, 7-05 Tisch Hall, Leonard N. Stern School of Business, New York University, 40 West 4th Street, New York, New York 10012 USA email: sseshadr@stern.nyu.edu

Vijay Srinivasan, IBM Corporation, Networking Architecture, P.O. Box 12195, Research Triangle Park, North Carolina 27709 USA email: vijay_srinivasan@vnet.ibm.com

Tatsuya Suda, Department of Information and Computer Science, University of California, Irvine, California 92717-3425 USA email: suda@ics. uci.edu

Carey L. Williamson, Department of Computer Science, University of Saskatchewan, 57 Campus Drive, Saskatoon SK Canada S7N 5A9 email: carey@cs.usask.ca

Editorial Board

Patrick Dowd, Department of Electrical Engineering, University of Maryland, A.V. Williams Building, College Park, Maryland 20743 USA email: dowd@eng.umd.edu, http://tebbit.eng.umd.edu/

Jason Lin, Department of Computer Science and Information Engineering, National Chiao Tung University, Hsinchu Taiwan R.O.C. email: liny@csie. nctu.edu.tw

Darrell D. E. Long, Department of Computer Science, University of California, 1156 High Street, Santa Cruz, California 95064 USA email: darrell@ece.ucsc.edu

Editors

Kallol Bagchi, Department of DIS/Business, Florida Atlantic University, Boca Raton, Florida 33431 USA email: kbag3046@fauvms.acc.fau.edu

Jean Walrand, Department of EECS, Cory Hall, University of California, Berkeley, California 94720-1770 USA http://www.eecs.berkeley.edu/~wlr

George W. Zobrist, Department of Computer Science, University of Missouri-Rolla, 1870 Miner Circle, Rolla, Missouri 65409-0350 USA email: zobrist@umr.edu

CHAPTER 1

WORMHOLE DATA ROUTING IN MULTIPROCESSORS: NETWORKS AND ALGORITHMS

Yen-Wen Lu

1.1 INTRODUCTION

In recent years many parallel architectures have been studied and built. Multiprocessors have provided very powerful computation capability for various applications. However, as technology and computation power continue to improve, communication between processors have become a performance bottleneck. The first key issue for inter-processors communication is the network interconnection. When we have more processing elements in a system, we want to have the performance scaled with the number of resources and the implementation should be feasible with reasonable cost.

The second issue for multiprocessor communication is the data routing scheme. Communication latency and throughput are the main metrics in a multiprocessor network. Fast and low cost routing schemes are attractive to be implemented to increase the efficiency of inter-processor communication and to improve performance of multiprocessor systems. Wormhole routing is becoming a popular routing scheme for parallel systems[7,18,5]. A packet is divided into a number of flow control digits, or *flits*, for transmission. As the header flit advances along the path, the remaining flits follow in a pipelined fashion. If the header is blocked, the following flits may either be blocked and distributed in the network or be collected in several nodes depending on the storage space in each node. Wormhole routing flow control has been adopted by most of the

1

new generation multiprocessors due to its low latency and low buffer cost.

The rest of the chapter is organized as follows. Sec. 1.2 gives the overview of network interconnection for multiprocessors. Different network topologies are given and compared. Sec. 1.3 describes some desired routing properties and routing flow control schemes, e.g., *store-and-forward*, *wormhole*, and so on. The virtual channel concept is also introduced. Sec. 1.4 introduces different classes of routing algorithms: deterministic, fully adaptive, and partially adaptive algorithms. We describe some representative routing algorithms proposed in recent years and show how they prevent deadlock.

1.2. NETWORK INTERCONNECTION

A multiprocessor network is composed of nodes and communication channels, and can be represented by a uni-directional graph $G = (N, C)$, with vertices $N = \{n_1, n_2, \ldots, n_m\}$ corresponding to the nodes and edges $C = \{c_1, c_2, \ldots, c_n\}$ corresponding to the communication links between nodes. An efficient network for multiprocessors should be able to utilize the hardware resources effectively. Network performance is usually measured by latency and throughput: Latency is the time required for a message to be delivered from source to destination. Throughput is the data rate which is maintained in the network. Both latency and throughput are strongly dependent on the network topology and routing algorithm. In this section, we will describe some properties of a network and introduce different network topologies.

1.2.1. Properties of Network Topology

There are several network properties which are directly related to network performance and complexity[13]. We will describe these network properties in this section and compare these properties for different networks in the next section.

Network Diameter

The network diameter is the maximum shortest path between any two nodes in the network. The diameter is the indication of latency in the worst case when the traffic load is low. A designer should keep the network diameter small to reduce latency.

Bisection Width

The network bisection width is the minimum number of channels required to be removed to cut the network into two equal parts. Therefore, the bisection width is related to the maximum communication bandwidth supported between two separated parts in the network.

Number of Links

The total number of links is related to the maximum total bandwidth provided in a network. In an ideal case, all the links can be used for transmitting data at the same time and give the peak throughput of the network. So the number of links is an indication of degree of concurrency of communications. The number of links also affects the cost of the network interconnection.

Node Degree

The node degree is the number of IO ports associated with each node in the network. When we design a scalable network, we would like to have the node degree independent of the network size to reduce the cost. Limited wire density and pin count in the current VLSI packaging technology restrict the node degree in a feasible network.

Symmetry

A network is symmetric if it is isomorphic to itself with any node as the origin. In a symmetric network, the network is the same seen from any node. For uniform traffic, a symmetric network has the same traffic loading in all channels, and "hot-spot" effects, which may occur in an asymmetric network, are reduced.

Network Mapping

No matter what form of network we design, we need to map the network onto a two- or three-dimensional space for implementation. This network mapping directly determines the physical channel width and wire length. Thus propagation delay, clock speed, and transmission power all depend on the network mapping.

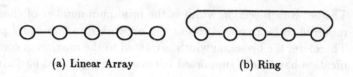

(a) Linear Array   (b) Ring

Figure 1.1: Linear Array and Ring

Data Routing

Data routing is the basic function performed by a network. Different network topologies have different properties as described above, different node addressing, communication paths, and channel dependency. Therefore, we need to develop different data routing algorithms to match the topologies.

Scalability

Ideally, the network performance should be linearly scaled with an increasing number of processors employed. For example, the network bisection width should be scaled with the network size to support sufficient communication bandwidth for the increased traffic. For a scalable network, the node degree should be constant, the network mapping should be compact, and the data routing should be identical for different size of networks.

1.2.2. Network Examples

In this section, we will give a brief description of some popular networks and compare their characteristics as defined in the previous section.

Linear Array and Ring

Fig. 1.1 shows the topology of a linear array and ring. Linear arrays and rings are very simple and low-cost, but long diameter and low bisection width causes the latency to increase exponentially as the number of nodes increases, due to traffic contention.

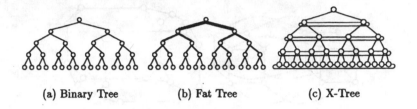

(a) Binary Tree   (b) Fat Tree   (c) X-Tree

Figure 1.2: Tree Networks

Tree

A binary tree is shown in Fig. 1.2(a). A tree is composed of a root, intermediate nodes, and leaves. Long distances between leaves on different branches and low bisection width are the main drawbacks of a tree network. Fat trees (Fig. 1.2(b)) were proposed to increase the bandwidth as we ascend from leaves to the root and then reduce traffic contention near the root. Another variation of the tree structure is the "X-tree" (Fig. 1.2(c)). In an X-tree network, all the nodes at the same level are also connected in a ring to reduce the communication across levels and the bottleneck near the tree root. All the tree structures are not only limited to binary connections. The structures can be extended to multiway trees.

Hypercube and Cube-Connected Cycle (CCC)

In general, a hypercube is an n-cube with $N = 2^n$ nodes. There are n dimensions with two nodes per dimension. An order n hypercube can be constructed from two order $n - 1$ hypercubes, but the node degree increases from $n - 1$ to n (Fig. 1.3(a)). The property that the node degree depends on the network size makes hypercubes unscalable. A cube-connected cycle (CCC) is a variation of hypercubes. An n-dimensional CCC is a n-cube in which each vertex is replaced by a cycle of n nodes. Therefore, an n-CCC has $N = n2^n$ nodes, and a longer network diameter, but a constant node degree of 3. Fig. 1.3(b) shows a 3-cube topology.

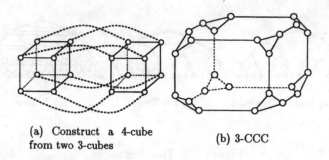

(a) Construct a 4-cube
from two 3-cubes

(b) 3-CCC

Figure 1.3: Hypercube and CCC

2-D Mesh and Torus

Fig. 1.4 shows the topology of a 2-D mesh and torus. A torus is basically a mesh with wrap-around connections in each row and column to reduce the network diameter. A folded torus shown in Fig. 1.4(c) can be easily laidout without the long wrap-around connections which increase the propagation delay. 2-D meshes and tori are becoming popular due to their simplicity, regularity, scalability, and feasibility.

k-ary n-cube

This is a very general network topology with n dimensions and k nodes per dimension. Linear arrays, rings, hypercubes, meshes, and tori all belong to this family. Several researchers have provided the results in favor of low-dimensional networks. Under the assumption of constant wire bisection width, Dally has shown that two-dimensional k-ary n-cube networks can offer the minimum latency with a linear wire delay model[4]. Agarwal also showed that three or four-dimensional networks perform best under some other constraints, *e.g.*, fixed node size, considerable switching delay, and so on[1]. Several new generation multiprocessors have chosen the k-ary n-cubes family as their interconnects.

Shared Bus

A shared bus is a very simple way to connect several hosts together (Fig. 1.5(a)). A bus is usually heavily loaded, has long

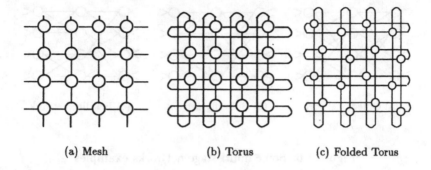

(a) Mesh   (b) Torus   (c) Folded Torus

Figure 1.4: 2-D Mesh and Torus

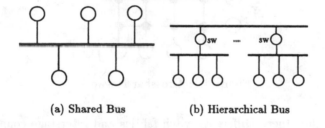

(a) Shared Bus   (b) Hierarchical Bus

Figure 1.5: Bus Networks

propagation delay, and consumes more energy. Bus arbitration needs to be considered because only one processor at a time can use the bus. Therefore, the bus architecture is not very scalable, and cannot support a large number of processors. A hierarchical bus structure has been proposed to increase utilization and bandwidth, and to reduce contention (Fig. 1.5(b))[16].

Multi-stage Network

A multi-stage interconnect network (MIN) consists of more than one stage of switch elements which can be set up dynamically according to traffic requests. Processing nodes (or memory) are located at the ends of the MIN, and traffic is routed from one end

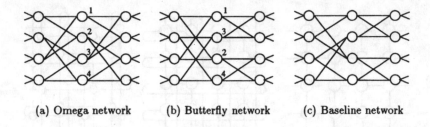

(a) Omega network   (b) Butterfly network   (c) Baseline network

Figure 1.6: Some multi-stage networks examples

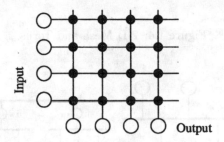

Figure 1.7: Crossbar Network

to the other. Different switch fabrics and interstage connections have been proposed for different MINs[9,21]. Some examples are the *Omega (or Shuffle-Exchange)*, *Butterfly*, *Baseline* networks, etc. (Fig. 1.6) We should note that some multi-stage networks are actually equivalent, for instance, Fig. 1.6 (a) is equivalent to (b) with some nodes in the middle stage re-ordered. All the paths in a MIN have the same latency, so the designer cannot take advantage of data locality in most applications.

Crossbar

A crossbar switch is an interconnection in which each input is connected to each output through a path that contains a single switching node (Fig. 1.7). It offers the least traffic contention, but has the highest complexity. The cost is proportional to N^2 where N is the network size. Because of the high cost, the crossbar network is not very scalable in a large system.

Network	size	diameter	bi-section width	number of links	node deg	sym-metry
Linear array	N	$N-1$	1	$N-1$	2	No
Ring	N	$\lfloor N/2 \rfloor$	1	N	2	Yes
Binary tree	$N = 2^n - 1$	$2(n-1)$	1	$N-1$	3	No
Hypercube	$N = 2^n$	n	2^{n-1}	$nN/2$	n	Yes
CCC	$N = n2^n$	$2n-1$ $+\lfloor n/2 \rfloor$	2^{n-1}	$3N/2$	3	Yes
2-D Mesh	$N = k^2$	$2(k-1)$	k	$2(N-k)$	4	No
2-D Torus	$N = k^2$	$2\lfloor k/2 \rfloor$	$2k$	$2N$	4	Yes
k-ary n-cube	$N = k^n$	$n\lfloor k/2 \rfloor$	$2k^{n-1}$	nN	$2n$	Yes
Shared Bus	N	1	1	1	1	Yes
Omega	N procs $(N \lg N)/2$ sw	$\lg N + 1$	$N/2$	$N(\lg N + 1)$	4	No
Crossbar	N proc N^2 sw	2	N	N	2	Yes

Table 1.1: Summary of network properties

Table 1.1 provides a summary of network characteristics, showing the relation between those properties and network size for different network topologies. Table 1.2 surveys the topologies used in some parallel systems. Most of the recent multiprocessor systems have chosen the low dimensional k-ary n-cube as the network interconnection because of their scalability for high bandwidth, regularity for easier data routing, and simplicity for efficient implementation.

1.2.3. Network Category

Networks also can be categorized based on interconnection status or node functionality. A network interconnection can be either *static* or *dynamic*. Static networks such as meshes and k-ary n-cubes have all their connections fixed without changing during execution. On the other hand, dynamic networks may change their channel configuration during the running time depending on data routing requirement, for example, multi-stage networks.

A network can also be either *direct* or *indirect*. In a direct network,

Machine	Year	Topology	Remarks
CMU/C.mmp	1972	Crossbar	16 processors × 16 memory.
Caltech/ Cosmic Cube	1983	Hypercube	64 nodes connected in a binary 6-cube.
Intel/iPSC	1985	Hypercube	7 I/O ports form a 7-dim hypercube.
IBM/RP3	1985	Omega	512 processors. The interconnect consists of 2 networks. A network with 128 ports (4 levels of 4 × 4) and a combining network with 64 ports (6 levels of 2 × 2).
TMC/CM-2	1987	Hypercube	CM-2 is made of 8 subcubes. Each subcube contains 16 matrix boards. A matrix board has 512 processors.
Cray/Y-MP	1988	Multi-stage Crossbar	8 processors and 256 memory modules connected by 4 × 4 and 8 × 8 switches and 1 × 8 demux.
BBN/ Butterfly	1989	Butterfly	A 3-stage 512 × 512 butterfly network constructed by 8 × 8 switches.
TMC/CM-5	1991	Fat tree	32 to 1024 processors (max. 16384 proc) bisection width of 1024 nodes is 5GB/s
KSR-1	1991	Fat tree	2 levels of ALLCACHE Engine hierarchy with the fat tree topology. Eng:0 has bandwidth 1GB/s, Eng:1 has 1, 2, or 4GB/s
Intel/Paragon	1991	2-D Mesh	link bandwidth: 175MB/s full duplex max bisection width: 5.6GB/s
Stanford/ DASH	1992	2-D Mesh	16 clusters (4 × 4 mesh) Each cluster has 4 PEs May extend to 512 clusters
MIT/ J-Machine	1992	3-D Mesh	1024-node (8 × 8 × 16). Max. addressing limit: 65536 nodes (32 × 32 × 64)
Caltech/ Mosaic C	1992	2-D Mesh	64 Mosaic chips are packaged in an 8 × 8 array on the circuit board. These boards can construct arbitrarily large 2-D arrays of nodes
Cray/T3D	1993	3-D Torus	2048 processors with peak 300 Gflops

Table 1.2: Topologies of existing parallel systems

all the nodes are the processing units as well as switching elements, *i.e.*, the communication channels connect processors directly. Unlike direct networks, indirect networks have some intermediate nodes which are only used for switching. Messages between processing nodes are routed through the paths set up by switching nodes.

A dynamic network is usually an indirect network. For example, a multi-stage network often has its processors (or memory) at both ends of the network, and has the intermediate stages as switches only. But a dynamic network can also be a direct network; for example, the reconfigurable mesh may change its connections to the neighbors while all the nodes are the processing units. Similarly, a static network can be either a direct or indirect network. For instance, a static tree network is a direct network if all the nodes are processors, or is an indirect network if only the leaves of the tree are processors.

1.3. ROUTING FLOW CONTROL

Data routing is one of the most important factors in a high performance multiprocessor network. In many situations, communication between processors has become the performance bottleneck. For example, in a shared memory system, processors may wait for the memory responses which need to travel across the network. Therefore, designing an efficient routing flow scheme and routing algorithm is crucial to improving overall system performance.

1.3.1. Desired Routing Properties

There are three basic types of data routing faults in any kind of network: *deadlock, livelock, and starvation*. In a network system, all messages compete with each other for limited resources. Unless the routing conflicts are resolved satisfactorily, one of these faults will occur. A desirable routing flow control will be deadlock-free, livelock-free, and starvation-free.

Deadlock

There are four necessary conditions for deadlock to occur: *mutual exclusion, no preemption, hold and wait, and circular wait*[20]. In other words, a resource may be occupied by a process, and this process is requesting another resource which is occupied by another process. If the resource cannot be released until the new request has been granted, and there is a circular request dependency among the processes, then deadlock arises (Fig. 1.8). In data routing, the resources may be buffers (in a store-and-forward network) or channels (in a wormhole network) depending on the routing flow control scheme (Sec. 1.3.2). When the circular waiting condition occurs, no message can move forward, and deadlock results. Avoiding deadlock is critical in the data routing problem. We will discuss deadlock avoidance methods in Sec. 1.4.

Livelock

The livelock situation occurs when a packet circulates in a network forever and never arrives at its destination. In the livelock situation, packets which are circulating in the network consume channel bandwidth and increase traffic contention. If all packets take only the shortest paths to their destinations, *i.e.*, every hop decreases the distance to the destination, then livelock cannot occur because all the packets will take finite steps to reach the destinations. Livelock can occur in the non-minimal routing algorithms where packets detour away from their destinations when they encounter traffic contention.

Starvation

A packet may wait for a resource indefinitely when it is competing with other packets. Starvation is caused by unfair arbitration of resources. For example, a low priority packet might not gain access to a channel which is always requested by other higher priority packets. One solution to the problem of starvation is *aging*. In order to prevent unlimited waiting, aging increases the priority of packets which have waited in the network for a certain time. Aging also increases the overhead of data routing in the form of the extra hardware required to calculate the age of a packet, and the additional data field required to store the age, etc.

1.3.2. Routing Flow Control Schemes

Flow control is the scheme for allocating communication channels and buffers, and determining the steps to advance messages[3]. In a message-

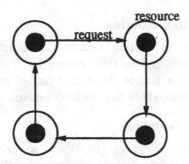

Figure 1.8: Deadlock: circular dependency

passing network, a message is divided into several *packets* for transmission in the network. Each packet contains its own header on routing information and can be routed independently. A packet is further divided into several flow control digits or *flits*. A flit is the basic unit for transmission. Only the header flit contains the routing information. The rest of flits follow the header and cannot be routed independently.

Several routing control schemes have been proposed and implemented in parallel machines. In this section, we will describe and compare these different schemes.

Store-and-Forward Routing

Early multiprocessors used store-and-forward as the routing flow control. A packet was treated as an indivisible entity in a store-and-forward network. When a packet reached an intermediate node, the entire packet was buffered in the node. Then the packet was forwarded to the next node on the path to the destination only when the next node had sufficient buffers to hold the packet and the channel was free.

Wormhole Routing

In a wormhole network, only the header flit carries the route information. As the header advances along the path, all the remaining flits follow in pipeline fashion. The intermediate nodes can begin to forward the message as soon as the header has been decoded and the next node on the route has been decided. If the header is blocked, the following flits are distributed in the intermediate nodes along the path.

Virtual Cut-Through Routing

Virtual cut-through routing is similar to wormhole routing in that the flits are pipelined in the network[14]. But when the header is blocked, all the flits of the stalled packet are collected by the intermediate node where the blocking occurs.

Pipelined Circuit Switching

Pipelined circuit switching (PCS)[10] is a variation of wormhole routing. In PCS, data flits do not immediately follow the header into the network. The header travels alone to find the path to its destination. When the header finally reaches the destination, an acknowledge flit returns to the source. Then data flits can be pipelined along the established path in the network.

The first difference among these routing flow control schemes is their latency. Let L_p be the packet length, L_f be the flit length, B be the channel bandwidth, and D be the distance between the source and destination.

The latency for a *store-and-forward* network is

$$T_{SAF} = \frac{L_p}{B} \times (D + 1) \tag{1.1}$$

The latency for a *wormhole* network is

$$T_{WH} = \frac{L_p}{B} + \frac{L_f}{B} \times D \tag{1.2}$$

The latency for a *pipelined circuit switching* network is

$$T_{PCS} = \frac{L_p - L_f}{B} + 3 \times \frac{L_f}{B} \times D \tag{1.3}$$

Fig. 1.9 provides a comparison of the latency for the different routing flow schemes. L_p is usually larger than L_f, therefore the latency of *store-and-forward* is larger than the latency of *wormhole* family. When $L_p \gg L_f$, the latency of wormhole routing is less sensitive to the distance D.

Secondly, the buffer requirement is different for these three schemes. *Store-and-forward* and *virtual cut-through routing* require buffering of the entire packet, so they need storage memory for at least an entire packet inside each node. In contrast, *wormhole* and *pipelined circuit*

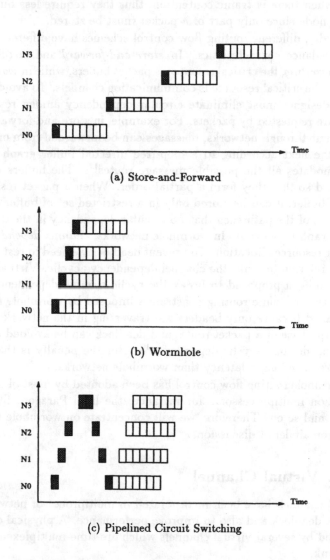

(a) Store-and-Forward

(b) Wormhole

(c) Pipelined Circuit Switching

Figure 1.9: Latency Comparison of different flow control schemes

switching routing allow a packet to be distributed in the intermediate nodes when there is traffic contention, thus they require less buffering in each node since only part of a packet must be stored.

Thirdly, different routing flow control schemes have different deadlock avoidance characteristics. In *store-and-forward* and *virtual cut-through routing*, the critical resource is packet buffers, while in *wormhole* routing, the critical resource is communication channels. To avoid deadlock a designer must eliminate circular dependency among resources which are requested by packets. For example, in store-and-forward and virtual cut-through networks, messages can be forwarded from one buffer to the next according to a loop-free directed buffer graph which accommodates all the possible message routes[17]. The buffers can be organized so that they form a partial order. When a packet resides in a given buffer, it can be stored only in a restricted set of buffers in the next node of the path such that no circular dependency in the directed buffer graph may occur. In wormhole networks, *channel dependency* is used for resource allocation. To prevent deadlock we need to restrict the routing relation to make the channel dependency acyclic. Virtual channels have been proposed to break the cyclic channel dependency[5]. In PCS networks, some routing constraints imposed by wormhole routing are relaxed because only headers are traversing in the network during the setup phase of a packet route, and deadlock can be avoided as long as the header has acyclic dependency[10]. But the penalty is that PCS networks have longer latency than wormhole networks.

Wormhole routing flow control has been adopted by most of the new generation multiprocessors: for instance, the Intel Paragon, Stanford DASH, and so on. Therefore, we will concentrate on wormhole routing in the remainder of discussion.

1.3.3. Virtual Channel

Virtual channels have been incorporated in multiprocessor networks to prevent deadlock and also to improve performance. A physical channel is shared by several virtual channels which are time-multiplexed on the same link.

A virtual channel consists of a buffer which can store one or more flits of a packet. Instead of having a deep FIFO, we may organize the buffers into several independent lanes, *i.e.*, virtual channels (Fig. 1.10). The buffer in each virtual channel can be allocated independently of

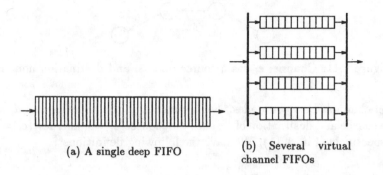

(a) A single deep FIFO

(b) Several virtual channel FIFOs

Figure 1.10: FIFO queue configurations.

other virtual channels, but the virtual channels which are associated with the same physical channel will compete with each other for the channel bandwidth.

When one virtual channel is blocked due to traffic contention, other virtual channels can still use the physical channel without being idle. Therefore, virtual channels can improve the network throughput substantially for heavily loaded traffic. Adding virtual channels and restricting the routing relation among some virtual channels can eliminate the circular channel dependency to avoid deadlock (Sec. 1.4). Many wormhole routing algorithms are based on virtual channels for deadlock avoidance. We will describe the channel dependency and some routing algorithms in detail in Sec. 1.4.

1.4. WORMHOLE ROUTING ALGORITHMS

In this section, we will give the theoretical background and definitions required to understand wormhole data routing. We then develop the routing algorithms in the following sections.

A routing algorithm decides where to send a packet according to its source, destination, and possibly local traffic conditions. An interconnection network, as defined in Sec. 1.2 , is a uni-directed graph $G = (N, C)$, with vertices $N = \{n_1, n_2, \ldots, n_m\}$ corresponding to the nodes and edges $C = \{c_1, c_2, \ldots, c_n\}$ corresponding to the communica-

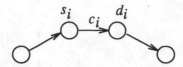

Figure 1.11: Channel c_i has a source node s_i and destination node d_i

tion channels between nodes. For a channel c_i, the nodes s_i and d_i are the source and destination of c_i, such that source$(c_i)=s_i$ and dest$(c_i)=d_i$, respectively (Fig. 1.11). We have the following definitions[8]:

Definition 1 *Routing Function R*

A routing function $R : N \times N \to P(C)$, where $P(C)$ is the set of communication channels C, provides a set of alternative output channels to send a packet from the current node n_c to the destination n_d, i.e., $R(n_c, n_d) = \{c_{c_1}, c_{c_2}, \ldots, c_{c_p}\}$, where source$(c_{c_i})=n_c$.

A routing function defines all the permissible movements which can prevent deadlock and guarantee correct delivery according to the current position and destination. For an adaptive routing, we may have more than one possible output channel supplied by the routing function if $n_c \neq n_d$. On the other hand, for a deterministic routing, there is only one possible output channel given any pair (n_c, n_d) if $n_c \neq n_d$.

Definition 2 *Local traffic F*

Local traffic F specifies the traffic conditions of the output channels in a node.

The local traffic variable F may be very simple. For example, it might only indicate whether the output channel is busy or not busy. It may also be complicated. For example, we may have the traffic load of each output channel, *e.g.*, available buffers left at the receiver, as the local traffic variable F.

Definition 3 *Selection function S*

A selection function $S : P(C \times F) \to C$ considers the traffic conditions of all candidate routings to select an output channel from the set supplied by the routing function R.

The selection function will have effect on performance. For example, choosing a lightly loaded output to avoid traffic contention. The selection function also needs to be fair. When an output channel is the candidate of the routing function of several packets, the choice of which packet is granted to use this output channel has to be fair in order to ensure that starvation will not occur.

Definition 4 *Channel Dependency*
For a given network and routing function R, the channel dependency graph $D = (C, E)$ is defined as: the channels C are the vertices of D, and the edges E are the pairs of channels connected by R:
$E = \{(c_i, c_j) \mid c_i \in R(s_i, n) \text{ and } c_j \in R(d_i, n) \text{ for some destination } n \in N\}$

We call the above definition of channel dependency *direct* dependency because we can use c_j immediately after c_i to transmit data by the path $(c_i, c_j, \ldots)$ to the destination n. The channel dependency is very important for the deadlock issue in data routing.

Theorem 1 *A routing function R for a given network is deadlock-free if there is no cycle in the direct channel dependency graph D* [8].

Virtual channels (Sec. 1.3.3) have been used in many routing algorithms to break the cycles in the channel dependency graph to prevent deadlock. An example of deadlock avoidance by virtual channels is shown in Fig. 1.12. By adding virtual channels and restricting the routing function, for example, if a packet at node n0 was coming from channel C3, then it has to use channel V0 instead of C0 to node n1, we can break the circular channel dependency as in Fig. 1.12(b).

Because of the importance of k-ary n-cube networks in the recent development of multiprocessors, we will describe some specific routing algorithms for the general k-ary n-cube networks in the following sections.

1.4.1. Deterministic Routing

In deterministic routing, the routing path is only dependent on the source and destination. When a packet is injected into a network, a unique path has been determined by its source and destination. In a k-ary n-cube network, the most commonly used routing algorithm

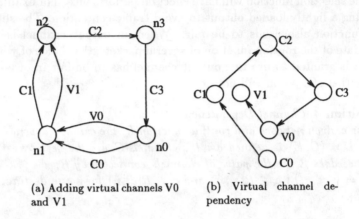

(a) Adding virtual channels V0   (b) Virtual channel de-
and V1   pendency

Figure 1.12: Deadlock avoidance by adding virtual channels. V0 is used
instead of C0 when C3 is the previous channel.

is the *e-cube* algorithm, *i.e., dimension-order routing* algorithm[7]. The
dimension-order routing algorithm has been implemented in most wormhole router designs due to its simplicity and low cost. In the dimension-
order routing algorithm, messages are routed in a strictly ascending
order of dimensions. Each packet is routed in one dimension at a time:
it takes hops in *dim0* (if any), then in *dim1* (if any), and so on until it reaches its destination. Therefore, there is only a pre-determined
path between any pair of source and destination nodes. If there is no
wrap-around connection in each dimension, then the dimension-order
routing is deadlock-free because only lower dimensional channels can
wait for higher dimensional channels, but higher dimensional channels
do not wait for any lower dimensional channel. Channels in the same
dimension will not have circular wait since there are no wrap-around
connections in all dimensions. So there is never a cycle in its channel
dependency.

However, if there are wrap-around connections, then deadlock may
occur potentially. Dally has developed a deadlock-free routing algorithm
for k-ary n-cubes with wrap-around connections by adding virtual channels [7]. Each physical channel is divided into two virtual channels: lower
and upper channels. A packet generated in a source node starts from

a lower channel in the lowest dimension on its path to the destination. The packet continues in the lower channels until it goes through the wrap-around connection if necessary. It jumps to upper channels after it takes the wrap-around connection. The packet returns to lower channels when it is routed to a higher dimension.

Theorem 2 *In a k-ary n-cube with wrap-around connections, two virtual channels per physical link can provide deadlock-free dimension-order routing.*

Proof: We label each virtual channel as $c_{(a_0,a_1,...,a_{n-1}),dir,dim,vc}$, where $(a_0, a_1, \ldots, a_{n-1})$ is the coordinate of the source node of this link, dir is the virtual channel direction (+ or -), dim is the current dimension (from 0 to $n-1$), and vc indicates it is a lower ($vc = 0$) or upper ($vc = 1$) virtual channel. Then we can assign a value V to each virtual channel based on its label:

$$V(c_{(a_0,a_1,...,a_{n-1}),dir,dim,vc}) =$$
$$\begin{cases} 2k \cdot (dim - 1) + k \cdot vc + a_{dim} & \text{if } dir = + \\ 2k \cdot (dim - 1) + k \cdot vc + (k - 1 - a_{dim}) & \text{if } dir = - \end{cases} \quad (1.4)$$

The channel dependency of the dimension-order routing function R have the following possible relations:

$$\left(c_{(a_0,a_1,...,a_{dim},...,a_{n-1}),+,dim,0}, \quad c_{(a_0,a_1,...,a_{dim}+1,...,a_{n-1}),+,dim,0} \right)$$
$$\left(c_{(a_0,a_1,...,a_{dim}=k-1,...,a_{n-1}),+,dim,0}, \quad c_{(a_0,a_1,...,a_{dim}=0,...,a_{n-1}),+,dim,1} \right)$$
$$\left(c_{(a_0,a_1,...,a_{dim},...,a_{n-1}),-,dim,0}, \quad c_{(a_0,a_1,...,a_{dim}-1,...,a_{n-1}),-,dim,0} \right)$$
$$\left(c_{(a_0,a_1,...,a_{dim}=0,...,a_{n-1}),-,dim,0}, \quad c_{(a_0,a_1,...,a_{dim}=k-1,...,a_{n-1}),-,dim,1} \right)$$
$$\left(c_{(a_0,a_1,...,a_{dim},...,a_{n-1}),\pm,dim,(0 or 1)}, \quad c_{(a_0,a_1,...,a_{dim},a_{dim+1}+1,...,a_{n-1}),+,dim+1,0} \right)$$
$$\left(c_{(a_0,a_1,...,a_{dim},...,a_{n-1}),\pm,dim,(0 or 1)}, \quad c_{(a_0,a_1,...,a_{dim},a_{dim+1}-1,...,a_{n-1}),-,dim+1,0} \right)$$

Based on the assignment by Eq. 1.4, all the channel dependency only increases the virtual channel value V when a packet travels from the source to destination. Therefore, there is no cycle in the channel dependency graph, and it is deadlock-free. □

Fig. 1.13 shows examples of the dimension-order routing in a 2-D torus. For the path $(3,1) \rightarrow (0,1) \rightarrow (0,0) \rightarrow (0,3)$, the virtual channel values V defined by Eq. 1.4 are $3 \rightarrow 10 \rightarrow 11$, *i.e.*, in a strictly ascending order. Because the maximum distance between the source and

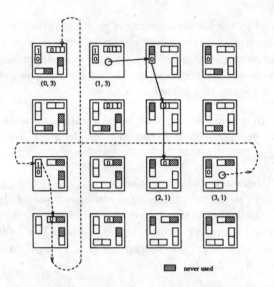

Figure 1.13: Examples of Dimension-order routing in a 2-D torus. Only input buffers are shown. Some buffers are omitted for simplicity. Packets are routed from node (3,1) to (0,3) and from (1,3) to (2,1). Half of the upper channels are never used (shaded buffers) because the maximum packet distance is half the torus size due to wrap-around connections.

destination in any dimension is half of the torus size, half of the higher level virtual channels will never be used (shaded buffers in Fig. 1.13). In spite of the simplicity of the dimension-order routing algorithm, it performs considerably well under the uniform random traffic condition. However, the performance degrades quickly if there are some hot spots in the traffic patterns. Furthermore, there is no fault-tolerance capability in the dimension-order routing algorithm.

1.4.2. Fully Adaptive Routing

In a multiprocessor network, there are usually multiple paths from a source to a destination. In adaptive routing, the routing function R may have more than one output channel as a candidate, and the selection function S will choose one of them based on the local traffic condition F. If a routing algorithm can use all possible shortest paths between any pair of source and destination nodes, then it is a fully adaptive routing algorithm. On the other hand, if a routing algorithm can only use a subset of the possible paths, then it is a partially adaptive algorithm. We will describe some fully adaptive routing algorithms in this section, and partially adaptive routing algorithms in the next section.

1.4.2.1. Virtual Network Algorithm

Deadlock-free adaptive routing can be achieved by partitioning a physical network into several virtual networks[15]. A virtual network is a collection of sets of virtual channels in which there is no cyclic channel dependency. When a packet is generated, we can decide which virtual network will be used based on its source and destination, and this virtual network can provide all possible paths of adaptive routing for this packet without deadlock.

We can define a virtual network as follows:

Definition 5 *Each virtual network is identified by a vector VN, where $VN = \{d_1, d_2, \ldots, d_{n-1}\}$, and $d_i = \{$ 0 or 1 $\}$ for $i \in [1, n-1]$. A virtual network vn_{VN} is defined as*

$$
vn_{VN} = \begin{cases} \text{the channels in dimension } d_i \text{ that point exclusively in} \\ \quad \text{the positive direction if } d_i = 1 \\ \text{the channels in dimension } d_i \text{ that point exclusively in} \\ \quad \text{the negative direction if } d_i = 0 \end{cases}
$$

Fig. 1.14 shows the example of virtual networks for a 2-D torus. In shortest-path routing, a packet never changes the direction, *e.g.*, from positive to negative, in any dimension on its path. Therefore, a packet stays in the same virtual network once it is injected. If there is no wrap-around connection, then these virtual networks are sufficient to provide deadlock-free adaptive routing. For an n-cube, there are at most n wrap-around connections which a packet may take. Thus we expand each virtual network into $n + 1$ levels. A packet starts at level 0, and moves to a higher level whenever it takes a wrap-around link. Fig. 1.15 shows the three level construction of the negative virtual network in a 2-D torus. We label a virtual channel as $c_{VN,L,(a_0,\ldots,a_{n-1}),dir,dim}$, where $VN = \{d_1, d_2, \ldots, d_{n-1}\}$ is the virtual network identification, L is the level for wrap-around connections, $(a_0, a_1, \ldots, a_{n-1})$ is the coordinate of the source node of this link, dim is the current dimension (from 0 to $n - 1$), and dir is the virtual channel direction ($dir = d_{dim}$ if $dim > 0$).

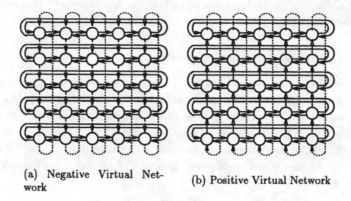

(a) Negative Virtual Network

(b) Positive Virtual Network

Figure 1.14: Two virtual networks in a 2-D torus

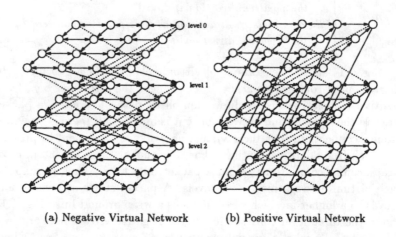

(a) Negative Virtual Network   (b) Positive Virtual Network

Figure 1.15: Expanding a virtual network to three logical levels in a 2-D torus

Theorem 3 *In a k-ary n-cube with wrap-around connections, the virtual network adaptive routing is deadlock-free.*

Proof: Similar to the proof of dimension-order routing, we can assign a value to each virtual channel such that all the channel dependency is in strictly ascending order.

$$V(c_{VN,L,(a_0,...,a_{n-1}),dir,dim}) = L \cdot k^n$$
$$+ \sum_{i=1}^{n-1} \begin{cases} a_i \cdot k^i & \text{if } d_i = 1 \\ (k-1-a_i) \cdot k^i & \text{if } d_i = 0 \end{cases}$$
$$+ \begin{cases} k & \text{if } dim \neq 0 \\ a_0 & \text{if } dim = 0 \text{ and } dir = + \\ (k-1-a_0) & \text{if } dim = 0 \text{ and } dir = - \end{cases} \qquad (1.5)$$

Where d_i is the vector element of VN. Based on the adaptive routing function R, we have the following channel dependency:

$$\left(c_{VN,L,(a_0,...,a_{n-1}),\pm,0}, \quad c_{VN,L,(a_0\pm1...,a_{n-1}),dir,dim} \right)$$
$$\left(c_{VN,L,(a_0=k+1,...,a_{n-1}),+,0}, \quad c_{VN,L+1,(a_0=0,...,a_{n-1}),dir,dim} \right)$$
$$\left(c_{VN,L,(a_0=0,...,a_{n-1}),-,0}, \quad c_{VN,L+1,(a_0=k+1...,a_{n-1}),dir,dim} \right)$$
$$\left(c_{VN,L,(a_0,...,a_{n-1}),d_i,i}, \quad c_{VN,L,(a_0,...,a_i+1,...,a_{n-1}),dir2,dim2} \right) \quad \text{if } d_i = 1$$
$$\left(c_{VN,L,(a_0,...,a_{n-1}),d_i,i}, \quad c_{VN,L,(a_0,...,a_i-1,...,a_{n-1}),dir2,dim2} \right) \quad \text{if } d_i = 0$$
$$\left(c_{VN,L,(a_0,...,a_i=k+1,...,a_{n-1}),d_i,i}, \quad c_{VN,L+1,(a_0,...,a_i=0,...,a_{n-1}),dir2,dim2} \right) \quad \text{if } d_i = 1$$
$$\left(c_{VN,L,(a_0,...,a_i=0,...,a_{n-1}),d_i,i}, \quad c_{VN,L+1,(a_0,...,a_i=k+1,...,a_{n-1}),dir2,dim2} \right) \quad \text{if } d_i = 0$$

Based on the assignment by Eq. 1.5, all the virtual channel values are increased as a packet travels from the source to destination for all possible routes. Therefore, there is no cycle in the channel dependency graph, and it is deadlock free. □

Fig. 1.16 shows the routing examples of the virtual network adaptive routing. For the path $(2,1) \rightarrow (3,1) \rightarrow (3,0) \rightarrow (0,0) \rightarrow (0,3)$, the virtual channel values V defined by Eq. 1.5 are $10 \rightarrow 12 \rightarrow 15 \rightarrow 32$. We can also view the path on the expanded virtual network graph (Fig. 1.16). The packet goes to a different logic level when it takes a wrap-around link.

The drawback of the virtual network approach is that it requires a large number of virtual channels because none of the virtual networks can share any virtual channels. For a k-ary n-cube network, there are

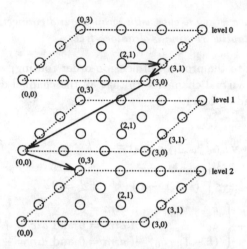

Figure 1.16: A packets is routed from (2,1) to (0,3) on the negative virtual network in a 2-D torus. The packet goes to a different logic level when it takes a wrap-around link.

2^{n-1} virtual networks, and each virtual network has $(n+1)$ levels. Therefore, the total number of virtual channels required per port is $(n+1)2^{n-1}$ for dimension 0 and $(n+1)2^{n-2}$ for other dimensions, which may not be feasible in a high dimensional network. The other disadvantage of the virtual network algorithm is that the virtual channel utilization of higher level networks is very low because the probability that a packet will take many wrap-around links on its path is small.

1.4.2.2. Dimension Reversal Algorithm

The dimension reversal (DR) number of a packet is the count of the number of times that this packet has been routed from a higher dimension to a lower dimension, which is the reverse of the dimension order. All packets are initialized with $DR = 0$. Whenever a packet has a dimension reversed route, the DR of the packet is incremented. Dally and Aoki developed an adaptive routing algorithm based on keeping track of the dimension reversal numbers of packets[6].

The virtual channels associated with a physical channel are divided into two classes: adaptive and deterministic channels. A packet is generated in the adaptive channels. While in the adaptive channels, a packet may be routed in any direction. A packet labels a virtual channel with its current DR when it acquires this channel. In order to prevent dead-lock, a packet with $DP = p$ cannot wait for a busy virtual channel with label $DR = q$ if $q \leq p$. If a packet reaches a node where all output channels are busy and have equal or lower DR labels, then this packet is forced to switch to the deterministic channels and follow the dimension-order routing on the rest of the path to its destination, and is not allowed to jump back to the adaptive channels.

Theorem 4 *The dimension reversal adaptive routing algorithm is dead-lock free*[6].

Proof: Assuming the network is deadlocked, then there is a set packets P in the cyclic channel dependent situation. There exists a packet p_{max} with a maximum $DR(p_{max})$. If p_{max} is waiting for some channel c occupied by packet p_j with $DR = r$ in set P, then $r \leq DR(p_{max})$. But p_{max} is not allowed to wait for a channel with equal or lower DR label. Therefore, there is contradiction and no deadlock. $\square$

When a packet is in adaptive channels, there is no restriction on the direction to route the packet. So a packet may take a hop which will increase the distance to its destination if all output channels on the shortest paths are busy, *i.e.*, non-minimal routing. In non-minimal routing, the livelock problem may arise (Sec. 1.3.1). In practice, we have to put a limit on the maximum number of DR due to counter width, storage space, etc. When a packet reaches its DR limit, it cannot take more dimension reversals and has to enter the deterministic channels for dimension-order routing, and it will be delivered to the destination eventually. Strictly speaking, the dimension reversal adaptive routing algorithm is not really a fully adaptive routing algorithm in the sense that a packet loses freedom of adaptivity in some situations where it has to take the deterministic channels for the rest of its path. In or-der to support more adaptivity, we have to increase the upper limit of DR and use more adaptive virtual channels. If the number of adaptive virtual channels is too small, packets are easily congested in those ad-aptive channels and converted to the deterministic channels, and the DR algorithm will behave more like the dimension-order routing algorithm.

1.4.2.3. Star-Channel Algorithm

The Star-Channel algorithm is a fully adaptive, minimal wormhole rout-ing algorithm which requires a small constant number of virtual chan-

nels per bi-directional link independent of the size and dimension of the
k-ary n-cube networks[2].

There are two kinds of virtual channels: *star* channels and *non-star*
channels. The *star* channels are used when packets are routed on the
dimension-order paths. When a packet takes some path which is not allowed by the dimension-order routing, it will use the *non-star* channels.
Therefore, for a physical channel between node $(a_0, \ldots, a_i, \ldots, a_{n-1})$
and $(a_0, \ldots, (a_i + 1) \bmod k, \ldots, a_{n-1})$, there are three virtual channels
associated with it:

$$c^*_{(a_0,\ldots,a_i,\ldots,a_{n-1}),+,i,0} \; , \; c^*_{(a_0,\ldots,a_i,\ldots,a_{n-1}),+,i,1} \; , \; c_{(a_0,\ldots,a_i,\ldots,a_{n-1}),+,i}$$

Similarly, for a link between $(a_0, \ldots, a_i, \ldots, a_{n-1})$ and $(a_0, \ldots, (a_i -
1) \bmod k, \ldots, a_{n-1})$, we may have

$$c^*_{(a_0,\ldots,a_i,\ldots,a_{n-1}),-,i,0} \; , \; c^*_{(a_0,\ldots,a_i,\ldots,a_{n-1}),-,i,1} \; , \; c_{(a_0,\ldots,a_i,\ldots,a_{n-1}),-,i}$$

Where c^* channels are defined as the same as the dimension-order
routing in Sec. 1.4.1. Assume a packet is transmitted on dimension i.
If dimension i is the lowest dimension which the packet needs to be
transmitted in all of its minimal paths, then it goes through the star
channel c^*_i in this dimension, otherwise it uses the non-star channel c_i
because dimension i is not the lowest dimension and it is not allowed
by the *dimension-order* routing. Each star channel c^*_i is partitioned
into two levels: $c^*_{i,0}$ and $c^*_{i,1}$. If the packet has taken a wrap-around link
along dimension i, then it uses $c^*_{i,1}$, if it has not, then it chooses $c^*_{i,0}$ [2]. A
packet will enter a star channel when the current dimension is the most
significant dimension defined by the *dimension-order* routing, and it is
allowed to correct any other dimensions along a minimal path through
non-star channels (Fig. 1.17).

Theorem 5 *The Star-Channel routing algorithm is fully adaptive and
deadlock free.*

Proof: All the possible minimal paths are allowed in the routing function R, so it is fully adaptive. The formal proof of deadlock-free property can be found in reference 15. Here we will give an intuitive ex-
planation. There is no cycle among the star channels because they are
defined by the *dimension-order* routing as in Sec. 1.4.1. A star-channel
never waits for a particular non-star channel indefinitely because there

always exists a star-channel which can be used in the next step on one of the possible shortest paths. Similarly, a non-star channel also never waits for another non-star channel indefinitely. Therefore, no unlimited waiting for non-star channels will occur under any condition. This implies that based on an acyclic star-channel dependency, the non-star channels will not introduce indefinite waiting cycles. Thus it is deadlock free.   □

There are cycles in the direct channel dependency (Definition 4) of the star-channel routing algorithm. The star-channel routing algorithm is a special case of the *extended* channel dependency[8]. The key point is to build an adaptive routing algorithm based on a deadlock-free routing with acyclic channel dependency. We will discuss a more formal construction and properties of the *extended* channel dependency in the next section. The most important property of the star-channel routing is that although a packet can use a non-star channel at any time, it never waits for a non-star channel indefinitely and there is always a star channel chosen by the routing function. If a packet is directed to a non-star channel, it must be handled in finite time in the non-star channel buffer in order to prevent deadlock. Therefore, the non-star channel buffer must be empty before it can accept any new packet, otherwise cyclic waiting may occur and packets may sit in the middle of queues forever. This more restricted rule is applied to for non-star channels but not star channels in order to avoid deadlock in the star-channel routing algorithm.

1.4.2.4. Extended Channel Dependency

Theorem 1 states that if there is no cycle in the direct channel dependency graph, then there is no deadlock. This is a sufficient condition for deadlock-free data routing. In this section, we will introduce the concept of the *extended* channel dependency graph which is based on both *direct* and *indirect* channel dependency and give a more relaxed deadlock-free condition[8].

The definition of direct channel dependency was given in Definition 4. Before we give the definition of indirect channel dependency, we will define the routing subfunction first, then define the *extended* channel dependency graph and give a theorem for deadlock-free data routing.

Definition 6 *Routing Subfunction*

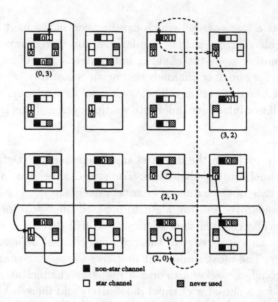

Figure 1.17: Examples of Star-Channel routing in a 2-D torus. Packets
are routed from (2,0) to (3,2) and from (2,1) to (0,3).

A *routing subsection* R_1 *for a given routing function R and a channel subset $C_1 \subset C$ is defined as*

$$R_1 : N \times N \to P(C_1)$$
$$R_1(x,y) = R(x,y) \cap C_1 \quad \forall x, y \in N$$

Definition 7 *Indirect Channel Dependency*
 *For a given network $G=(N, C)$, a routing function R, a subset chan-
nel $C_1 \subset C$ which defines a routing subfunction R_1, and a pair of channels c_i, $c_j \in C_1$, there is an indirect dependency from c_i to c_j if and
only if*

$$\exists \bar{c}_1, \bar{c}_2, \ldots, \bar{c}_k \in \bar{C} = C - C_1 \, such \, that$$

$$\begin{cases} c_i \in R_1(s_i, n) \\ \bar{c}_1 \in R(d_i, n) \\ \bar{c}_{m+1} \in R(\bar{d}_m, n) \quad m = 1, \ldots, k-1 \\ c_j \in R_1(\bar{d}_k, n) \end{cases}$$

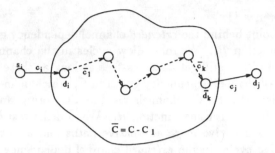

Figure 1.18: Indirect channel dependency from c_i to c_j. Solid lines $\in C_1$, and dashed lines $\in \bar{C} = C - C_1$

where s_i and d_i are the source and destination nodes of link c_i, respectively, and n is a node in N.

We can construct a path from node s_i to d_j for a packet destined to node n. Between s_i and d_j, c_i and c_j are the first and last channels and the only ones belonging to C_1. All other channels used between them belong to $\bar{C} = C - C_1$ (Fig. 1.18). Therefore, c_j will be used by a packet after using c_i and other channels in $\bar{C}$. So there is an *indirect* dependency of channel c_i and c_j.

Based on the definition of *indirect* channel dependency, we may define the *extended* channel dependency graph which has more freedom of adaptive routing while still guaranteeing deadlock free.

Definition 8 *Extended Channel Dependency Graph*

For a given network and routing subfunction R_1 of a routing function R, the extended channel dependency graph $D_E = (C_1, E_E)$ is defined as: the vertices of D_E are the set of channels C_1 which defines R_1, and the edges E_E are the pairs of channels $(c_i, c_j) \in C_1$ such that there is either a direct or indirect dependency from c_i to c_j.

A very important theorem proven by Duato shows that we may have a more relaxed rule for deadlock-free data routing[8].

Theorem 6 *A routing function R for a given network is deadlock-free if there exists a channel subset $C_1 \subset C$ that defines a routing subfunction R_1 which is connected such that there is no cycle in the extended channel dependency graph D_E.*

Proof: Reference 11.

The key point behind the *extended* channel dependency graph is the routing subfunction R_1. We may allow cycles in the channel dependency graph in C but still get deadlock-free as long as there is no cycle in the *extended* channel dependency graph in C_1 which defines the routing subfunction R_1. So C_1 channels are like the core channels which are deadlock-free by routing function R_1. We add the rest of channels $\bar{C} = C - C_1$ which give more alternative paths and adaptivity while not introducing cycles in the *extended* channel dependency graph. As mentioned in Sec. 1.4.2.3, the star-channel algorithm is an example of the *extended* channel dependency graph where the star channels and the dimension-order routing function are C_1 and R_1, respectively. The non-star channels belonging to $\bar{C} = C - C_1$ are used to add adaptivity on top of the star channels. We may check that there are no cycles in the *extended* channel dependency graph of the star channels, therefore it is deadlock-free. The other very important rule is that there is no indefinite waiting for the channels in $\bar{C}$ so as to make sure that no waiting cycles will occur in all channels. Thus the buffers of channels in $\bar{C}$ have to be empty before they accept new packets.

1.4.3. Partially Adaptive Routing

In a partially adaptive routing algorithm, the routing freedom is restricted to a subset of possible paths from a source to a destination. By this restriction, deadlock avoidance is easier and cheaper to implement in hardware.

1.4.3.1. The Turn Model

The turn model has been proposed to avoid deadlock by prohibiting some turns to break all possible cycles in the channel dependency without adding virtual channels[11]. The basic idea is to limit the smallest number of turns to prevent cycles while remaining as adaptive as possible. In fact, the dimension-order routing algorithm is a special case of the turn model where the turns from a higher dimension to a lower dimension are not allowed. Obviously, the dimension-order routing algorithm prohibits more than necessary turns and loses its adaptivity. Different combinations of turns might need to be eliminated in order to break cycles. For example, for a 2-D mesh, Fig. 1.19 shows two

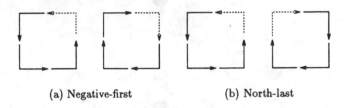

(a) Negative-first   (b) North-last

Figure 1.19: Two different possible ways to break cyclic dependency in a 2-D mesh, where the dotted turns are prohibited

different possible ways to break cyclic dependency. In the *negative-first* routing, a negative direction channel can be followed adaptively by either a negative or positive direction channel in any dimension, but a positive direction channel is not allowed to be followed by any negative direction channel. Thus by prohibiting one quarter of all possible turns, we can prevent deadlock in an n dimensional mesh without wrap-around connections.

Based on which turns are prohibited, there is a different degree of adaptivity for different pairs of sources and destinations. For example, in the *negative-first* routing on a 2-D mesh, if the destination is at the right-upper side of the source ($x_d > x_s$, $y_d > y_s$), then it is fully adaptive from the source to destination (Fig. 1.20 (a)). On the other hand, if the destination is at the left-upper side of the source ($x_d < x_s$, $y_d > y_s$), then it is strictly deterministic if only the shortest path can be taken, or partially adaptive if non-minimal path is allowed (Fig. 1.20 (b)). In Fig. 1.20, path (c) is not allowed because it violates the *negative-first* principle.

In an n dimensional mesh without wrap-around connections, restricting the *positive* to *negative* turns in the *negative-first* routing is sufficient to avoid deadlock. However, an n-cube with wrap-around connections requires a more complex approach to prevent deadlock. One way is to recognize the *logic* direction of a wrap-around link. For example, if the wrap-around link between node $(k - 1, y)$ and $(0, y)$ is labeled as a negative direction channel, then we can apply the *negative-first* routing as described above. This approach, however, will reduce adaptivity and utilization of those wrap-around channels.

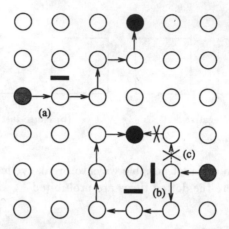

Figure 1.20: Examples of paths for the *negative-first* algorithm of the Turn model in a 2-D mesh

1.5. CONCLUSION

In this chapter, we have given an overview of network interconnection. Most of the recent multiprocessor systems have chosen the low-dimensional k-ary n-cube family as the network topology because of their scalability for high bandwidth, regularity for easier data routing, and simplicity for efficient implementation.

Different routing flow control schemes were introduced and compared. Wormhole routing has the lowest latency compared with store-and-forward and pipeline circuit switching. In addition to the latency advantage, wormhole routing also requires less buffer storage than store-and-forward. Therefore, wormhole routing has been adopted by most of the new generation multiprocessors as the routing flow control scheme.

Several wormhole routing algorithms including deterministic, fully adaptive, and partially adaptive algorithms, were described in detail. The channel dependency graph is a key concept for deadlock-free wormhole routing. Virtual channels were used to break the cycles in the channel dependency graph to eliminate deadlock. Different algorithms have different routing capability and adaptivity, and also have different virtual channel requirement and complexity. These are design tradeoffs between routing performance and hardware cost.

REFERENCES

1. A. AGARWAL, "Limits on Interconnection Network Performance", IEEE Trans. on Parallel and Distributed Systems, 2(4), 398-412 (1991).

2. P. E. BERMAN, L. GRAVANO, G. D. PIFARRE, and J. L. C. Sanz, "Adaptive Deadlock- and Livelock-free Routing with All Minimal Paths in Torus Networks", in Proc. 4th ACM SPAA, 3-12 (1992).

3. W. J. DALLY, "Network and Processor Architecture for Message-driven Computers", in VLSI and Parallel Computation, edited by R. Suaya and G. Birtwistle (Morgan Kaufmann, 1990), 140-222.

4. W. J. DALLY, "Performance Analysis of K-ary N-cube Interconnection networks", IEEE Trans. on Comput., C-39(6), 775-785 (June 1990).

5. W. J. DALLY, "Virtual-channel Flow Control", IEEE Trans. on Parallel and Distributed Systems, 3(2), 194-205 (Mar. 1992).

6. W. J. DALLY and H. AOKI, "Deadlock-free Adaptive Routing in Multicomputer Networks Using Virtual Channels", IEEE Trans. on Parallel and Distributed Systems, 4(4), 466-475 (Apr. 1993).

7. W. J. DALLY and C. L. SEITZ, "Deadlock-free Message Routing on Multiprocessor Interconnection Networks", IEEE Trans. on Comput., 36(5), 547-553 (May 1987).

8. JOSE DUATO, "A New Theory of Deadlock-free Adaptive Routing in Wormhole Networks", IEEE Trans. on Parallel and Distributed Systems, 4(12), 1320-1331 (Dec. 1993).

9. T. Y. FEN, "A Survey of Interconnection Networks", IEEE Computer, 12-27 (Dec. 1981).

10. P. T. GAUGHAN and S. YALAMANCHILI, "A Family of Fault-tolerant Routing Protocols for Direct Multiprocessor Networks", IEEE Trans. on Parallel and Distributed Systems, 6(5), 482-497 (May 1995).

11. C. J. GLASS and L. M. NI, "The Turn Model for Adaptive Routing" , in Proc. 19th Int. Symp. on Comput. Arch., 278-287 (1992).

12. L. GRAVANO, G. D. PIFARRE, P. E. BERMAN, and J. L. C. SANZ, " Adaptive Deadlock-and Livelock-free Routing with All Minimal Paths in Torus Networks", IEEE Trans. on Parallel and Distributed Systems, 5(12), 1233-1251 (Dec. 1994).

13. K. HWANG, Advanced Computer Architecture (McGraw-Hill, 1993).

14. P. KERMANI and L. KLEINROCK, "Virtual Cut-through: a New Computer Communications Switching Technique", Computer Networks, 3(4), 267-286 (1979).

15. D. H. LINDER and J. C. HARDEN, "An Adaptive and Fault Tolerant Wormhole Routing Strategy for K-ary N-cubes", IEEE Trans. on Comput., 40(1), 2-12 (Jan. 1991).

16. S. M. MAHNUD, "Performance Analysis of Multilevel Bus Networks for Hierarchical Multiprocessors", IEEE Trans. on Comput., 43(7), 789-805 (July 1994).

17. P. M. MERLIN and P. J. SCHWEITZER, "Deadlock Avoidance in Store- and-forward Networks I: Store-and-forward Deadlock", IEEE Trans. on Commun., 28(3), 345-354 (Mar. 1980).

18. L. M. NI and P. K. MCKINLEY, "A Survey of Wormhole Routing Tech- niques in Direct Networks", IEEE Computer, 26(2), 62-76 (Feb. 1993).

19. G. D. PIFARRE, L. GRAVANO, S. A. FELPERIN, and J. L. C. SANZ, " Fully Adaptive Minimal Deadlock-free Packet Routing in Hypercubes, Meshes, and Other Networks: Algorithms and Simulations", IEEE Trans. on Parallel and Distributed Systems, 5(3), 247-263 (Mar. 1994).

20. A. SILBERSCHATZ, J. PETERSON, and P. CALVIN, Operating System Concepts (Addison Wesley, third edition, 1991).

21. F. A. TOBAGI, "Fast Packet Switch Architectures for Broadband Integrated Services Digital Networks, <u>Proceeding of the IEEE</u>, 78(1), 133-167 (Jan. 1990).

CHAPTER 2

REUSABILITY TECHNIQUES FOR BUILDING A SIMULATION ENVIRONMENT AND MODELING COMMUNICATION SYSTEMS

Atika Cohen and Radouane Mrabet

2.1. INTRODUCTION

The dynamic expansion of communication networks has grown considerably during the past two decades to meet the increasing demand of sophisticated users. The widespread use of LANs and the advent of new technologies such as ATM and frame relay are creating new problems for both managers and designers of telecommunication networks. Indeed, the design, analysis, and optimization of performance of such systems is a nontrivial task.

Nowadays, simulation plays an important role in computer-aided analysis, design, and management of communication networks. In fact, simulation technology is maturing and has been successfully applied during the design, development, and operational phases. It constitutes the only possible way to provide the network engineer with detailed information, when he has to decide regarding performance.

"Simulate before you buy or build" is becoming the norm, particularly for the OSISIM (Open Systems Integrated Simulator) project. This four-year research project was initiated by the "Université Libre de Bruxelles", represented by "Service Télématique et Communication", and by SAIT Systems, a Belgian company specialized into radio and satellite communication. The two main objectives of this project are : i) to set up an environment to model and simulate communication systems, and ii) to

39

define a methodology to model, in a generic way, mechanisms, protocols, and services related to communication systems.

One of the most significant criticisms on traditional simulation modeling has been the lack of reusability. However, the cost of using simulation technology can be reduced through the extensive application of model reusability. In addition, reusability is widely believed to be a key to improving development productivity and quality[1,2]. Therefore, reusability has been the key-word along the development of this work.

We address the question of reusability at three levels[3]: 1) reusability for creating new software systems from developed and tested software rather than from scratch, 2) reusability for creating complex models from building blocks already modeled, and 3) reusability for composing common functional elements to create building block models.

The first level of reusability, which can be considered as a coarse grain of reusability, is applied extensively to build an environment for modeling and simulation. As we will see later on, a prototype of this environment is based on four existing packages which have proved their usefulness in their respective field.

Another approach to reusability is to create components expressed in a simulation language and to group them into a library. Thus, a library can be defined as a database of reusable components. The issues which have to be considered when designing such a library are: what is the granularity and domain of application of the library?, how are components created, inserted, and maintained?, which relations among components may be expressed?, and what kind of knowledge is needed to build composite components from the library, while leaving the components unchanged in the course of their reuse?

This type of reusability is adopted to define the second and third levels of reusability. The main difference between the two levels is the granularity of components. For the second level, components are network elements, such as buses, rings, protocols, traffic sources, bridges, satellite repeaters, etc. While, the third level of reusability, which is considered as the fine grain of reusability, considers the functionalities of a protocol as reusable units, such as flow control, error recovery, segmenting, and rate control functions.

This chapter will address these three reusability levels in the three following sections. Section two focuses on AMS (Atelier for Modeling and Simulation), which is the simulation environment developed in the context of the OSISIM project. Section three describes the communication network model unit, called DBM for Detailed Basic Model. Section four describes the protocol entity modeling unit which is the function. A conclusion is drawn in the last section.

2.2. SIMULATION ENVIRONMENT : AMS

We apply the first level of reusability to design a simulation environment for modeling and simulating communication systems. This environment is called AMS for Atelier for Modeling and Simulation[4,5], and it is designed in a modular fashion to allow the integration of several existing software.

AMS mainly differs from existing tools like OPNET[6] (Optimized Network Engineering Tool), TOPNET [7] (Tool for the Object oriented, Petri net based Network Evaluation and Test), and BONeS[8] (Block Oriented Network Simulator), in the formal methods and in the way it is used to describe the internal structure of the modeled components. OPNET is based on a graphical description of an extended finite state machine, and on the C language. With TOPNET, a modeled component is described by a class of timed Petri nets named PROT networks. BONeS has developed a block oriented paradigm. The blocks are graphically assembled and primitives written in C are at the lowest level of abstraction.

Unlike these approaches, ours is based on queueing networks. Indeed, queueing network models have come into widespread use as a modeling paradigm for deriving analytical as well as simulation based performance measures. They are especially effective in modeling computer communication systems, including point-to-point communication, broadcast systems, distributed multiple access systems, etc. QNAP2[9] (Queueing Network Analysis Package 2) has been selected to be the modeling and simulation language. It is a package for describing, handling and solving large and complex discrete event flow systems. It contains an object oriented specification language which is used for the description of the models and the control of their resolution.

In order to provide a wide range of features that facilitate modeling of communications networks, AMS includes on one side a library of basic models from which the end-user can construct a large number of transmission systems and networks, and on the other side several tools to edit the architecture, to simulate and to present results.

The two following subsections are organized as follows. The former describes in more details the functional structure of AMS, while the later presents the prototype we developed and which is based on this structure.

2.2.1 Functional Structure of AMS

AMS is designed in a modular manner. The main modules constituting AMS are structured in four phases, each of them is handled by one or several processes. These phases are the editing phase, ADL (Architecture Description Language) phase, simulation phase and presentation phase. Figure 2.1 illustrates this structure. Furthermore, the atelier is based on the library of basic models constructed in a very modular fashion to allow more flexibility.

Editing Phase: In this phase, the end-user constructs graphically a communication system using the basic models from the AMS library. The editing phase is managed by a dedicated process called the graphical editor which corresponds to the world view of the network designer, with icons that represent rings, buses, bridges, protocols, etc. Several instances of basic models can be created and connected by links for a specific architecture. The editor has the ability to provide substantial user interaction for either simple parameter changes or major reconfigurations of systems, and to permit the provision of hierarchical modeling capability for extremely large and complex models. On the other hand, an end-user without graphical capabilities has to describe his architecture directly in the ADL language.

ADL Phase: This phase mainly consists of translating the description written in ADL language into a QNAP2 simulation language. In addition, the aim of this phase is to fulfill several objectives mainly the definition of a clear border between the editing phase and the simulation phase. This separation will enforce the independence between the interactive part of the atelier represented by the editor and the computational part represented mainly by the simulator. This phase permits the design of the editor separately from the design of the computational part of the atelier, so that modifications in either tend not to cause changes in the other.

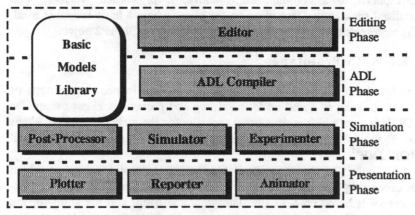

FIGURE 2.1 : AMS STRUCTURE

Simulation Phase: The main objective of this phase is to assess the performance of a previously edited system. This phase is handled by three processes which are the experimenter, the simulator and the post-processor. The experimenter goal is to help formalizing a proper experimental design to obtain the maximum information with the minimum number of experiments. The simulator process compiles and executes the QNAP2 code generated by the ADL process. The execution depends on the experiments defined by the end-user. At the end of the execution, all the desired rough results are produced. The recorded results of the simulation can be statistically analyzed with the post-processor, so that, aggregate parameters of interest can be reported.

Presentation Phase: This phase is meant to allow different presentations of the simulation results. It offers the end-user the possibility of supervising the simulation by visualizing its executions. In other words, it offers a high level animation showing, for instance, messages passing through the simulated architecture. This phase is handled by three processes which are the plotter, the animator and the reporter.

Library of Basic Models : The core of the AMS is the library of basic models which includes standard networks such as popular LAN technologies (Ethernet, Token Ring, FDDI, etc.), WANs (X25, TCP/IP), satellites (TDMA, FDMA, etc.), radio networks, and special network components like routers, bridges and gateways. Each basic model corresponds to a communication entity; it is studied, verified, and validated separately. Depending on the phase where a basic model is used, it is represented by an icon, an ADL object, or by a QNAP2 object.

2.2.2 AMS Prototype

The first level of reusability is extensively applied. Indeed, a prototype of AMS is developed based on four existing and proven packages except the ADL language which is developed specially for the atelier. These packages are : QNAP2, GSS[10] (Graphical Support System), S-PLUS[11] and MODLINE[12].

Figure 2.2 shows the available tools in the prototype and on which packages they are based. The simulator is based on QNAP2, the post-processor is based on S-PLUS. The graphical editor and the animator are based on GSS which provides generic graph edition facilities to make the development of graphical performance modeling tools easier. The textual editing of an architecture can be done using ADL. The Reporter, Plotter, and Experimenter processes are based on MODLINE, a modeling environment conceived to assist in all stages of the performance analysis. On the other hand, AMS integrates all these packages through MODLINE which provides its graphical user's interface to the atelier. A prototype of the atelier has been developed on a SUN machine running the SunOs operating system. It is developed in C language. At present time, about 15000 lines have been coded.

2.3. COMMUNICATION NETWORK MODELING UNIT : DBM

So far, we said that the library is composed of basic models. More precisely, each basic model is to be detailed so as to reflect its exact behavior, and in the following it will be called DBM for Detailed Basic Model. We applied the second level of reusability, and DBM will be considered as a reusable unit for modeling communication network components. Accordingly, it has to implement, as precisely as possible, the operations performed by the target component, the component which is modeled by means of a DBM.

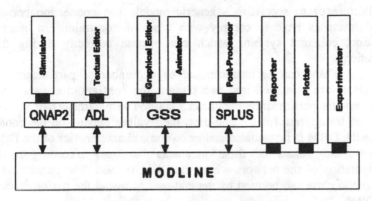

FIGURE 2.2 : AMS PROTOTYPE

A DBM can be used either as a component of a communication network or as a component of a generic model (for example complex network component). Thus, a DBM should be constructed in a very modular fashion, in order to achieve easily and efficiently this high degree of composition between DBMs.

A DBM is composed of three blocks : the Behavior Engine Block (BEB), the Interfaces Block (IB) and the Measurements Block (MeB). The structure is designed to meet the following fundamental objectives :

- Each DBM is self-contained, namely the behavior of the target component is modeled inside the DBM, and all the interactions with the outside world take place through interfaces.
- We keep in mind that each DBM may be a component of a communication system. Hence, a DBM must be connected to other DBMs; connections are made via interfaces. Interfaces have another important role, which is to free the BEB of messages exchange between the DBM and the outside world. This intends that the BEB has to handle only the behavior of the target component and not the issue of how to structure the messages.
- The main objective of modeling is performance assessment. Hence, statistical results are required. They will be processed during the simulation phase. Each DBM is intended to offer one or several measurements, which must be meaningful to an end-user.

DBMs are designed as objects which can be instantiated several times. The instances are linked together so as to mimic a given network architecture or to specialize a generic model. The connection between DBM instances have to comply with a set of constraints, in order to construct coherent systems which can operate correctly during their execution.

A DBM can be characterized by a number of parameters. The parameters are classified into two classes, the configuration parameter's class and the performance parameter's class. The parameters of the first class are transparent for the end-user, their values depend on the context where the DBM is instantiated and/or on some characteristics of the DBM. Namely, the values of these parameters are set according to the configuration of the network where the DBM is used. The parameters of the second class can be used by the end-user to assess the performance of the DBM.

The following sub-sections explain the internal structure of a DBM more thoroughly.

2.3.1 Behavior Engine Block

The behavior of a target component is modeled within the BEB of its associated DBM. The BEB is an open network of stations. Each station includes a queue with limited or unlimited capacity, and one or several servers. The network of stations is open because it receives from and/or sends to the outside, through the interfaces, different messages. The configuration of the network of stations and the services offered by each station are left to the responsibility of the modeler. The complexity of the network of stations heavily depends on the complexity of the target component.

2.3.2 Interfaces Block

The interfaces block is an important part of a DBM for several reasons. The modularity aspect of a DBM is reinforced by its presence. It allows the modeler to develop a DBM independently of any system of which it can be a component. Well-defined interfaces also promote the reuse of the global model. Finally, it frees the BEB of the task of message exchange with the outside world.

A DBM can have several interfaces. Their number can either be a fixed value known during the modeling phase or it can vary. In the later case, the modeler can progressively add new interfaces to the DBM. A given interface can be instantiated one or several times if an instance of the current DBM is connected to one or several instances of a DBM through this given interface.

An interface is represented by means of two stations (figure 2.3), each station is composed of a queue and a server. The station Qin receives messages from the outside, which are meant to be sent later to the BEB.

Qout receives messages from the BEB to be sent later to another DBM, which is connected to it. The services inside Qout and Qin both depend on the type of DBM connected to the current DBM as well as the type of messages to be handled by the current DBM.

2.3.3 Measurements Block

The measurements block contains two types of measures. The first type reflects the behavior of a DBM, and it is associated with the BEB. The second type is associated with the interfaces, and it mainly shows the data flow entering and exiting the DBM.

The modeler of a DBM defines a list of measurements. The measurements must be meaningful to an end-user who is not specialized in the field of queueing networks. All the aspects related to this field are transparent. These measurements must be related to some metrics currently used in the field of communication systems, e.g. throughput, response delay, etc.

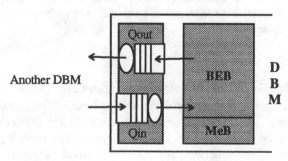

FIGURE 2.3 : A STANDARD INTERFACE

2.4. PROTOCOL ENTITY MODELING UNIT : FUNCTION

The fine grain unit of reusability is the concept of function. A function is defined in OSI RM[13], as part of the activity of a protocol entity, knowing that most protocol entities can be expressed in terms of functions. Based on this concept, we have developed a methodology[14,15] to model protocol entities as DBMs, especially, their behavior engine blocks. Presently, only the internal structure of a DBM has been defined and not the way to describe the BEB. This leaves to the modeler the hard task of its description.

Each function will be separately developed as a reusable unit, which will facilitate its implementation, verification, and if necessary its maintenance. Based on these reusable units, which interact in a simple and well-defined way, the modeler can rapidly build well-structured models of protocol entities. Thus, the proposed methodology will help the modeler to partly fill the gap between specifying and modeling protocol entities.

On the other hand, a high degree of service flexibility can be provided. Indeed, applications can use efficient communication subsystems tailored to their individual needs. Clearly, a protocol entity pattern will be composed of a sub-set of functions selected from a library called LoF, for Library of Functions. The selection is driven by the application's needs and the services offered by the underlying sub-networks.

This approach is pursued in many other projects, specially to design the new generation of high speed transport protocols for high speed communication systems[16,17,18,19,20].

2.4.1 Function Concept

The Library of functions (LoF) is a set of simple functions. LoF = {f_1, f_2, ..., f_n} with n≥2. A simple function is defined as a function performing one task, provided this task is atomic, i.e. it does not need the cooperation of other functions to be achieved. A cooperation between functions is possible when all or part of the functions are asked to provide a given service. Henceforward, only the term "function" will be used instead of "simple function".

Three types of functions are considered : Prerequisite, Selected and Pulled functions. A function is defined as prerequisite, if and only if, it is always present in a protocol entity pattern, whatever the service required. A "selected function" is a function which is chosen initially by the modeler to be present inside the pattern of a protocol entity. As a rule, a selected function has to be present inside the pattern of the protocol entity. A "pulled function" is a function which is chosen by the "pattern protocol determination process" and which is neither a prerequisite function nor a selected function. This type of function has to be present in a protocol entity pattern in order to make the pattern consistent.

Each function f_i can perform its task in different ways, which implies that it has to be associated with different algorithms (the term mechanism is also used). Let us denote :

- Δ_i : the set of algorithms associated with f_i ($\Delta_i \neq \varnothing$)
- Π_i : a sub-set of Δ_i including at least one algorithm ($\Pi_i \subseteq \Delta_i$ and $\Pi_i \neq \varnothing$)
- Furthermore, we write f_i/Π_i to denote that function f_i is associated with a sub-set of its algorithms. Π_i may contain only one algorithm A_{ij} (jth algorithm of f_i).

A function f_i/A_{ij} is modeled as a module with well-known boundaries represented, in our case, by sets of inputs and outputs. $Sin(f_i, A_{ij})$ is the set of the object attributes whose values can be used by a function f_i/A_{ij} during its execution. Clearly, the values of these object attributes may be read by the function f_i when the algorithm A_{ij} is executed. $Sin(f_i, A_{ij})$ is never empty, because when a function is triggered by an event, and has to perform a certain job, it has to know at least the type of the event and/or the context where this event occurs.

$Sout(f_i, A_{ij})$ is the set of the object attributes whose values are updated by f_i during the execution of the algorithm A_{ij}. As for $Sin(f_i, A_{ij})$, it may happen that not all the object attributes of $Sout(f_i, A_{ij})$ are updated. $Sout(f_i, A_{ij})$ is never empty.

The functions of LoF can be partitioned into non-empty sub-sets. The partitioning is based on the class of events processed by the protocol entity, which can be classified into essentially three classes. The first class is defined by the arrival of messages from the application layer, the layer which asks for a service. The second class is defined by the arrival of segments from the sub-network which is beneath the protocol entity layer, while the third class is defined by the expiration of timers. This partitioning will allow to define a partial order between the functions belonging to the same part, while it does not exclude the existence of relations between the functions belonging to different parts.

2.4.2 Relations Between Functions

A function may be related to the other functions by means of two graph types, precedence graphs and $\mathcal{E}$-Graph. In the first type of graph, the partial order between functions is captured, while in $\mathcal{E}$-graph, mutual presence of functions in a protocol is captured. Hereafter, a formal description of these two types of graphs.

1. Precedence Graph. A partial order between the functions belonging to the same part of LoF is defined as the acceptable order in which operations can be performed. The reason for dependencies could be viewed as some sort of shared information, manipulated by a function and required by another one. So, the necessary condition for function f_i/A_{ip} to precede function f_j/A_{jq} is : $Sout(f_i/A_{ip}) \cap Sin(f_j/A_{jq}) \neq \varnothing$. Two main types of precedence are defined : *strong precedence* and *weak precedence*.

- *Strong Precedence* : Function f_j/A_{jq} is preceded strongly by function f_i/Π_i ($i \neq j$) means that if f_j/A_{jq} has to be part of a protocol entity pattern then f_i also has to be part of this pattern with one algorithm belonging to Π_i (let it be A_{ip}). The statement "a function has to be part of a protocol entity pattern" is a general statement which means indirectly that a function is either a prerequisite, selected or pulled function.

- *Weak Precedence* : Let us assume that function f_j/A_{jq} has to be part of a protocol entity pattern. If f_j/A_{jq} is preceded by function f_i/Π_i ($i \neq j$) by means of a weak-arc, then f_j/A_{jq} will always be executed even if f_i will not be part of this pattern. In the case where f_i has to be part of the pattern then it has to be associated with an algorithm belonging to Π_i.

    Definition : A precedence graph G_i, associated with a sub-set F_i, is a digraph. The vertices of G_i are the functions of F_i. The G_i arcs represent the precedence relation between the functions. An arc is either a "strong-arc" or a "weak-arc". Each arc is labeled. If it connects functions f_i and f_j, the label is denoted L_{ij}^{pq} (f_i/A_{ip} precedes f_j/A_{jq}). G_i has two special vertices, the "Begin" vertex and the "End" vertex. The former is not preceded by any other vertex, and the later does not precede any vertex.

2. $\mathcal{E}$-Graph. An $\mathcal{E}$-Graph is a graph which may have arcs and edges. A connector is either an arc or an edge. The vertices of an $\mathcal{E}$-Graph are the functions of LoF. The two extremities of a connector have to belong to two different parts of LoF. A connector linking two functions f_i and f_j is labeled either by the symbol Γ or the symbol Λ.

If f_i/Π_i is connected to f_j/Π_j by a Γ-labeled (respectively, Λ-labeled) connector and the function f_i has to be part of a protocol entity pattern with an algorithm belonging to Π_i then the function f_j has also to be part of this protocol entity pattern (respectively, the peer protocol entity pattern) associated with an algorithm belonging to Π_j. The opposite is not true in the case where the connector is an arc.

2.4.3 Protocol Entity Pattern

A protocol entity has to be modeled as a DBM to be added to the AMS Library. Therefore, the internal structure of a DBM has to be taken into account. Figure 2.4 shows the structure of a protocol entity and mainly the queueing network modeling the Behavior Engine Block. Actually, the BEB is composed of three stations and a specific process, TiM for Timers Manager, which is dedicated to the management of timers. The service of each station executes the selected functions of a given part.

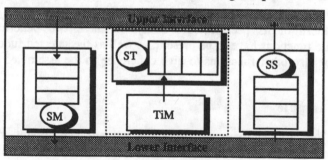

FIGURE 2.4 : BEB STRUCTURE OF A PROTOCOL ENTITY

As if the structure of a BEB is simple, it is efficient for two main reasons: i) the modeler can recognize in which station service a given function should be used, ii) the number of stations is limited to only three stations, thus the interactions between the stations are also limited, which leads to a reduction of the simulation time of the model.

Concerning the measurements, they are related to the function concept. A measurement will be seen as a hook on a function or a sub-set of functions. A function can be associated with zero, one or more than one measurement(s). In the case where at least one measurement is associated with one function, this measurement will be used to assess the behavior of this function. If a measurement is associated with a group of functions, then it will be computed only if all the functions of the group are chosen to be part of the pattern of the protocol entity.

The pattern of a protocol entity will be tailored according to the application needs. So, building up a pattern of a protocol entity is driven by the required service. A given service can be seen as a set of functions which have to be implemented by a protocol entity. External constraints which generally come from the sub-network have to be taken into account by the modeler when he makes his selections. Indeed, these constraints either require to select additional function(s) or on the contrary, to cancel the pre-selected function(s).

We have developed a specific process, called PPDP for Protocol Pattern Determination Process. It is used to construct a pattern of a protocol entity from LoF which will provide a given service. PPDP uses the precedence graphs and the $\mathcal{E}$-graph defined for the available functions into LoF. PPDP constructs at the same time a pattern of a protocol entity and a pattern of its peer-protocol entity. In these two patterns, the prerequisite functions have to be present, as well as the selected functions, and maybe also other functions to give coherence to the assembled set of functions.

2.4.4 Example

XTP[21] is one of the most promising full-featured light-weight transfer protocols; it provides the functionalities of Network Layer and Transport Layer. XTP can provide a full range of services needed to support distributed systems. The features of XTP include rate control, selective retransmission, no-error mode, etc.

We model XTP using the function-based methodology described above. The functions which are modeled are stored in LoF and are partitioned into three parts : Fmsg, Fpack and Ftimer. Each part is associated with an event class, arrival of messages, arrival of segments or expiration of timers. Figure 2.5 shows the precedence graphs associated with Fmsg. Figure 2.6 depicts the $\mathcal{E}$-Graph, where only the connected vertices are shown. We assume that each function is associated with only one algorithm.

LoF = {fragmentation, flow control, rate control, padding, numbering, retention, transfer DT, go-back-n on wtime, coalesce, un-padding, resequencing, selective retransmission, rtt estimation, transfer CNTL}

Fmsg = {fragmentation, flow control, rate control, padding, numbering, retention, transfer DT}

Ftimer = {go-back-n on wtime}

Fpack = {coalesce, un-padding, resequencing, selective retransmission, rtt estimation, transfer CNTL}.

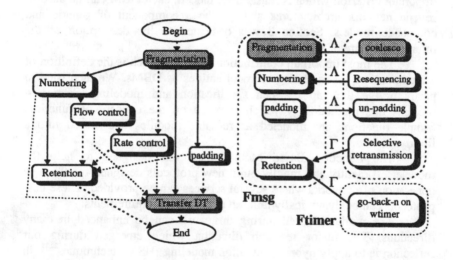

FIGURE 2.5 : PRECEDENCE GRAPH OF FMSG

FIGURE 2.6 : THE $\mathcal{E}$ GRAPH

2.5. CONCLUSIONS AND FUTURE DIRECTIONS

This work has been accomplished in the context of the OSISIM project. The main contribution is the emphasis put on the reusability concept, on one side, for designing a simulation environment, and on the other side, for defining two different levels of granularity for reusable network component libraries. In retrospect, one can clearly see the positive potential influence that reusability is having on the development of high quality software and models.

The design of our simulation environment, called AMS, was based on existing pieces of software, which proved their usefulness in their respective fields. In order to carry out this integration efficiently, a modular structure of the atelier was proposed.

The kernel of the AMS is its library of Detailed Basic Models (DBMs). Each DBM was designed in order to comply with the most important criterion which is reusability. Indeed, each DBM can be used in several network architectures and can be a component of generic and composite models. Section 3 was dedicated to the description of the internal structure of a DBM.

The most important contribution of this research is the definition of a methodology for modeling protocol entities as DBMs. We then tried to partly bridge the gap between specification and modeling. Section 4 presents this methodology which is based on the concept of function. Simple functions are modeled as reusable modules and stored into a library.

The Function Based Methodology was designed to help the modeler efficiently and rapidly build new protocols designed for the new generation of networks where several services can be provided. These new protocols can be dynamically tailored to the user's requirements.

The work achieved during this work can be enhanced in many directions. The major research direction which emerged during our reflection is to apply hybrid simulation modeling (HSM) techniques[22,23] in order to tackle the main disadvantage of simulation which is the slowness of the execution. The goal of HSM is to build models which are, on one side, more representative than pure analytical models and, on the other side, that lead to a substantial reduction of execution time with respect to pure simulation models. The HSM techniques were already used for particular situations but reusability was not taken into account.

In order to define more formally HSM, we refer to the classification introduced by Shanthikumar and Sargent[24], that distinguishes four classes of HSM by considering four different interaction ways between simulation and analytical models. Specifically, two of these classes (I and II) include the combination over time of simulation and analytical solutions either in parallel or through a joint solution procedure. The other two classes (III and IV) consider either a pure analytical or simulation model of the total system and use, respectively, a simulation or an analytical solution to represent a portion of the system. In our case and for reusability purposes, the fourth class of HSM has to be studied more thoroughly. Actually, the total system can only be resolved by simulation with one or several parts modeled analytically.

2.6. REFERENCES

[1]   W. TRACZ, Software Reuse: Emerging Technology (IEEE Computer Society Press, 1990).

[2]   E.T. SAULNIER and B.J. BORTSCHELLER, "Simulation Model Reusability", IEEE Communications Magazine, 32, 64 (1994).

[3]   R. MRABET, "Reusability and Hierarchical Simulation Modeling of Communication Systems for Performance Evaluation. Simulation Environment, Basic and Generic Models, Transfer Protocols." Ph.D. Thesis, Applied Sciences Faculty, Université Libre de Bruxelles, Brussels, Belgium, June 1995.

[4]   A. COHEN and R. MRABET, "AMS : An Integrated Simulator for Open Systems", Proceedings of IEEE GLOBECOM'93 Conference, (Houston, Texas, 29 November - 2 December 1993), 656.

[5]   COHEN and R. MRABET, "An environment for Modelling and Simulating Communication Systems, Application to a System Based on a Satellite Backbone", The International Journal of Satellite Communications, 13, 147 (1995).

[6]   F.H. DESBRANDES, S. BERTOLOTTI, and L. DUNAND, "OPNET 2.4: An Environment for Communication Network Modeling and Simulation", Proceedings of European Simulation Symposium, (Delft, The Netherlands, October 1993), 609.

[7]   M. A. MARSAN, G. BALBO, G. BRUNO, and F. NERI, "TOPNET : A Tool for the Visual Simulation of Communication Networks", IEEE Journal on Selected Areas in Communications,

8, 1735 (1990).

[8]   K. S. SHANMUGAN, V. S. FROST, and W. LARUE, "A block-Oriented Network Simulator", Simulation, 83 (1992).

[9]   SIMULOG S.A. "QNAP2 User's Manual", Version 10, (1992).

[10]   SIMULOG S.A. "GSS User's Guide", Version 4, (1992).

[11]   MATHSOFT INC. STASCI, "S-PLUS User's Guide", Version 3.2, (1993).

[12]   SIMULOG S.A "MODLINE User's Guide", Version 3.3, (1995).

[13]   ISO International Standard 7498, "Information processing systems — Open Systems Interconnection : Basic Reference Model", (1984).

[14]   A. COHEN and R. MRABET, "Function-based Methodology to Model Communication Protocols for Performance Evaluation", Proceedings of International Conference on Communication Systems, (Singapore, 14-18 November 1994), 90.

[15]   A. COHEN and R. MRABET, "Modeling Function-Based Communication Protocols Entities for Performance Assessment, Application to XTP", Proceedings of Twelfth International Conference on Computer Communication, (Seoul, South Korea, 21-24 August 1995), 75.

[16]   D.D. CLARK and D.L. TENNENHOUSE, "Architectural Considerations for a New Generation of Protocols", Computer Communications Review, **20**, 200 (1990).

[17]   Z. HASS, "A Protocol Structure for High-Speed Communication over Broadband ISDN", IEEE Network Magazine, **5**, 64 (1991).

[18]   M. ZITTERBART, "High-Speed Transport Components", IEEE Network Magazine, **5**, 54-63 (1991).

[19]   D.C. FELDMEIER, "A Framework of the Architectural Concepts for High-Speed Communication Systems", IEEE Journal on Selected Areas in Communications, **11**, 480 (1993).

[20]   D.C. SCHMIDT and T. SUDA, "Transport System Architecture Services for High-Performance Communications Systems", IEEE Journal on Selected Areas in Communications, **11**, 489 (1993).

[21]   Protocol Engine Inc., Xpress Transfer Protocol, Version 4.0 (1995).

[22]   V.S. FROST, W.WOOD LARUE, and K.S. SHANMUGAN, "Efficient Techniques for the Simulation of Computer

Communications Networks", IEEE Journal on Selected Areas in Communications, **6**, 146 (1988).

[23]   S. BALSAMO, M. CAPPUCIO, L. DONATIELLO, and R. MIRANDOLA, "Some Remarks on Hybrid Simulation Methodology", Proceedings of Summer Computer Simulation Conference, (Calgary, Canada, 16-18 July 1990), 30.

[24]   J.G. SHANTHIKUMAR and R.G. SARGENT, "A Unifying View of Hybrid Simulation/Analytic Models and Modeling", Operations Research, **31**, 1031 (1983).

CHAPTER 3

REDUCTIONS IN GSPN AND SWN: AN OVERVIEW AND AN EXAMPLE OF APPLICATION

M. Ajmone Marsan, S. Donatelli
G. Franceschinis, F. Neri

3.1. INTRODUCTION

The stochastic modeling approaches used for the performance analysis of different types of real systems (distributed computer architectures, telecommunication networks, flexible manufacturing systems, etc.) can be divided in two large families: analysis and simulation. Both of them are plagued with an enormous complexity increase with the model growth, which is essentially due to the so-called "state space explosion problem", i.e., to the extraordinary increase in the number of possible states in the model.

When state spaces become extraordinarily large, simulation becomes costly, since the exploration of the state space requires enormous CPU times, specially when many of the states are visited very seldom (as it happens quite often). Analytical approaches, instead, become difficult to apply because they typically require the solution of equation systems that comprise one equation for each state.

59

The only area of stochastic modeling that is partly immune from this largeness problem comprises product-form queueing networks. This is the reason why product-form queueing networks are so widely used, and are adopted as a modeling paradigm whenever possible. However, it is well-known that many important features of systems cannot be captured by product-form queueing network models (synchronization, passive resources, customer splitting and merging, some types of blocking and loss, etc.). When this happens, the analytical approach to performance modeling is often based either on a direct Markovian system description, or on the representation of the system characteristics with some version of Stochastic Petri Nets (SPNs).

The advantages of SPNs over the direct approach are in a graphical description of the system dynamics, and in the availability of a *structure*, which can be exploited for the proof of some qualitative properties of the model. However, for the derivation of quantitative performance results, an SPN model must be converted into an equivalent Continuous-Time Markov Chain (CTMC); this CTMC is then solved with standard techniques, and the desired aggregate performance indices can be computed from its solution.

The availability of a *structure* in the SPN model can also be exploited in a preliminary phase of the solution step in order to originate a smaller CTMC that will provide exactly the same aggregate performance predictions as the original one. This can be achieved through the application of *reduction rules,* which allow the simplification of the SPN structure, and a corresponding reduction in the number of states, equivalent to a lumping of the original CTMC.

In this chapter we overview the reduction rules known for GSPNs (Generalized SPNs) and SWNs (Stochastic Well-formed Nets — a type of colored SPNs). The reduction rules are based on the exploitation of symmetries in the model and on the elimination of immediate transitions.

GSPN and SWN models of a symmetrical random polling system are used as running examples: reduction rules are applied to both, showing the effectiveness of the reduction approach.

In our presentation we assume that the reader has some, at least preliminary, knowledge of the GSPN and SWN modelling formalisms. Readers can find in the literature the original definition of GSPNs[1], and the second version of the GSPN definition[2,11], that allows a net-level specification of the probabilistic parameters. Tutorials on GSPNs are also available[3,4]. A more vast presentation of the subject is provided by a recent book by Ajmone et al.[6]. A definition of the SWN formalism can be found in Chiola et al.[12].

The original works reporting on reduction techniques for GSPNs were published by Chiola et al.[9], and by Simone et al.[18]. The first application of GSPN reduction techniques to models of random polling systems was presented by Ajmone et al.[5]. The first papers describing reductions performed on SWN models were published by Chiola et al.[7,10].

Part of the reduction techniques used in this chapter are novel. Some of the simpler rules for GSPNs have been known for a long time, but are explicitly presented here for the first time. Structural decolorization approaches in SWNs were previously defined only for untimed models, and the rules for their application also in a timed domain are presented here for the first time. In this chapter we also present two new rules for the partial decolorization of a color component. Similarly, the rules for the elimination of immediate transitions were defined only for nets without colors, and they are extended here also to colored models.

All the GSPN and SWN models described in this chapter were developed and solved by means of the GreatSPN1.7 package[13].

The chapter is organized as follows. Section 3.2 overviews the most useful GSPN reduction techniques, and Section 3.3 provides an example of application of the GSPN reduction rules to the analysis of a symmetrical random polling GSPN model. Section 3.4 briefly reviews the SWN formalism, and presents the SWN reduction rules; Section 3.5 shows how a SWN model of a random polling system can be reduced through the application of the SWN reduction rules. Section 3.6 concludes with a comparison of the GSPN and SWN reduction approaches, and with an indication about the possibility of automating the SWN reduction process as a useful intermediate step in the solution of SWN models.

3.2. GSPN REDUCTIONS

In order to provide the reader with a first flavor of the issues that are addressed in this chapter we can use a very simple example. Consider the two SPN models in Fig. 3.1. They provide two representations of the dynamics of three switches, that remain open and closed for

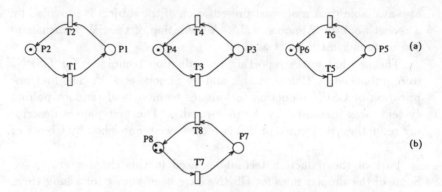

FIGURE 3.1. Two models of three switches

exponentially distributed random periods of time. We assume that the probabilistic description of the behaviors of the three switches are identical: the system is thus highly symmetrical.

The SPN at the top, marked (a), shows a model where the identity of each switch is explicitly represented, and associated with one of the three replicas of the elementary description of the dynamics of one switch. On the contrary, the SPN at the bottom, marked (b), shows a model where the identity of the switches is lost. The server semantics[6] of transitions T_1 through T_6 is irrelevant, while transitions T_7 and T_8 are of infinite-server type, to correctly represent the possibility for more than one switch to remain open (or closed) at the same time. From the evolution of model (a), it is possible to know how many switches are open, and which ones are open. From the evolution of model (b), it is only possible to know how many switches are open, not their identities. However, for the computation of performance indices, given the symmetry of the system, the identity of the open switches is irrelevant. It may thus be sufficient to use model (b) for the description of the dynamics of our system, specially if by so doing something is gained.

What we gain is obviously a reduction in the state space size, due to the elimination of one of the combinatorial elements that make the number of states grow. Denoting by N the number of switches ($N = 3$ in our case, but the result can be extended to any N), the cardinality of the state spaces (i.e., of the reachability sets RS_a and RS_b) of the two models is:

$$|RS_a| = 2^N = 8$$
$$|RS_b| = N + 1 = 4$$

Although in this very simple example we just gain a factor 2, the reader should observe that the law that governs the state space growth in case (a) is exponential, whereas in case (b) it is linear.

From the point of view of the underlying Markov process, we can easily understand that the CTMC generated by model (b) corresponds to a lumping[16] of the CTMC obtained from model (a).

The simplicity of the system that we used as a first example might induce the reader to believe that: i) the reduction approach is applicable only to very simple and special cases; ii) the application of reduction rules is trivial. In this chapter we instead show that reduction rules can indeed be quite powerful, but sometimes tricky to apply. Moreover, we show that reduction rules can produce drastic reductions of the model state space.

Our overview of the GSPN reduction rules is quite informal, due to the nature of this chapter, and quite concise, due to space limitations; readers desiring more details and formal definitions are referred to the original papers[9,18].

RR_1: Deletion of implicit places

Rule RR_1 eliminates a place p, and all of its input and output arcs, if the place can be recognized as implicit, i.e., if its marking is a deterministic function of the markings of other places, and it never concurs in determining the net evolution, or in influencing the enabling degree of its output transitions[17,14] (see rule $R1$ in Simone[18]).

RR_2: Deletion of timed transitions that do not modify the marking

Rule RR_2 deletes a timed transition T, and all of its input and output arcs, if the timed transition firing does not modify the marking of the GSPN, i.e., if the transition input set coincides with the transition output set.

RR_3: Deletion of redundant immediate transitions

Rule RR_3 eliminates an immediate transition t that has only one input place, for which it is the only output transition, and that has only one output place whose tokens enable transitions of priority not higher than that of t; the input and output places of t are merged into one.

RR_4: Reduction of non-conflicting timed transitions

Rule RR_4 (numbered $R2$ in Simone[18]) considers a timed transition T with infinite-server semantics that is not in conflict with other transitions, and that has just one input place. This place is the only output of k immediate transitions $t_1, \ldots, t_k$ that are persistent (a transition is said to be *persistent* if once it becomes enabled, it cannot be disabled before firing).

The timed transition T and the k immediate transitions $t_1, \ldots, t_k$ are substituted with k timed transitions $T_1, \ldots, T_k$, each one having the input set of the corresponding immediate transition (T_1 corresponds to t_1, etc.), and the output set of T. Each of the timed transitions $T_1, \ldots, T_k$ has infinite-server semantics, and the same rate as T.

RR_5 : Reduction of apparent conflicts

Rule RR_5 reduces sets of conflicting transitions $u_1, \ldots, u_k$ (immediate of equal priority, or timed with either single-server or infinite-server semantics) with weights $w_1, \ldots, w_k$ to only one transition u, if all transitions have the same set of input and output places, and the same input and output arc weights.

The only remaining transition u, has weight $W(u) = \sum_{i=1}^{k} w_i$.

RR_6 : Reduction of sets of mutually exclusive transitions

Rule RR_6 reduces sets of mutually exclusive transitions $u_1, \ldots, u_k$ (immediate of equal priority, or timed with either single-server or infinite-server semantics) with identical weights w to only one transition u, if the following conditions hold: i) all transitions induce the same modification in the marking; ii) the enabling condition of each of the k original transitions can be expressed as $\Phi_i \wedge \Psi, i = 1, \ldots, k$ and $\vee_{i=1}^{k} \Phi_i = TRUE$ and $\forall i, j : i \neq j, \Phi_j \wedge \Phi_i = FALSE$ (Φ_i and Ψ are expressed as a conjunction of conditions on the marking of places).

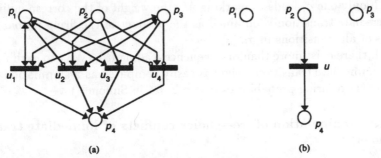

FIGURE 3.2. The application of rule RR_6 – a) original subnet – b) reduced subnet

The only remaining transition u, has weight w, and its input, output and inhibitor arcs are such that it induces the same modification in the marking as the originating transitions $u_j, j = 1, \ldots, k$, and its enabling condition is Ψ.

Fig. 3.2 shows an example of application of this rule where $\Phi_1 = (p_1 > 0) \wedge (p_3 > 0)$, $\Phi_2 = (p_1 = 0) \wedge (p_3 > 0)$, $\Phi_3 = (p_1 > 0) \wedge (p_3 = 0)$, $\Phi_4 = (p_1 = 0) \wedge (p_3 = 0)$, and $\Psi = (p_2 > 0)$.

In case transitions u_i are timed with infinite-server semantics, it might be necessary to transform the rate of the new timed transition u into a marking-dependent rate, in order to take into account the fact that some input places may be disconnected from the transition, so that its enabling degree may be affected by the reduction.

RR_7: Reduction of immediate subnets

Rule RR_7 reduces a subnet of immediate transitions that has an unique enabling marking, to an (extended) free-choice conflict of immediate transitions. This is done by explicitly considering all possible paths followed within the immediate subnet.

Consider an open subnet A, whose border transitions are connected to the rest of the net through places $q_1, \ldots, q_r$ in input, and through places $p_{11}, \ldots, p_{ks_k}$ in output (note that some of the p_{ij} can coincide with some of the q_h, and that the p_{ij} need not be all different).

The reduced net comprises one immediate transition t_i for each sequence σ_i of immediate transitions leading from the (unique) initial marking (M_{0A}) of the input interface places $q_1, \ldots, q_r$, to each possible final marking M_i.

If only one σ_i leads to marking M_i, the weight of the corresponding immediate transition is obtained as the product of the firing probabilities of all transitions in σ_i.

If there exist more than one sequence leading from M_{0A} to each M_i, the immediate transition weight is easily computed as a summation of products of firing probabilities (see rule $R4$ in Simone[18]).

RR_8: Manipulation of free-choice conflicts of immediate transitions

Rule RR_8 transforms a free-choice conflict of immediate transitions preceded by timed transitions into free-choice conflicts of timed transitions, like in Fig. 3.3, where transitions $T_1, \ldots, T_n$ are timed and transitions $t_1, \ldots, t_k$ are immediate with identical priorities.

Place p plays the role of a buffer that receives and sends the same amount of tokens whatever transition puts or gets tokens to/from it.

All the new transitions are timed with the following rates:

$$W(X_{ji}) = W(T_j)\, \frac{W(t_i)}{\sum_{h=1}^{k} W(t_h)}$$

Also in this case, an infinite-server semantics for timed transitions is permissible (see rule $R5$ in Simone[18]).

RR_9: Manipulation of non-free-choice conflicts of immediate transitions

Rule RR_9 transforms a non-free-choice conflict of immediate transitions preceded by timed transitions into non-free-choice conflicts of timed transitions. In Fig. 3.4 an example of this type of transformation is shown, where transition T is timed and transitions t_1, t_2 are immediate with the same priority. If several timed transitions put tokens into the input places (or withdraw tokens from the inhibitor places) of the immediate transitions, the rule must be applied to each timed transition before the immediate transitions can be removed from the net.

Each possible evolution of the immediate transitions in the non-free-choice conflict following the firing of the timed transitions must be considered, and results in one timed transition in the reduced net. The rate of the newly created timed transition is the product of the rate of the original timed transition and the probability of the associated firing sequence.

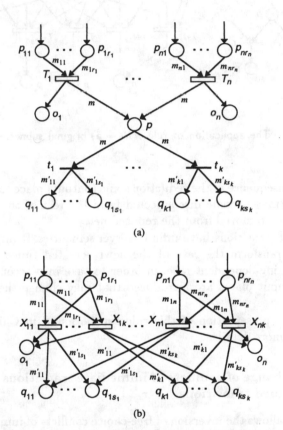

(a)

(b)

FIGURE 3.3. The application of rule RR_8 – a) original subnet – b) reduced subnet

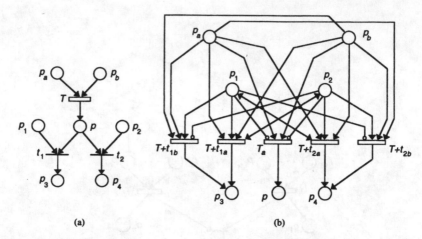

FIGURE 3.4. The application of rule RR_9 – a) original subnet – b) reduced subnet

As a consequence of the reduction some (output) place (of the timed transition) may become disconnected from the rest of the net: these places can be removed from the reduced net.

If timed transitions have infinite-server semantics, it might be necessary to transform the rate of the newly created timed transitions into a marking-dependent rate, in order to take into account the fact that new input places are introduced that may change the transition enabling degree.

The first presentation of this rule can be found in Chiola et al.[9], with some more details.

RR_{10}: Exchange of conflicts of immediate transitions with conflicts of timed transitions

Rule RR_{10} allows the inversion of free-choice conflicts of immediate and timed transitions, implicitly recognizing and eliminating some symmetries of the underlying stochastic process. This is equivalent to a lumping of the CTMC underlying the GSPN.

Rule RR_{10} manipulates combinations of free-choice conflicts of immediate and timed transitions like in Fig. 3.5. Transitions t_i are immediate of equal priority, whereas transitions T_{ij} are timed, and the n timed transitions in any of the k free-choice timed conflicts have the

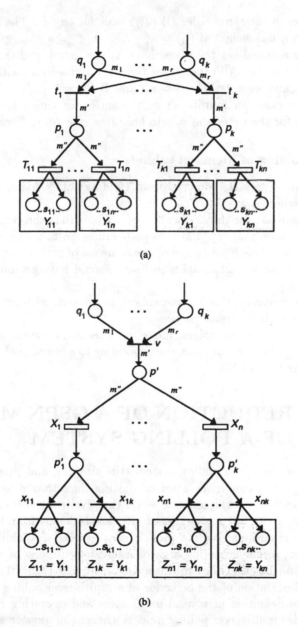

(a)

(b)

FIGURE 3.5. The application of rule RR_{10} – a) original subnet – b) reduced subnet

same rates in the same order $(W(T_{ij}) = w_i$ for any $j)$. The immediate transition t_i has weight $W(t_i) = w_i'$.

In the reduced net the transitions X_j are timed, and their weights are $W(X_j) = w_j$. All other transitions are immediate, with identical priorities, and weights $W(x_{ji}) = w_i'$, and $W(v) = 1$.

In this case, an infinite-server semantics for timed transitions is necessary for the reduction rule to hold (see rule $R6$ in Simone[18]).

RR_{11}: Folding of identical subnets

Rule RR_{11} allows the superposition (folding) of N identical subnets into a single one.

Precondition for the application of RR_{11} is that the N subnets are state machines, that input arcs to each subnet go to a single place and that arcs out of each subnet go to the same set of places, common to all replicas. Moreover all timed transitions should have an infinite-server semantics.

In the reduced net only one subnet is present, with all input arcs going to the single input place.

Also this rule recognizes and eliminates some symmetries of the underlying stochastic process, corresponding to a lumping of the CTMC underlying the GSPN.

3.3.   REDUCTION OF A GSPN MODEL OF A POLLING SYSTEM

A single-server cyclic polling system (the simplest and most common polling system) comprises a set of waiting lines that receive arrivals from the external world, and one server that cyclically visits the queues, providing service to customers that afterwards depart from the system.

While traditional polling models consider the availability of only one server, a new emerging area of interest is the one of *multiserver* polling models, also called multiserver multiqueue (MSMQ) systems.

The description of the behavior of a multiserver polling system requires the definition of several parameters and operating rules. Here we consider multiserver polling models where: the *number of queues* is equal to N (≥ 1); the *storage capacity* at each queue is equal to 1, so that no more than one customer can be at a queue at any time; the customer *arrival process* at each queue is Poisson with rate λ, with interruptions due to the limited storage capacity; the *number of servers* is equal to S $(1 \leq S \leq N)$; the customer *service times* are independent, exponentially distributed random variables with mean $1/\mu$ at each queue, and for each server; the *polling order* is random: the next queue to be visited is selected according to a uniform distribution encompassing all queues, including the one just visited; the server *walk times* from one queue to the next are independent, exponentially distributed random variables with mean $1/\omega$.

The queuing discipline (normally FCFS), the service discipline (normally limited, gated or exhaustive), and the server utilization policy (i.e., the maximum number of servers that can be simultaneously providing service at a queue) need not be specified, due to the storage capacity limit of one customer.

Fig. 3.6 shows a GSPN model describing a multiserver random polling system with four queues. It is clearly composed of four replicas of the queue submodel, connected through the submodels describing the queue selection and the server walks. We shall use the superscript (q) to indicate that a place (or a transition) belongs to the model of queue q. The initial marking (with S tokens in place $p_p^{(0)}$ and one token in places $p_a^{(q)}$, $q = 0, 1, 2, 3$) defines the number of servers in the system, as well as their initial position and the initial states of the individual queues.

Consider the subnets that describe the internal organization of each individual queue. Transition $T_a^{(q)}$ models the customer arrival process at queue q $(q = 0, 1, 2, 3)$. Customers waiting for a server are queued in place $p_q^{(q)}$, while a token in place $p_p^{(q)}$ represents the server when polling queue q. Transition $t_s^{(q)}$ fires if the server finds a waiting customer when it polls the queue, so that service can be provided; if the server finds no waiting customers, then $t_w^{(q)}$ fires, and the server moves to the next queue. One token in place $p_s^{(q)}$ represents a customer of queue q being served, as well as the server when providing service at queue q. $T_s^{(q)}$ is timed with a delay equal to the customer service time. The server moves to the routing place $p_r^{(q)}$ at the end of the visit at queue q (after the service completion represented by the firing of $T_s^{(q)}$, if a waiting customer was found; after the firing of $t_w^{(q)}$ if no waiting customer was found).

Consider now the subnets describing the choice of the next queue to be visited and the movement towards that queue. A server that

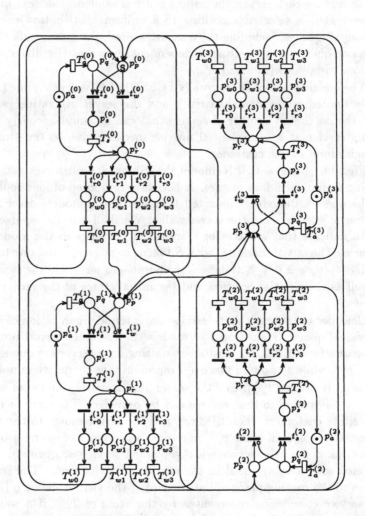

FIGURE 3.6. The first GSPN model of a multiserver random polling system

transition	weight	priority/semantics
$t_s^{(q)}$	1	1
$t_w^{(q)}$	1	1
$t_{rp}^{(q)}$	1	1
$T_a^{(q)}$	λ	irrelevant
$T_s^{(q)}$	μ	irrelevant
$T_{wp}^{(q)}$	ω	infinite-server

TABLE 3.1. Characteristics of the transitions in the first GSPN model of a multiserver random polling system ($p, q = 0, 1, 2, 3$)

leaves queue q is modelled by a token in place $p_r^{(q)}$; the choice for the next queue is modelled by the free-choice conflict comprising the four immediate transitions $t_{r0}^{(q)}, t_{r1}^{(q)}, t_{r2}^{(q)}$, and $t_{r3}^{(q)}$. The firing of transition $t_{rp}^{(q)}$ corresponds to the selection of the queue with index p as the next queue to be visited. Since the next queue to be visited must be selected according to a uniform distribution encompassing all queues, the four immediate transitions have identical weights. After the next queue has been selected, the server walks to the chosen queue. The timed transitions $T_{wp}^{(q)}$, $p = 0, 1, 2, 3$ model the walk times to reach queue p from queue q; since they have infinite-server semantics, in a marking M they are assigned a rate equal to $M(p_{wp}^{(q)})\omega$, where ω^{-1} is the mean walk time required to move from one queue to the next, and $M(p)$ is the number of tokens in place p.

The characteristics of timed and immediate transitions in the GSPN model in Fig. 3.6 are summarized in Table 3.1. The last column gives the priority in case of immediate transitions and the service semantics in case of timed transitions; this specification is irrelevant for transitions $T_a^{(q)}$ and $T_s^{(q)}$, since their enabling degree is at most one.

The symmetries in the GSPN model of Fig. 3.6 can be exploited for the model reduction. This reduction can often be obtained by applying the reduction rules that were presented above; other times the intervention of the modeler is required.

As a first step, it is possible to apply rule RR_{11} to the GSPN model in Fig. 3.6, to fold the subnets describing the choice of the next queue and the movement towards that queue. By so doing, we obtain the GSPN model in Fig. 3.7, where place p_r is the folded equivalent of places $p_r^{(0)}, p_r^{(1)}, p_r^{(2)}$, and $p_r^{(3)}$, and each one of the four immediate transitions that in Fig. 3.7 represent the choice of the next queue is obtained by folding four immediate transitions of Fig. 3.6; for instance, t_{r0} represents the choice of queue 0 and derives from the folding of $t_{r0}^{(0)}, t_{r0}^{(1)}, t_{r0}^{(2)}$, and $t_{r0}^{(3)}$. An analogous folding is done for timed transitions and places.

It is now possible to apply to the GSPN model in Fig. 3.7 the reduction rule RR_{10}, to obtain the GSPN model in Fig. 3.8. For the application of rule RR_{10}, we must consider the simpler case in which only one place q_i is present, namely place p_r, and the role of transitions t_i is played by t_{rq}, with $q = 0, 1, 2, 3$. Each set of transitions T_{ij} then comprises only the timed transition T_{wi}.

In Fig. 3.8, transition T_w is the only transition of type X_i, and the role of transitions x_{ij} is played by transitions t_{ri}. Note that, since only one place q_i is present, transition v that results from the application of RR_{10} is eliminated through RR_3.

From the model perspective, the last reduction step has anticipated the server walk *before* the selection of the next queue: since a server leaving a queue must walk, and the walk time is independent of the next queue, the selection of the next queue can be performed *after* the walk.

The second, third, and fourth columns in Table 3.2 show the cardinalities of the tangible and vanishing state spaces for the three GSPN models in Figs. 3.6, 3.7, and 3.8, in the case of two servers ($S = 2$) and for an increasing number of queues. Although in the three cases the growth of the total number of states with N is always combinatorial, the exploitation of symmetries yields very significant reductions, particularly for larger values of N (for $N = 6$ the reduction is more than one order of magnitude).

Note that all the models we have presented so far are parametric in S, the number of servers, but not in N, the number of queues in the system; indeed, in order to change the value of S we only need to change the initial marking, while in order to change the value of N, the structure of the net must be modified.

Since the system is completely symmetric, i.e., since all queues can be characterized with the same parameters, and the selection of the next queue is made on the basis of a uniform probability distribution, it is possible to produce a very compact model in which queues are not modelled individually. This produces a GSPN model featuring the remarkable property of being parametric with respect to the number of

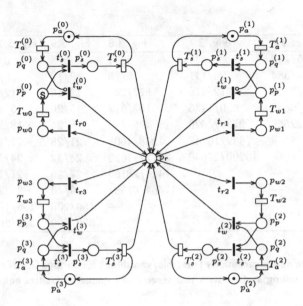

FIGURE 3.7. GSPN model obtained applying rule RR_{11} to the GSPN model in Fig. 3.6

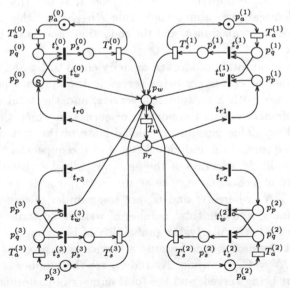

FIGURE 3.8. GSPN model obtained applying rules RR_{10} and RR_3 to the GSPN model in Fig. 3.7

N	Fig. 3.6	Fig. 3.7	Fig. 3.8	Fig. 3.9	Fig. 3.10
2	57/62	21/34	9/24	6/8	6/5
3	474/384	90/141	26/80	9/12	9/7
4	2712/1744	312/476	72/240	12/16	12/9
5	12480/6640	960/1435	192/672	15/20	15/11
6	49776/22560	2736/4026	496/792	18/24	18/13
7	—	7932/10745	1248/4608	21/28	21/15
8	—	19200/27640	3072/11520	24/32	24/17
9	—	—	7424/28160	27/36	27/19
10	—	—	17664/67584	30/40	30/21
50	—	—	—	150/200	150/101
100	—	—	—	300/400	300/201

TABLE 3.2. State space cardinality (tangible/vanishing) for various GSPN models of a random polling system with two servers and queue capacities equal to one

queues as well.

Note that, despite the fact that the subnets that describe a single station are identical, we cannot apply rule RR_{11}, since the identical subnets are not state machines, and the reduction process is therefore non automatic.

Due to the assumption of storage capacity equal to 1 at all queues, the total number of *customers* being served in the system equals the number of *queues* with a customer in service, and the total number of waiting *customers* equals the number of *queues* in which there is a customer waiting. This permits the global state of the system to be identified as the sum of the individual states of the queues.

The equally likely selection of the next queue to be visited allows the probability of providing service at the next queue to be written as $N_q/N = C_q/N$, where N_q and C_q are the number of queues with waiting customers, and the total number of waiting customers in the system, respectively. Similarly, the probability of being unable to provide service at the next queue because a service is in progress can be written as $N_s/N = C_s/N$, where N_s and C_s are the number of queues with customers being served, and the total number of customers being served in the system, respectively. Finally, the probability of being unable to provide service at the next queue because the buffer is empty

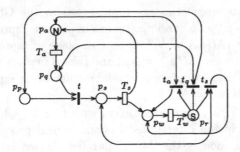

FIGURE 3.9. Abstract GSPN model of the symmetric multiserver random polling system

transition	weight	priority/semantics
t	1	2
t_a	$M(p_a)/N$	1
t_q	$M(p_q)/N$	1
t_s	$M(p_s)/N$	1
T_a	λ	infinite-server
T_s	μ	infinite-server
T_w	ω	infinite-server

TABLE 3.3. Characteristics of the transitions in the compact GSPN model of a symmetric multiserver random polling system

can be written as $N_a/N = C_a/N$, where N_a and C_a are the number of queues with empty buffer and the total number of empty buffers in the system, respectively.

A compact GSPN model of the symmetric multiserver random polling system with N queues can be constructed as depicted in Fig. 3.9. The characteristics of the transitions in this GSPN model are summarized in Table 3.3.

The global system state is defined by three quantities: the number of queues with empty buffer (N_a), the number of queues with a waiting customer (N_q), and the number of walking servers. Note that the number of queues being attended by a server (N_s) is simply the complement to N of the sum of the first two quantities ($N_s = N - N_a - N_q$), which also equals the number of busy servers.

These aggregate quantities are represented in the GSPN by the markings of places p_a, p_q, p_w and p_s. Tokens in place p_a represent queues with empty buffer $(M(p_a) = N_a)$, tokens in place p_q represent queues with a waiting customer $(M(p_q) = N_q)$, and tokens in place p_w represent walking servers. Tokens in place p_s model queues being served, as well as busy servers $(M(p_s) = N_s)$.

Consequently, T_a is a timed transition with rate $M(p_a)\lambda$, modelling the superposition of the interrupted Poisson arrival processes, T_s has rate $M(p_s)\mu$, and models the $M(p_s)$ parallel service activities, and T_w has rate $M(p_w)\omega$ to model the server walks that are currently in progress.

Place p_r is the place where the decision about the queue to be visited next is made: the choice is implemented by firing one of the three conflicting immediate transitions t_a, t_q, or t_s (all with priority 1), corresponding to the choice of a queue with an empty buffer, of a queue with a waiting customer, or of a queue with a service in progress, respectively.

The initial parametric marking of our GSPN model of a multiserver random polling system with N queues and S servers has N tokens in place p_a and S tokens in place p_r.

The rationale of the model is as follows. When a server terminates a service at a queue (firing of T_s), it must execute a walk (firing of T_w), and this can be done before choosing the next queue to visit, as previously noted. In this abstract model, queues are not modelled individually, so that instead of explicitly modelling the choice of the next queue to be visited, we model the causes and the consequences of the choice (this is the only relevant information from the point of view of the underlying stochastic model). A server chooses a queue with a waiting customer with probability $M(p_q)/N$. This choice is conditioned on the existence of at least one queue with a waiting customer, and it is modelled in the GSPN by immediate transition t_q, whose weight (probability) is $M(p_q)/N$. As a consequence of this choice a customer will be served; therefore the number of waiting customers $M(p_q)$ is decremented by one, while the number of queues being served $M(p_s)$ is incremented by one (by the firing of the immediate transition t with priority 2), and a new service can start (timed transition T_s is enabled). Alternatively, a server may choose a queue where the buffer is empty with probability $M(p_a)/N$, or it may choose a queue at which a service is in progress with probability $M(p_s)/N$. The first choice is modelled by transition t_a, while the second is modelled by transition t_s. Again, both choices are conditioned on the presence of at least one queue in the required situation, i.e., on the presence of at least one token in the appropriate place, and this explains the presence of test arcs connecting t_a to p_a and t_s to p_s (as well as t_q to p_q). The consequence of both choices is that the server must execute another walk (return to place p_w to execute T_w), and then repeat the choice of the next queue to be visited (coming back to the decision place p_r).

The reduction in the state space size with respect to the models in which queues are individually described is shown in Table 3.2. The differences in the number of states become drastic for larger values of N, due to a linear growth with N, which can be expected by the elimination of the combinatorial growth of the possible symmetric combinations of individual queue states. It is also interesting to note that the resulting model is parametric in both the number of queues and the number of servers. The parametrization is a result of the exploitation of the system symmetries, which however does not result from an automatic application of the reduction rules, but requires the intervention of the modeler.

It is possible to further reduce the abstract GSPN model of Fig. 3.9 by applying rule RR_7 to the subnet formed by the two immediate transitions t_q and t, that always fire in a row. Places p_r and p_q play the role of the input interface places q_i; p_p is the unique internal place, t_q and t are the internal transitions, and finally p_s plays the role of the output interface places p_{ij}. The initial marking M_{0A} to be considered for the transformation is $p_r + p_q$; the unique final marking is p_s. Fig. 3.10 shows, with a rearranged layout, the GSPN model after the reduction.

We are now in a position to cope with the non-free-choice conflict of immediate transitions comprising the three immediate transitions (t_a, t_q, t_s) that remove from p_r tokens that were deposited by the firing of timed transition T_w.

The application of reduction rule RR_9 eliminates the three immediate transitions and produces the SPN model shown in Fig. 3.11, where one timed and three immediate transitions have been replaced by twelve timed transitions (three groups of four replicas), and the vanishing place p_r has been removed (note that the removal of p_r requires a different definition of the initial marking, placing the S tokens that represent servers in place p_w).

The states of this SPN are isomorphic to the *tangible* states of the

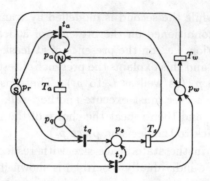

FIGURE 3.10. GSPN model obtained from that of Fig. 3.9 by applying rule RR_6

GSPN model in Fig. 3.10, so that the total number of states has been reduced at the price of cluttering the resulting SPN with timed transitions and arcs.

We can now continue in the reduction by applying rule RR_6 to each group of replicas, since all transitions in the same set of replicas have the same rate, and modify the SPN marking in the same way, as they actually correspond to the firing of the same transition.

Consider the rates of transitions in the first set of replicas. Denoting by $W(T_x)$ the rate of transition T_x, we have

$$W(T_{wa1}) = M(p_w)\,\omega\,\frac{M(p_a)}{M(p_a)} = M(p_w)\,\omega\,\frac{M(p_a)}{N}$$

$$W(T_{wa2}) = M(p_w)\,\omega\,\frac{M(p_a)}{M(p_a) + M(p_q)} = M(p_w)\,\omega\,\frac{M(p_a)}{N}$$

$$W(T_{wa3}) = M(p_w)\,\omega\,\frac{M(p_a)}{M(p_a) + M(p_s)} = M(p_w)\,\omega\,\frac{M(p_a)}{N}$$

$$W(T_{wa4}) = M(p_w)\,\omega\,\frac{M(p_a)}{M(p_a) + M(p_q) + M(p_s)} = M(p_w)\,\omega\,\frac{M(p_a)}{N}$$

where $M(p_w)\omega$ is the firing rate of T_w, and the first expression provides the rates assigned by the algorithm, while the second is how the rate can be rewritten by exploiting P-invariants. For example, the first equation is true because T_{wa1} is enabled only when both t_q and t_s are not enabled, and therefore p_a must contain N tokens, so that $M(p_a) + M(p_q) = 1$. Similar considerations hold for the other two sets of replicas.

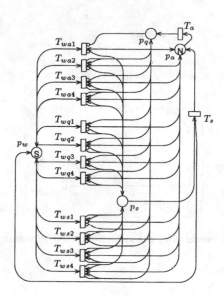

FIGURE 3.11. SPN model equivalent to the GSPN in Fig. 3.10

We can therefore apply rule RR_6, and substitute the four transitions with just one, with the same rate. The SPN obtained with this substitution is shown in Fig. 3.12.

A further simplification of the SPN in Fig. 3.12 can be obtained by observing that the two timed transitions T_{wa} and T_{ws} have preconditions equal to the postconditions, so that their firing does not modify the SPN marking. They can therefore be removed from the model through the application of rule RR_2. We thus come to the net shown in Fig. 3.13(a).

The covering of the net by the two P-semiflows $p_a + p_q + p_s$ and $p_s + p_w$ is obvious in this very compact model. P-invariants help us to further simplify the model, producing the final SPN shown in Fig. 3.13(b). To make this final step we take advantage of the fact that the sum of tokens in p_s and p_w is always equal to S, so that we can translate the test for at least one token in p_w (input arc from p_w to T_{wq}) into a test for less than S tokens in p_s (inhibitor arc with weight S from p_s to T_{wq}). The rate of transition T_{wq} is changed accordingly from $[M(p_w)]\omega M(p_q)/N$ to $[S - M(p_s)]\omega M(p_q)/N$.

At this point, both the enabling of T_{wq} and its firing rate are independent of the marking of p_w which can therefore be removed by applying rule RR_1.

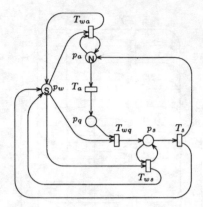

FIGURE 3.12. SPN model after the reduction of timed transitions according to rule RR_6

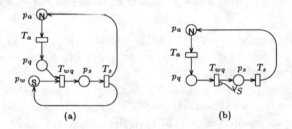

FIGURE 3.13. Two further simplifications of the SPN model

The striking simplicity of the final model in Fig. 3.13(b) deserves a few remarks. First of all, note that the SPN model is parametric both in N and in S, but the initial marking only comprises N tokens in place p_a: the dependency on S is embedded into the arc weights and transition rates. Second, note that servers have disappeared from the model; the server utilization policy is not obvious, as it is not obvious that servers can perform several walks in a row. Third, note that we ended up with three transitions and three places arranged in a circle; that two of the transitions have infinite-server rates, while the rate of the third one is a marking-dependent function that accounts for the number of servers in the system and the number of tokens in the transition output place.

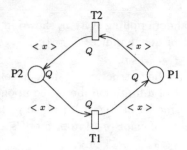

FIGURE 3.14. The SWN model of three switches

Finally, a few words are needed to comment on the numerical results in Table 3.2, which reports the cardinality of the tangible and vanishing state spaces of the various GSPN models presented so far, in the case of two servers ($S = 2$), for an increasing number of queues.

While a linear growth with N was already achieved with the model in Fig. 3.9, that already exhibits a tangible state space cardinality equal to $3N$, the reduction of immediate transitions allows the elimination of vanishing markings, so that the cardinality of the whole state space of the final model equals $3N$. This is extraordinarily less than the number of states of the original simple GSPN model we started with!

3.4.   SWN REDUCTIONS

In Colored Petri Nets[15] (CPNs), tokens have an identity called "color". Many different types of CPNs were defined in the literature. We consider here Stochastic Well-Formed Nets (SWNs)[8]. In the following we provide a brief introduction to SWNs, with a particular attention to those aspects of the formalism that are more relevant in this context; the style is very informal, mainly based on examples, like the SWN model of a set of three switches given in Fig. 3.14, and the one of the random polling model given in Fig. 3.15. Readers can refer to the literature[12,8] for a complete definition of the formalism and for a study of the relationships between SWNs and other colored nets.

Each place of a SWN model has an associated set, called *color domain*. Given a place p, its color domain $C(p)$ identifies the permissible colors of the tokens in place p. In the SWN model of the three switches shown in Fig. 3.14, both places $P1$ and $P2$ have the same associated color domain $Q = \{q_1, q_2, q_3\}$, the set of all switch identities. In the

SWN model of the random polling system, shown in Fig. 3.15, the color domains are: the set of queue indices $Q = \{q_1, \ldots, q_N\}$, and the set of server indices $R = \{r_1, \ldots, r_S\}$.

Color domains can be "structured", i.e., a color domain can be the Cartesian product of a finite number of components or sets (called "color sets"). In the model of Fig. 3.15, place p_s has a color domain equal to $Q \times R$: a token of color (q, r) in p_s models a customer of queue q being served by server r.

Also transitions have an associated color domain; in the switch example of Fig. 3.14 all transitions have color domain Q. The firing of transition $T1$ for color $q \in Q$, represents the fact that switch q changes its state from open to closed. We say that "$T1$ has fired for color instance q", and that "the color of the transition instance is q".

In non-colored nets, the input and output arcs of a transition define the enabling condition of a transition and the modification that the transition firing induces on the state. In SWNs the specification of enabling and firing is augmented with functions (associated with input and output arcs). The color of the transition instance can be related in a complex way to the color of the tokens that are removed from input places and that are added to output places, but in this chapter we only need to use "simple" functions. A function from the color domain of transition t to the color domain of place p, or viceversa, is said to be *simple* if it is either the identity, or the projection over some of the components of the color domains. In the SWN of Fig. 3.14, transition $T1$ is enabled for color q when there is a token of that same color in $P2$, and the firing of $T1$ removes a token of color q from $P2$ and puts a token of color q in place $P1$. The identity function is denoted in the switch example as $< x >$ on both the input and output arcs of $T1$.

More complex combinations of input and output function can be found in the model of Fig. 3.15. Consider for example transition t_r, of color $Q \times Q \times R$, that models the choice of the next queue. The firing of t_r for color instance (q, p, r) models the choice of server r leaving queue q to visit queue p. The function on the input arc is $< x, z >$, while the one on the output arc is $< x, y, z >$. To fire t_r for (q, p, r) the variables x, y, z are instantiated to the values $x = q$, $y = p$, $z = r$, therefore a token of color (q, r) is deleted from place p_r, and one of color (p, q, r) is added to place p_w. Observe that the variable y can assume any value in Q, and therefore t_r represents what in GSPN terminology is a free-choice conflict.

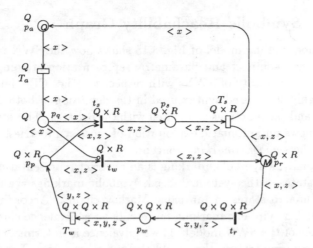

FIGURE 3.15. An SWN model of a random polling system

As another example of the use of functions, consider transition t_s in Fig. 3.15, which models a synchronization between tokens in places p_p and p_q. For transition t_s to fire for color (q, r), variable x should be bound to q and variable z to r. Since the variable x is present on both input arcs of t_s, then there should be a token of color (q, r) in p_p, and one of color q in p_q. Observe that when a token of color q is in place p_q, and two tokens of colors, say, (q, r_1) and (q, r_2) are in place p_p, then transition t_s can fire for two color instances (q, r_1) and (q, r_2), in conflict.

In SWNs, transitions can have an associated predicate that enriches the enabling definitions given by the arc functions. For example to model a system in which a server that leaves a queue deterministically comes back to the same queue, we can add to transition t_r in Fig. 3.15 the predicate $x = y$.

The initial marking of an SWN model is of course expressed in terms of colored tokens, and, more generally, as a function of the color sets. The initial marking of the net in Fig. 3.15 assigns the color set Q of queues to place p_a, representing a customer arriving at each queue, and marking $M = (R, 1)$ to place p_r, representing the servers of the color set R, initially all sitting in queue 1.

3.4.1. Symbolic Reachability Graph

The random polling model of Fig. 3.15 shows how the SWN paradigm
allows a very compact and parametric representation of complex systems. The peculiarity of SWNs with respect to other CPN formalisms
is the highly structured syntax used in the definition of both the color
domains and the functions associated with the net arcs. This structured
syntax allows an automatic exploitation of most symmetries, achieved
through the *symbolic marking* concept.

Informally, a symbolic marking is an abstract representation of one
or more states of the system: indeed, symbolic markings are the analogous of macro states in lumpable Markov chains. According to its
definition[12], a symbolic marking represents an equivalence class on the
state space of the SWN model. The equivalence is in terms of the possible color permutations that yield the same behavior. The interesting aspect of SWNs is that, instead of building the whole reachability
graph (RG), and then aggregating states into macrostates, which is
the standard procedure for lumpability, it is possible to directly build
the aggregate reachability graph, the so-called *Symbolic Reachability
Graph* (SRG), in such a way that each symbolic state of the graph is
a macrostate that represents a set of "ordinary" states with a common behavior (we term as ordinary the states of the equivalent GSPN
model obtained from the SWN model through unfolding, that is to say
through appropriate replication of the SWN structure as many times
as required by the cardinality of the color classes). The aggregation
performed in this way is such that the strong lumpability condition
of Markov chains is satisfied[16]. Moreover, all states in a macrostate
are equally probable[12]; therefore, all performance indices that can be
computed on the ordinary RG can also be computed on the SRG.

3.4.2. Goal of reductions in SWN systems

To explain the issues concerning the reduction of SWN models, we
can again go back to the three-switches example, and compare the two
models of Fig. 3.1 [net (a) and net (b)] and the model of Fig. 3.14 [net
(c)]. Net (a) showed a GSPN model of the system where the identity
of each replica is kept, net (b) showed a GSPN model that does not
keep the identity of the replicas, while net (c) is an SWN model of the
system. All places and transitions of the SWN model are of color class
$Q = \{q_1, q_2, q_3\}$.

The state space size for the SWN model must be computed for the case of both ordinary and symbolic markings, obtaining

$$|RS_c| = 2^N = 8$$
$$|SRS_c| = N + 1 = 4$$

where RS denotes the ordinary reachability set and SRS denotes the symbolic reachability set. We can then observe that, if we consider ordinary markings, nets (a) and (c) are perfectly equivalent, in the sense that whatever is computed and defined in (a) can be computed and defined in (c), and vice-versa: indeed (a) is the unfolding of (c), and (c) is the folding of (a) over the set of switches. Instead, if we consider symbolic markings, the reachability set of net (c) becomes perfectly equivalent to that of net (b).

Since the SRG construction is expensive, and its complexity depends on the colors associated with places and transitions, when a color component is not strictly required it is advisable to eliminate it from the net specification. The operation of deciding that a color component is "redundant" and its elimination from (part of) the net is called *decolorization* and it will be extensively used in the reduction process.

3.4.3. SWN reduction rules

The SWN reduction techniques used in this chapter are: i) SWN *structural decolorization*, defined in the literature[7,10] only for the untimed case, and extended here with two new rules that allow to partially decolorize a color component and to preserve the timed behavior; and ii) elimination of immediate transitions (and therefore of vanishing states), as defined for GSPNs, and extended here to SWNs.

Structural decolorization is a purely structural method, that considers only the net, and the definition of colors and functions; it consists in recognizing and removing parts of the color specification, when they do not influence the behavior of the model.

CRR_1: Elimination of a redundant color component

This rule simplifies the color structure of a model in the case of an overspecification. To identify the color domains that can be simplified we need to introduce the concept of *color component*[7,10], which is based on the definition of a dependency relation $\mathcal{R}$ between color classes in the color domains of nodes (places or transitions) that are connected through any type of arc. This relation is easy to check by looking at the (structured) functions on the arcs. For example, consider transition t_r and place p_r in the SWN model of Fig. 3.15, and a generic instance of t_r identified by the tuple of variables x, y and z (where, of course, the first two variables are of color Q and the third is of color R). If $C(t) \downarrow_i$ denotes the i-th color class in $C(t)$, then we have $C(t_r) \downarrow_1 \ \mathcal{R} \ C(p_r) \downarrow_1$, and $C(t_r) \downarrow_3 \ \mathcal{R} \ C(p_r) \downarrow_2$, meaning that the first component of the color domain of t_r is mapped into the first component of the color domain of p_r, and that the third component of the color domain of t_r is mapped into the second of p_r.

Note that relation $\mathcal{R}$ is symmetric and reflexive, and its transitive closure allows the partition of the components of the color domains of an SWN model into equivalence classes called *color components*.

According to its definition[7,10], a color component is considered *redundant* when it is never used to decide about a synchronization.

As an example of color component used to decide of a synchronization, consider the subnet identified by places p_p and p_q, and by transition t_s. $C(p_p) \downarrow_1 \ \mathcal{R} \ C(t_s) \downarrow_1$, $C(p_q) \downarrow_1 \ \mathcal{R} \ C(t_s) \downarrow_1$, hence $C(p_p) \downarrow_1$, $C(t_s) \downarrow_1$ and $C(p_q) \downarrow_1$ belong to the same color component, moreover this color component is used to decide whether a token in p_p (a server polling a station) can "synchronize" with a token in p_q (a customer waiting for a server) through the firing of an instance of t_s (the two tokens can synchronize only if the unique component of the token in p_q is the same as the first component of the token in p_p). Similar considerations apply to transition t_w, for which p_q is now an inhibitor place.

Redundant colors can be removed, producing equivalent SWNs with a simplified color structure that usually originate a smaller SRG.

In the work by Chiola et al.[7,10] the definition of redundant color component does not take into account the timing aspects: for the extension to stochastic nets, in the structural decolorization it is necessary to first check the qualitative conditions (untimed aspect), and then show that the rate out of a symbolic state is equal to the rate out of the corresponding state after the decolorization, i.e., to show that the CTMC rates are preserved by the decolorization.

Several factors influence the rate out of a state: the set of enabled transitions, their enabling degree, the rates associated with the transitions and their associated semantics (single-, multiple- or infinite-server). Since the set of enabled transitions is preserved by the rules defined in the work for the untimed case[7,10], it is only necessary to check: i) the rate of each decolored transition - there should be no dependency of the transition rates from a specific color; ii) the semantics of each decolored transition - there should be no semantics defined on the specific color.

For example, in the SWN of Fig. 3.14, if we want to decolor place $P1$ and transition $T2$, then the rate of $T2$ should be independent of the specific color instances for which $T2$ can fire. This means that a rate of $T2$ equal to μ when exactly one token is in place $P1$, and equal to ν when two or more tokens are in $P1$ is permissible, while a rate μ when $T2$ fires for color q_1 and ν for all other colors is not allowed. Moreover, since we cannot allow any dependency of transition semantics from a specific color value, we can allow a general infinite-server policy, with a transition rate that depends on the total number of tokens in $P1$, while it is clearly not possible to allow an infinite-server semantics with respect to different colors, but single-server within another color (from a modelling point of view, this would mean that one server is dedicated to each color).

Two new rules can be defined, that allow the elimination of portions of a color component rather than the whole component.

CRR_2: Elimination of a color if not immediately used

Rule CRR_2 applies when a new color is "created" by transition t but it is not immediately used in a synchronization. The creation of the new color can therefore be postponed.

This reduction is illustrated in Fig. 3.16: the color to be eliminated corresponds to variable x. This variable is "created" by t_1, since it appears only once in the function associated with the arc from t_1 to p, and it does not appear in the predicate of t_1. We are assuming that x appears only once in the input and output functions of p, and that this color is not used by transition t_2 in a synchronization: indeed t_2 has only one input arc from p, with an associated function that is simple and contains only one occurrence of x. This same variable appears in at least one output arc function of t_2. Moreover, the rate/weight of t_1 does not depend on the specific value assigned to x. We further assume, without loss of generality, that x corresponds to the first component in

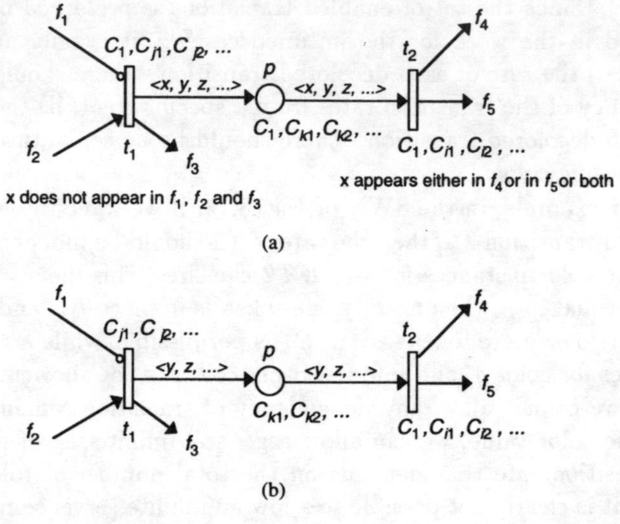

FIGURE 3.16. The effect of the color reduction rule CRR_2

the color domain of p.

The reduction removes the color from the color domain of t_1 and of p; as a consequence, variable x disappears from the input and output arc functions of p. The effect of this reduction is to "merge" all the color instances of t_1 with the same value of the variable x, and "merge" all the color instances of p with the same first component.

By observing the effect of the reduction on the unfolding, one can realize that the instances of t_1 that are merged were in free-choice conflict in the original net. If C_1 is the type of x, then the number of concurrently enabled instances of t_1 (in any marking) is reduced by a factor $|C_1|$ by the application of the rule. To compensate the loss of concurrency it is therefore necessary to multiply the weight/rate of (each instance of) t_1 by $|C_1|$.

On the contrary, by merging the instances of p, we may increase the number of (possibly) enabled instances of t_2 (x is no longer constrained by the marking of p). This is a problem only if t_2 is timed. In this case we require an infinite-server semantics for t_2, and divide its rate by the cardinality of the color class C_1 of x. The reason for dividing the rate by $|C_1|$ is that, after the reduction, t_2 makes a (free) choice of a value for x among the objects in C_1 and we assume a uniform probability distribution over C_1.

CRR_3: **Elimination of a color "swallowed" by a transition**

Rule CRR_3 applies when a color is "destroyed" (or swallowed) by a transition, but it could have been already eliminated before by the firing that put tokens into the input place of the transition. The reduction anticipates the color elimination of one step.

The reduction is illustrated in Fig. 3.17: the color to be eliminated corresponds to variable x. We are again assuming (without loss of generality) that x corresponds to the first component in the color domain of p (the input and output arc functions of p are simple functions, and x appears only once in all of them). The variable x is "swallowed" by t_2 (it doesn't appear in any output arc function), however, since it is not used by t_2 (the only output transition of p) in a synchronization, and provided that the rate/weight function associated with t_2 does not depend on the specific color assigned to variable x, it can be removed from the color domain of t_2; as a consequence, the corresponding color component of p should be removed as well. After the reduction, x may be "swallowed" by some input transition of p (all those transitions that do not have variable x in any output arc function). In Fig. 3.17 we consider a case in which x does not disappear from the color domain of the input transitions $(t_{11}, \dots, t_{1h})$ of p. Note that transitions $t_{11}, \dots, t_{1h}$ do not have necessarily the same number of input, output and inhibition places as the picture may suggest.

The effect of this reduction is to merge all the instances of p with equal first component, and all the instances of t_2 with the same value of x. If t_2 is timed with infinite-server semantics, then the timed behavior can be preserved by keeping the infinite-server semantics after the reduction. If t_2 is timed with single-server semantics, then the reduction is possible only if p is color-safe for any color in its color domain (a place p is *color safe* for color q if there can be at most one token of color q in p, in any reachable state): in this case the semantics of t_2 is changed to infinite-server in the reduced net. If t_2 is immediate, no problem arises, because the merged instances of t_2 are non-conflicting in the original net (conflicts exist neither among the different instances, nor with respect to other transitions). The transitions $t_{11}, \dots, t_{1h}$ are not affected by the reduction (their color domains and enabling conditions remain unchanged).

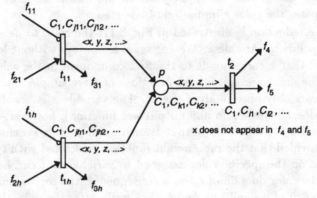

x appears either in f_{11} or in f_{21} or in f_{31}

x does not appear in f_4 and f_5

x appears either in f_{1h} or in f_{2h} or in f_{3h}

(a)

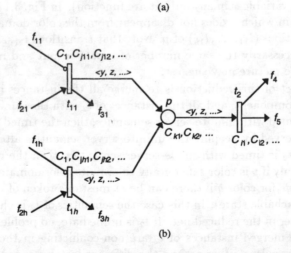

(b)

FIGURE 3.17. The effect of the color reduction rule CRR_3

CRR_4: **Manipulation of non free-choice conflicts of immediate transitions**

This reduction rule is an extension of rule RR_9 to the colored case. The rule can be applied when the structure of the subnet to be reduced is the same as that considered by rule RR_9, while all places and transitions have the same color domain and all arc functions are identity functions. Indeed, in this case the colored subnet is just a superposition of several identical (not connected) uncolored nets, and the reduction rule works on all the copies at the same time. The color domain of the new set of timed transitions that replace the timed transition and the conflicting immediate transitions in the original net is equal to the color domain of the originating transitions, and all arc functions are still identities.

For example, let us consider an SWN model with the same net structure as the GSPN model in Fig. 3.4(a), with color domain $C_1 \times C_2$ for all transitions and places, except for p_a and p_b that may have different color domains, and with function $< x, y >$ associated with all arcs in the net except for the input arcs of T that may be associated with any type of function, possibly containing occurrences of variables x and y. This means that there are $|C_1|\,|C_2|$ identical (and not connected) replicas of the net comprising T, t_1, t_2, p, p_1, p_2, p_3 and p_4. The SWN model obtained after the reduction has the same net structure of the GSPN model in Fig. 3.4(b), color domain $C_1 \times C_2$ for all places except p_a and p_b (that maintain their previous color domain) and for all transitions, and function $< x, y >$ associated with all arcs in the net (except those associated with the arcs out of p_a and p_b that remain unchanged).

Concerning the specification of the timing aspects, the same considerations already made in the uncolored case apply.

Observe that in the example above the identity functions on the input and output arcs of place p are actually expressed using the same tuple of variables. When all the input/output arc functions of the place are identity functions, but use different variables (e.g., if all the input/output arc functions of T in the example were $< a, b >$ instead of $< x, y >$), the reduction rule can still be applied after a renaming of the variables. Indeed, the behavior of an SWN model is not affected by a renaming of variables, provided that all occurrences of the same variable in the input, inhibition and output arc functions and in the predicate associated with the same transition are renamed consistently.

The same type of extension can be applied to reduction rule RR_8.

3.5.   REDUCTION OF THE SWN MO-DEL OF THE POLLING SYSTEM

The SWN model of a random polling system depicted in Fig. 3.15 considers servers and queues with identities, while the GSPN model presented in Section 3.3 keeps the identity of queues only. An SWN model with no server identities is presented in Fig. 3.18(a), where color R has been dropped. The reader may want to check that the model of Fig. 3.18(a) can be obtained from the model of Fig. 3.15 through application of rule CRR_1 on the color component of servers.

Transitions t_r and T_w and place p_w have color domain $Q \times Q$, meaning that each token is a pair (origin, destination), while all other places and transitions in the model have color domain Q, representing either the queue visited by a server, or the queue of a customer.

The model can be considered as the composition of the queue submodel with the server movement submodel. We describe the queue model first.

Transition T_a of color q models the customer arrival process at queue q ($q \in Q$); it is assigned a rate λ and a "single server per color" semantics, meaning that each transition instance has a single server semantics. Customers waiting for a server are queued in place p_q, while a token of color q in place p_p represents the server when polling queue q. Transition t_s fires for color q if a server of color q finds a waiting customer of color q when it polls the queue, so that service can be provided; if the server of color q finds no waiting customer with its same color, then t_w fires for color q, and the server moves to the next queue. One token of color q in place p_s represents a customer of queue q being served, as well as the server when providing service at queue q. T_s is timed with a delay equal to the customer service time. The delay is independent from the color. The server moves to place p_r at the end of the visit at queue q (after the service completion represented by the firing for color q of T_s, if a waiting customer was found; after the firing for color q of t_w if no waiting customer was found).

Consider now the subnet describing the choice of the next queue to be visited and the movement towards that queue. A server that leaves queue q is modelled by a token of color q in place p_r; the choice

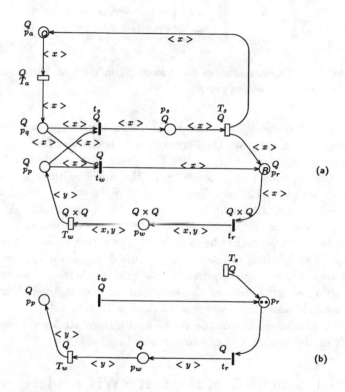

FIGURE 3.18. The first SWN model of a multiserver random polling system (a) and the result of the first reduction (b)

transition	weight	priority/semantics
t_s	1	1
t_w	1	1
t_r	1	1
T_a	λ	single-server per color
T_s	μ	single-server per color
T_w	ω	infinite-server per color

TABLE 3.4. Characteristics of the transitions in the first SWN model of a multiserver random polling system

for the next queue is modelled by immediate transition t_r. If a token of color q is in place p_r, then transition t_r is enabled for N instances, of color (q, q_i), for $i = 1, \ldots N$. The firing of transition t_r for color (q, p) corresponds to the selection of the queue with index p as the next queue to be visited. Since the next queue to be visited must be selected according to a uniform distribution encompassing all queues, the N instances of the immediate transition have identical weights. After the next queue has been selected, the server walks to the chosen queue. The instance of color (q, p) of timed transition T_w, models the walk time to reach queue p from queue q; since there can be more than one server walking between the same pair of queues, then all instances are assigned an infinite-server semantics, with rate ω.

The characteristics of the timed and immediate transitions in the SWN model in Fig. 3.18 are summarized in Table 3.4.

3.5.1. The SRG of the first SWN model

The second column of Table 3.5 shows the number of symbolic tangible markings obtained for the model in Fig. 3.18(a) with two servers, for a variable number of queues. In parentheses is shown the number of corresponding ordinary markings. The latter number is computed by the symbolic reachability graph algorithm as an additional information: the computation is based only on the cardinality of the color classes and on the structure of each symbolic marking, and it does not require the construction of the ordinary RG (this explains why numbers of the order of 10^9 can be handled). Note that the tangible and vanishing ordinary state spaces are identical to those generated by the GSPN model in Fig. 3.6.

The drastic difference between the number of symbolic and ordinary states is motivated by the great symmetry of the system: symmetries are automatically discovered and exploited in the SRG construction.

An analysis of the symbolic states reveals that the SRG construction is able to "forget" the queue index when it is not strictly necessary: indeed, each symbolic marking represents a set of ordinary states characterized by the same number of queues with a customer waiting, and the same number of queues with a customer in service.

3.5.2. Reduction of the SWN model

We now show how the SWN model in Fig. 3.18(a) can be progressively reduced through the application of the SWN reduction rules, until all colors are removed, and an equivalent GSPN model is obtained.

Observe that the portion of color component representing the origin of a walk (variable x on the path $T_s \rightarrow p_r \rightarrow t_r \rightarrow p_w \rightarrow T_w$) is "swallowed" by transition T_w, and that this color is not used in the path for a synchronization. We can thus apply rule CRR_3 to the subnet t_r, p_w, and T_w, and to the subnet t_w, T_s, p_r and t_r. Indeed, after the first reduction, transition t_r "swallows" the color corresponding to variable x, while after the second reduction the color is swallowed by t_w; the reduction rule cannot be applied further, because x is used in a synchronization by transition t_w. Note that the decolorization of p_r causes also a decolorization of the tokens in its initial marking.

After the reduction, the server movement submodel in Fig. 3.18(a) is transformed as shown in Fig. 3.18(b); observe that place p_r is now neutral, and it has therefore been initialized with S neutral tokens (in the figure $S = 2$). The numbers of symbolic and equivalent ordinary markings of the new model are given in the third column of Table 3.5.

We can now apply reduction rule CRR_2 to the subnet $t_r - p_w - T_w$ with respect to the color represented by variable y: this color is not used in a synchronization up to transitions t_s and t_w. Moreover, due to the system symmetries, the color is never used to assign a weight to the instances of the transitions involved in the reduction. Observe that the transformation requires, according to rule CRR_2, that the rate of T_w be divided by the number of queues (N).

This decolorization makes the (now) neutral immediate transition

N	Fig. 3.18 (a)	Fig. 3.18 (b)	Fig. 3.19	Fig. 3.20
2	31/31	12/18	6/13	6
	(57/62)	(21/34)	(9/24)	(9)
3	91/69	21/30	9/20	9
	(474/384)	(90/141)	(26/80)	(26)
4	161/107	30/42	12/27	12
	(2712/1744)	(312/476)	(72/240)	(72)
5	231/145	39/54	15/34	15
	(12480/6640)	(960/1435)	(192/672)	(192)
6	301/183	48/66	18/41	18
	(49776/22560)	(2736/4027)	(496/1792)	(496)
7	371/221	57/78	21/48	21
	(179424/70805)	(7932/10745)	(1248/4608)	(1248)
8	441/259	66/90	24/55	24
	(599808/209436)	(19200/27640)	(3072/11520)	(3072)
9	511/297	75/102	27/62	27
	$(1.9\,10^6/0.6\,10^6)$	(46384/69111)	(7424/28160)	(7424)
10	581/335	84/114	·30/69	30
	$(5.7\,10^6/1.6\,10^6)$	(119040/168950)	(17664/67584)	(17664)
20	–	174/234	60/139	60
	–	$(479\,10^6/660\,10^6)$	$(61\,10^6/242\,10^6)$	$(61\,10^6)$
30	–	264/354	90/209	90
	–	$(1.1\,10^9/1.5\,10^9)$	$(133\,10^9/532\,10^9)$	$(133\,10^9)$
100	–	894/1194	300/699	300
	–	(–)	(–)	(–)

TABLE 3.5. Symbolic state space cardinality (tangible/vanishing) for SWN models of a random polling system with two servers and queue capacities equal to one. Numbers in parentheses refer to the equivalent ordinary markings.

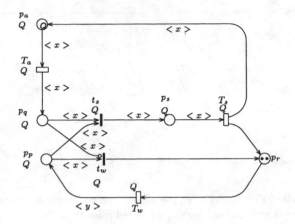

FIGURE 3.19. Reduced SWN model after the application of rule CRR_2

t_r obviously redundant, and it can therefore be removed through rule RR_3, reducing the subnet $p_r - t_r - p_w$ into place p_r.

The SWN model resulting from the application of the reduction rules to the SWN in Fig. 3.18(b) is depicted in Fig. 3.19. For this model the fourth column of Table 3.5 shows the number of symbolic and equivalent ordinary markings.

Observe that this reduction process can be interpreted as an exchange of the free-choice conflict of the N instances of the immediate transition t_r with the instances of the timed transition T_w, much along the lines of the GSPN rule RR_{10}.

Following the same process as for the GSPN model, we now remove immediate transitions in order to eliminate vanishing markings. Indeed we can apply rule CRR_4 to the subnet comprising the timed transition T_w, the two (conflicting) immediate transitions t_s and t_w, and the places p_p and p_q. Observe that being t_s and t_w mutually exclusive, and since one of the two must necessarily be enabled after the firing of T_w, then only two timed transitions are introduced by the reduction. Moreover, place p_p becomes disconnected from the rest of the net, and can be removed. Observe also that before applying the reduction rule we need to rename variable y of T_w to x.

The result of this reduction is the SWN model of Fig. 3.20(a). The number of symbolic states for this model is reported in the fifth column of Table 3.5.

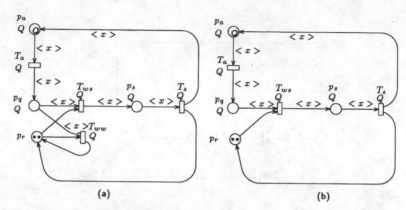

FIGURE 3.20. SWN Model after the elimination of immediate transitions (a), and after the removal of non significant timed transitions (b)

Observe that no instance of the timed transitions T_{ww} modifies the marking, hence this transition can be removed from the model by applying rule RR_2, that can be trivially extended to SWNs, yielding the SWN model depicted in Fig. 3.20(b).

As a final step, the SWN model in Fig. 3.20(b) can be completely decolored since the identity of the color is not essential in the model evolution. The model obtained by decoloring the SWN is actually a GSPN, with a number of states equal to the number of symbolic markings of the SWN in Fig. 3.20. The GSPN model that we obtain is the same that was obtained at the end of the reduction process of the GSPN model, and shown in Fig. 3.13(a).

3.6.   CONCLUSIONS

In this chapter we have presented in a common framework reduction rules for both GSPN and SWN models, as well as their application to the simplification of models of a symmetric multiserver random polling system.

Reductions for GSPN models are based on the elimination of immediate transitions, and on the simplification of subnets without altering the model behavior. Reductions for SWN models are based on the simplification of the color structure, and on the elimination of immediate transitions.

Some of the reduction techniques presented and used in this chapter are novel. Structural decolorization approaches in SWNs were previously defined only for untimed models, and their timed extension is presented here for the first time; new are also the two rules for the partial decolorization of a color component in SWNs. The rules for the elimination of immediate transitions in SWNs are a novel extension of rules known for GSPNs to the case of colored models.

It is quite interesting to observe that starting from either a GSPN model or an SWN model of the same multiserver random polling system, we have reached the same compact GSPN model. This may give the impression of an equivalent power in the reduction processes with the two formalisms. However, in the case of SWNs, the reduction process is entirely based on formalized reduction rules, while the ingenuity of the modeller is necessary in the case of GSPNs, where not all the reduction steps can be automated.

This difference indicates that the use of a more powerful formalism like SWN induces the modeller to embed in the representation a knowledge of the high-level behavior of the system, and in particular the description of its symmetries, that can be then automatically exploited to produce models with smaller state spaces.

This is quite an important point in favor of SWN models, and leaves hope for the possible integration of reduction as an automatic preliminary step in the model solution process. The problem that however still has to be solved concerns the decision about the sequence of application of the reduction rules. Indeed, nothing guarantees that the rules can be applied in any order, and that the final result be the same in all cases. More research in this direction is necessary before the reduction of a Petri net model can be made transparent to the user.

REFERENCES

1. M. AJMONE MARSAN, G. BALBO, G. CONTE, "A Class of Generalized Stochastic Petri Nets for the Performance Evaluation of Multiprocessor Systems", <u>ACM Transactions on Computer Systems</u>, **2**, 2 (May 1984).

2. M. AJMONE MARSAN, G. BALBO, G. CHIOLA, G. CONTE, "Generalized Stochastic Petri Nets Revisited: Random Switches and Priorities", <u>Proceedings of the second International Work-</u>

shop on Petri Nets and Performance Models (PNPM87), (Madison, Wisconsin, USA, August 1987).

3. M. AJMONE MARSAN, "Stochastic Petri Nets: an Elementary Introduction", in: G. ROZENBERG (editor), Advances in Petri Nets 1989, Lecture Notes in Computer Science **424**, (Springer Verlag, 1990).

4. M. AJMONE MARSAN, G. BALBO, G. CHIOLA, G. CONTE, S. DONATELLI, G.FRANCESCHINIS, "An Introduction to Generalized Stochastic Petri Nets", Microelectronics and Reliability, **31**, 4 (1991).

5. M. AJMONE MARSAN, S. DONATELLI, F. NERI, U.RUBINO, "On the Construction of Abstract GSPNs: An Exercise in Modeling", Proceedings of the fourth International Conference on Petri Nets and Performance Models (PNPM91), (Melbourne, Australia, December 1991).

6. M. AJMONE MARSAN, G. BALBO, G. CONTE, S. DONATELLI, G.FRANCESCHINIS, Modelling with Generalized Stochastic Petri Nets, (John Wiley & Sons, 1995).

7. G. CHIOLA, G. FRANCESCHINIS, "Colored GSPN Models and Automatic Symmetry Detection", Proceedings of the third International Workshop on Petri Nets and Performance Models (PNPM89), (Kyoto, Japan, December 1989).

8. G. CHIOLA, C. DUTHEILLET, G. FRANCESCHINIS, S. HADDAD, "On Well-Formed Colored Nets and their Symbolic Reachability Graph", Proceedings of the eleventh International Conference on Application and Theory of Petri Nets, (Paris, France, June 1990). [reprinted in High-Level Petri Nets. Theory and Application, edited by K. JENSEN and G. ROZENBERG, (Springer Verlag, 1991)]

9. G. CHIOLA, S. DONATELLI, G. FRANCESCHINIS, "GSPN versus SPN: What is the Actual Role of Immediate Transitions?," Proceedings of the fourth International Conference on Petri Nets and Performance Models (PNPM91), (Melbourne, Australia, December 1991).

10. G. CHIOLA, G. FRANCESCHINIS, "A Structural Color Simplification in Well-Formed Colored Nets", Proceedings of the fourth International Conference on Petri Nets and Performance Models (PNPM91), (Melbourne, Australia, December 1991).

11. G. CHIOLA, M. AJMONE MARSAN, G. BALBO, G. CONTE, "Generalized Stochastic Petri Nets: a Definition at the Net Level and its Implications," IEEE Transactions on Software Engineering, **19**, 2 (February 1993).

12. G. CHIOLA, C. DUTHEILLET, G. FRANCESCHINIS, S. HADDAD, "Stochastic Well-Formed Colored Nets and Symmetric Modelling Applications," IEEE Transactions on Computers, **42**, 11 (November 1993).

13. G. CHIOLA, G. FRANCESCHINIS, R. GAETA, M. RIBAUDO, "GreatSPN1.7: GRaphical Editor and Analyzer for Timed and Stochastic Petri Nets", Performance Evaluation: special issue on Performance Modeling Tools, **24**, 1-2 (November 1995).

14. J.M. COLOM, M. SILVA, "Improving the Linearly Based Characterization of P/T Nets", Proceedings of the tenth International Conference on Application and Theory of Petri Nets, (Bonn, Germany, June 1989).

15. K. JENSEN, Colored Petri Nets: Basic Concepts, Analysis Methods and Practical Use, (Springer Verlag, 1995).

16. J.G.KEMENY, J.L. SNELL, Finite Markov Chains, (Van Nostrand, 1960).

17. M. SILVA, Las Redes de Petri en la Automatica y la Informatica, (Ed. AC, Madrid, Spain, 1985).

18. C. SIMONE, M. AJMONE MARSAN, "The Application of EB-Equivalence Rules to the Structural Reduction of GSPN Models", Journal of Parallel and Distributed Computing, **15**, 3 (July 1992).

CHAPTER 4

TRAFFIC MODELING FOR ATM NETWORKS

Carey L. Williamson

4.1. INTRODUCTION

Workload modeling is a vital component of any simulation study. Outputs from a simulation model are highly dependent on the inputs provided to the model, and without realistic input workload models, the simulation results are of little value.

Many simulation studies use very simple network traffic models. Typical modeling assumptions include the assumption that packet arrivals are Poisson, that packet traffic is uniformly distributed among all the hosts on the network, and that all traffic streams are independent.

Measurement studies of packet traffic on real networks have shown that these assumptions do not hold in practice[1,2,3]. Packet arrivals are invariably bursty, and tend to be correlated over surprisingly long time intervals. Long range dependence and other non-Poisson behaviours have been identified in local area network (LAN) traffic[1], wide area network (WAN) traffic[2], and compressed video traffic[3]. Thus any simulation study that uses simplistic traffic modeling assumptions is unlikely to make accurate performance predictions. More realistic traffic models are required for accurate simulation studies[4].

The purpose of this chapter is to describe three non-trivial network traffic models that have been designed and implemented for use in network simulations[5,6,7]. In particular, these traffic models have been

built as part of the TeleSim project, the goal of which is to design
high performance parallel simulation tools for the design and analysis
of telecommunications networks. The traffic models are currently used
in a high fidelity cell-level ATM (Asynchronous Transfer Mode) network simulator, called ATM-TN (ATM Traffic and Network model),
developed by the TeleSim project participants[8].

The goal in the traffic modeling effort for the TeleSim project was
to design a small set of accurate and representative workload models
to use as inputs for the overall ATM-TN simulation engine. *Synthetic*
workload models were chosen to provide concise mathematical representations of the workload characteristics of existing network applications,
eliminating the need for lengthy packet-level traces as input to simulations (which are undesirable for reasons of flexibility, storage, and
simulation execution time).

Three specific input traffic types were chosen as representative examples of applications on high speed networks: MPEG (Motion Pictures Experts Group) compressed video, aggregate Ethernet LAN traffic, and Internet World Wide Web (WWW) traffic. Video traffic is
one of the most bandwidth-intensive applications on high speed networks, and variable bit rate video (i.e., compressed video) is one of the
most important classes of video to consider in the context of ATM networks. The MPEG video model is designed to model this compressed
video traffic. The Ethernet LAN traffic model is designed to model the
aggregate data packet traffic generated across an ATM backbone network connecting campus-area LANs. The Internet World Wide Web
model is designed to capture the workload characteristics of the application protocol that is the fastest-growing consumer of bandwidth on
the NSFNET backbone.

Each of the three workload models has its own specific workload
characteristics and parameters. To the extent possible, the construction
and parameterization of the workload models has been based on empirical network traffic measurement and workload characterization in our
own local area network environment. The models also draw upon network measurement results and innovative traffic modeling techniques
in the recent published literature[1,2,3,9,10].

The next three sections describe the design and construction of each
of these three models.

4.2. MPEG VIDEO TRAFFIC MODEL

4.2.1. Purpose

The MPEG video traffic model in ATM-TN is designed to model the unidirectional transmission of a single variable bit rate (VBR) compressed video stream in an ATM network, where the video source is compressed according to the MPEG standard. MPEG defines a standardized method for compressing full-motion video for storage as digital data. For viewing, this data is transmitted over a network as an MPEG stream and decoded at its destination.

4.2.2. Background

The MPEG standard is intended primarily for use with stored video applications (e.g., entertainment video), but it can also support some limited real-time (i.e., "live") video applications, such as desktop video-conferencing, depending on the compression hardware available. Because the encoding of an MPEG video sequence usually takes much longer than decoding, a video sequence is usually encoded only once and stored in compressed form. Playback can then be done as many times as desired. The decoding of MPEG video sequences can be done in real time.

The MPEG video stream consists of a sequence of images called *frames* that are displayed one after the other, at short periodic intervals (e.g., 30 frames per second). The MPEG standard defines three types of compressed frames:

I I (Intraframe) frames are encoded using only the image data available in one frame. Since I frames represent a complete image, they provide an absolute reference point for the other two image types in the MPEG sequence, which are encoded using interframe coding (i.e., they express the relative differences from one frame to the next).

I frames are compressed using Discrete Cosine Transform (DCT), similar to the JPEG (Joint Photographic Experts Group) standard for single image compression. I frames take the least time to compress, but have the least compression.

P In addition to DCT compressed data, P (Predictive) frames contain motion-compensated data predicted from the preceding (I or P) frame. P frames take longer to encode than I frames, are faster to decode than I frames, and achieve higher compression than I frames.

B B (Bidirectional interpolative) frames are similar to P frames, but they contain motion-compensated data from both the previous and the next frame (I or P). B frames take the longest time to encode, but offer the highest levels of compression.

An MPEG sequence thus consists of a pattern of I, P, and B frames, called a Group Of Pictures (GOP). The GOP pattern must be specified at the time of encoding, and must start with an I frame. The same encoding pattern is then used repeatedly for the duration of the video sequence, with each new I frame starting a new GOP. An example of a typical MPEG sequence is IBBPBBPBBIBBPBBPBBI..., where the GOP pattern is IBBPBBPBB. Significant correlations (i.e., autocorrelation and cross-correlation) have been observed in the sizes of the frames in an MPEG video sequence[9].

4.2.3. Modeling Methodology

The MPEG video sources are modeled using the Transform-Expand-Sample (TES) modeling methodology[9,10] developed by Melamed *et al.* TES provides a fast method to generate autocorrelated time series. In this particular case, TES is used to generate autocorrelated time series data that closely resembles the output of an MPEG stream.

Three separate TES processes are used, with one for each type of MPEG frame. The marginal distribution (i.e., frequency histogram) and autocorrelation function of frame sizes (done separately for I, P, and B frames) are the key inputs to the TES modeling process. These inputs have been used to derive a separate TES model for each frame type. Each of these models is saved in a TES model specification file that is used by the MPEG source model. The three frame types are then interleaved as determined by the GOP pattern. Dependence between frame types (as has been empirically observed in MPEG sequences) is created by duplicating the TES background variate of the I frame at the beginning of each GOP. The resulting cross-correlation between frame sizes increases the accuracy of the model[3,9]. Thus the final MPEG model is a composite TES model. The model has been parameterized based on empirical studies of MPEG sequences (i.e., using MPEG data provided with `testool`[9,10]).

4.2.4. Model Parameters

The final MPEG model has four parameters: (1) the GOP (Group of Pictures) structure of the MPEG stream; (2) a scaling factor for the average bit rate; (3) the frame rate for the displayed video; and (4) a smoothing parameter for shaping the video source.

4.2.5. Model Validation

The MPEG model in ATM-TN was validated by comparing its generated frame sizes to those of the sample MPEG data and models shipped with the testool software. Our MPEG model matched very closely with all three traces provided. A version of our MPEG model was also parameterized to generate traffic that closely matches the JPEG data available for the movie *Star Wars*[3]. The ability of our video traffic model to match both MPEG and JPEG empirical traces illustrates the power and generality of the TES modeling methodology.

4.2.6. An Example

An example of the frame size information generated by the MPEG model is illustrated in Figure 4.1. The graph shows 100 frames generated by the MPEG model, where the GOP is IBBPBBPBBI. Assuming a frame display rate of 30 frames per second, this video sequence corresponds to an average bit rate of 9 Mbps. The distinctive pattern of I frames, P frames, and B frames is easily discernible in the graph, as well as the significant correlation in the sizes of successive frames of the same type.

4.2.7. Summary

Compressed video traffic is likely to be one of the dominant traffic types on future high speed networks. Our MPEG traffic model in ATM-TN is capable of modeling the precise structure and correlation empirically observed in compressed video traffic streams.

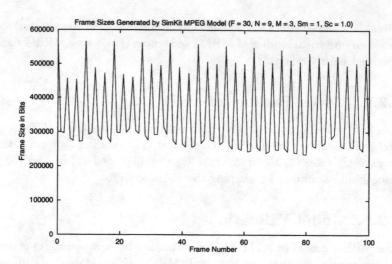

Figure 4.1: Example of Frame Sizes Generated by MPEG Model

4.3. ETHERNET LAN TRAFFIC MODEL

Recent research in network traffic measurement has established the "self-similar" nature of aggregate Ethernet LAN traffic[1], as well as the presence of self-similarity in Internet traffic[2] and video traffic[3] as well. This "non-Poisson" behaviour has serious implications on the performance of networks and systems that have been designed on the assumption of uncorrelated Poisson traffic.

Understanding the performance implications of self-similar traffic is thus important to network designers and planners, and is especially relevant in the context of ATM networks. The ATM-TN TeleSim project has thus incorporated a self-similar Ethernet traffic model into its set of synthetic workload models for the ATM-TN network simulator.

4.3.1. Purpose

The Ethernet LAN traffic model in the ATM-TN TeleSim project is designed to represent the workload characteristics of aggregate data packet traffic on existing local area networks, such as campus LANs. The model produces a unidirectional flow of ATM cells, with statistical characteristics matching those of aggregated traffic.

The Ethernet model is capable of generating self-similar traffic with various degrees of self-similarity, and various network utilizations. This model is useful as a background traffic generator for network backbone traffic, as well as a "worst-case" stress test for ATM switches and ATM networks.

4.3.2. Background

Modeling studies of Ethernet performance often make many simplifying assumptions, such as assuming that the packet arrival process is Poisson. The results of some recent measurement studies, however, have shown that traffic is very much *not* Poisson[1,2]. In particular, Ethernet LAN traffic has been found to have a "fractal" self-similarity property. Such behaviour has potentially serious implications on the design, control, modeling and analysis of high speed cell-based networks.

The paper[1] by Leland *et al.* demonstrates that Ethernet LAN traffic is statistically self-similar in the sense that there is no natural length of a burst: at time scales ranging from milliseconds to seconds to minutes, similar-looking traffic bursts are evident. Mathematically speaking, a stochastic time series process $X = (X(t) : t = 0, 1, 2, \ldots)$ is said to be self-similar with self-similar Hurst parameter H if the process is covariance stationary (that is, the process has constant mean and finite constant variance) and the corresponding aggregated process has the same correlation structure as the original process (exactly self-similar) or agrees asymptotically with the correlation structure of the original process (asymptotically self-similar) over large intervals.

The Hurst parameter H provides a measure of the degree of self-similarity in the traffic. The Hurst parameter expresses the behaviour of the rescaled adjusted range statistic (R/S statistic) for large sample sizes n. For many naturally occurring time series, including Ethernet traffic, $E[R(n)/S(n)]$ is proportional to n^H, with H typically about 0.7. For models with only short-range dependence, H is 0.5. This discrepancy is called the Hurst effect[1].

Self-similarity manifests itself in a number of ways. One manifestation is a slowly decaying variance. That is, if one takes the original time series X and computes a new smoothed time series by averaging every non-overlapping group of m observations to get a new time series $X^{(m)}$, then the variance of the sample mean for the new time series $X^{(m)}$ decreases more slowly than the sample size m (i.e., $Var(X^{(m)}) \approx am^{-\beta}$ as $m \to \infty$, where a is a constant, and $0 < \beta < 1$). On a log-log plot of the variance of $X^{(m)}$ versus m, the result is a straight line with (negative) slope β. The Hurst parameter H can be estimated using $H = 1 - \frac{\beta}{2}$. A second manifestation is a hyperbolically decaying auto-correlation function of the form $AF(k) \approx ck^{-\beta}$, for some constant c. If X is self-similar, then the autocorrelation function for $X^{(m)}$ is indistin-guishable from the autocorrelation function for X, for any value of m. A third manifestation is a straight line of slope β on a log-log plot of the R/S statistic.

Ethernet traffic has been found to have this self-similarity property, and the degree of self-similarity tends to increase with the load level on the Ethernet[1]. Furthermore, the self-similarity property has been found to hold both in the traffic within a LAN, as well as in the traffic leaving a LAN destined for the Internet. In short, the self-similarity property is pervasive enough to merit its inclusion in the traffic model · for aggregate LAN packet traffic.

4.3.3. Modeling Methodology

A synthetic workload model for self-similar Ethernet traffic was con-structed using a two step process.

The first step of the modeling process used an S program to generate a self-similar time series based on Fast Fourier Transform inversion[2]. The S program produces as output a zero-mean time series with self-similarity controlled by an input parameter H (the Hurst parameter). Time series were generated for five different values of H (namely, $H = 0.5, 0.6, 0.7, 0.8$, and 0.9). The output time series from the S program were then translated and scaled (within S) to produce non-negative Ethernet packet count time series with a specified mean network uti-lization U. These synthetically generated time series were then used as input to the second step of the modeling process.

The second step of the modeling process used the TES modeling methodology[9]. While TES cannot (yet) truly model self-similarity, TES provides a very general approach to modeling first-order (i.e., frequency histogram) and second-order (i.e., autocorrelation function) statistics of time series. In this case, the time series of interest is the "packet count per interval" time series from the first step above. The `testool`[10] program was used to construct an abstract TES model that had the same frequency histogram and autocorrelation function as the (syn-thetic) Ethernet time series. One TES model was constructed for each value of H considered. The resulting TES models were converted (automatically) to C^{++}, and incorporated into the ATM-TN simulator.

4.3.4. Parameters

The Ethernet traffic model in the ATM-TN simulator has two parameters:

- **H**: The Hurst parameter $0.5 \leq H < 1$ expresses the degree of self-similarity in the traffic. Data sets with higher self-similarity parameter H have higher "burstiness", in the intuitive sense.

  Empirical measurements of Ethernet traffic[1] suggest that the value of H for aggregated LAN traffic is $0.7 \leq H \leq 0.9$.

- **U**: The network utilization $0 \leq U \leq 1$ determines the average load level offered by the Ethernet LAN, as a fraction of its total 10 Mbps bandwidth. Most Ethernets operate at low to moderate levels of load (e.g., 1% to 30% utilization).

  The utilization U has been empirically observed to have an effect on the degree of self-similarity observed in the traffic[1]. The higher the network load, the higher the degree of self-similarity usually observed. Despite this observation in the literature, the Ethernet model in the TeleSim project treats H and U as two independent and orthogonal parameters.

4.3.5. Model Validation

The Ethernet traffic model was tested using the standard statistical methods described in the literature[1,2,3]. The main methods used in the analysis are variance-time plots, and time-domain analysis based on the R/S-statistic. The latter method subdivides a given sample of N observations into K non-overlapping blocks and computes the rescaled adjusted range statistic (R/S statistic)[1]. Graphical R/S analysis is used to estimate the Hurst parameter H from the graph's asymptotic slope. More detail about the testing of the Ethernet model is reported in a separate paper[6].

4.3.6. An Example

Figure 4.2 illustrates two examples of the synthetic Ethernet traffic generated by our model: one for $H = 0.5$, and one for $H = 0.9$. The traffic generated by each model is shown in the bottom row of graphs in Figure 4.2. The graphs illustrate several characteristics of the synthetically generated Ethernet traces, such as their burstiness and correlation.

Furthermore, Figure 4.2 shows the effects of aggregating (in the time domain) the Ethernet traffic time series, for different values of the Hurst parameter H, and different levels of aggregation M. These plots are shown in a format similar to Figure 4 in the paper by Leland *et al.*[1] When $H = 0.5$ in Figure 4.2 (i.e., the leftmost column), the time series aggregates to smooth traffic quite quickly as M increases from 1 to 1000. When $H = 0.9$ (i.e., the rightmost column), the traffic remains bursty across three or four orders of magnitude in the time domain, similar to the traffic in the Leland *et al.* paper[1]. Our traffic model becomes smooth sooner than their traffic because our TES model only approximates self-similarity. That is, our TES model captures the short range and medium range dependence in the traffic, but is unable to capture the very long range dependence observed in real traffic. Despite this deficiency, we believe that our synthetic workload model is a reasonably good generator of self-similar traffic.

4.3.7. Summary

This section has presented a synthetic workload model that is capable of approximating self-similar Ethernet traffic. The model captures the correlation and long range dependence that has been observed in recent measurements of Ethernet LAN traffic[1]. Self-similar traffic models are a valuable tool in network simulation, providing for "worst-case" stress testing of ATM networks.

4.4. WORLD WIDE WEB TRAFFIC MODE

The World Wide Web (also called WWW, or the Web) is a hypermedia-based globally distributed information system. A standard language called HTML (HyperText Markup Language) is used to define the content and structure of documents, called *Web pages*, and the links, called *hyperlinks*, from one Web page to the next. Web pages at a given site

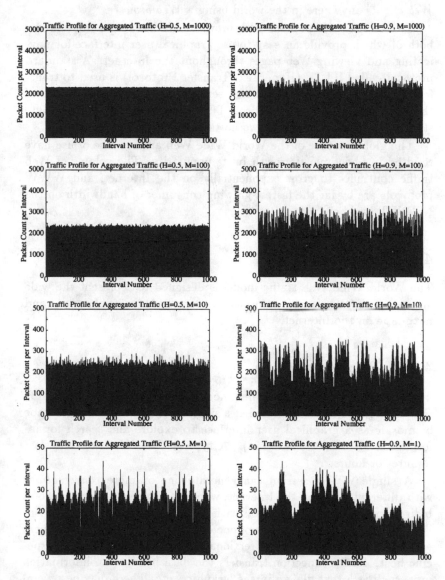

Figure 4.2: Effect of aggregation on Ethernet traffic model: $H = 0.5$ vs $H = 0.9$

are stored as files on a *Web server*, and these pages can be accessed by *Web clients* anywhere in the world using a *Web browser*.

Two of the most popular Web browsers are `netscape` and `mosaic`, both of which provide an easy-to-use graphical user interface for navigating and viewing Web pages throughout the Internet. A standard protocol called HTTP (HyperText Transfer Protocol) is used to transfer Web pages between clients and servers. HTTP is built on top of the Transmission Control Protocol (TCP), which provides reliable byte stream delivery between any two hosts on a TCP/IP internetwork.

The global nature of the World Wide Web and its ease of use have resulted in phenomenal growth in its popularity. The volume of Web traffic continues to grow exponentially on the Internet, and WWW protocols are by far the fastest growing consumer of bandwidth on the NSFNET backbone[5].

4.4.1. Purpose

The World Wide Web traffic model is designed to represent the wide area network (WAN) traffic workload generated by users of `mosaic` and `netscape` on the Internet.

4.4.2. Background

The key part of the WWW traffic model is modeling a WWW *session* (i.e., a single human user seated at a single workstation, using netscape or mosaic as a graphical user interface to explore and search for information all over the Internet). A typical WWW session may last minutes or hours.

A single WWW session can generate one or more *conversations* with different hosts on the Internet, where a conversation consists of a bidirectional exchange of packets with a single destination host. A conversation, in turn, may consist of one or more TCP *connections*, where each connection involves a bidirectional exchange of packets with a specific host. Each connection transfers the data bytes of an information unit, such as a text file, an image, graphics, etc. There may be several successive connections to the same destination host as part of a conversation. The next conversation may use the same destination host again, or a different one.

4.4.3. Modeling Methodology

Our WWW traffic model was constructed and parameterized based on network measurement and workload characterization of mosaic-generated Web traffic on a campus LAN, as reported in an earlier paper[5].

4.4.4. Model Parameters

The WWW traffic model has six parameters: (1) number of conversations per session; (2) conversation arrival model; (3) conversation destination model; (4) number of connections per conversation; (5) connection arrival model; and (6) number of bytes exchanged per connection.

These parameters are described in more detail as follows:

- **Number of conversations per session**.

  This parameter specifies the average number of conversations initiated during one WWW session. Because of the wide variability in the WWW sessions of individual users, it is extremely difficult to determine a proper setting for this parameter. For simplicity, our model assumes that the number of conversations is geometrically distributed, with a mean of 50 conversations per session.

- **Conversation arrivals**.

  Each conversation corresponds to a complete Web page. Once a conversation is complete, the arrival time of the next conversation must be determined. The next conversation may follow immediately after the previous conversation if the user is selecting successive links in a list of items, or is traversing links that have been previously explored. The next conversation may follow after a pause if the user takes some time to read the current document before selecting the next link, or if the user leaves the session idle, to return to it later.

  Empirical measurements have found both the conversation interarrival times (i.e., the time between the start of one conversation and the start of the next conversation) and the conversation gap times (i.e., the time between the end of one conversation and the start of the next conversation) to be exponentially distributed and independent. As a result, a simple Poisson arrival model is

used for conversations. The mean conversation gap time in our
model is 33 seconds.

- **Conversation destination**.

  When a conversation is to be started, the destination for the conversation must be determined. Several factors must be considered
  when making this choice.

  First, when a conversation is established with a particular destination, there is a strong possibility that there will be more conversations to the same destination within the near future. This
  phenomenon, called temporal locality or persistence in the literature, is common in many areas of computer systems.

  A second factor in determining the choice of the next destination
  is the distribution of network traffic workload across the Internet. Since the World Wide Web makes it easy to connect to sites
  across the Internet, and individual users have their own prefer-
  ences in what sites they visit, it seems reasonable to expect that
  WWW traffic from a single session will be widespread around
  the world. However, many studies of network traffic have identified the non-uniform distribution (i.e., concentration) of traffic
  on most networks. For example, since many users begin their
  WWW sessions with a default WWW page, there will be many
  references to common hyperlinks. As another example, certain
  ftp sites on the Internet tend to be more popular than others.

  Standard techniques for modeling persistence and concentration
  have been used to incorporate these characteristics into the WWW
  traffic model.

- **Number of connections per conversation**.

  This parameter specifies the average number of TCP connections
  per conversation (i.e., the number of separate files required for
  one Web page). In our model, the number of connections per
  conversation is geometrically distributed with a mean of 2.5.

- **Connection arrivals**.

  Each connection represents the transfer of one file, which may be
  part of a Web page. Within each conversation, the arrival time
  of each connection must be determined. The next connection

may follow immediately after the previous connection (e.g., the graphics to appear on a Web page are transferred immediately after the transfer of the text of the page), or may follow after a pause (e.g., when the user selects a link to another page on the same server). Only the former are modeled with connection arrivals. The latter are modeled as conversation arrivals.

As with the conversation arrivals, empirical measurements have found that connection arrivals are Poisson, and connection gap times (i.e., the time between the end of one connection and the start of the next connection) are exponentially distributed. Thus a simple Poisson arrival model is used for connection arrivals. The mean connection gap time in our model is 0.5 seconds.

- **Bytes exchanged per connection.**

Finally, the WWW traffic model needs to select the amount of information to be exchanged in each direction. Empirical measurements show that traffic is bidirectional. The source sends relatively few bytes (typically 1136 bytes plus or minus a few bytes), and the destination sends relatively more bytes (anywhere between a few hundred bytes and a few megabytes). Source bytes are modeled using a Normal distribution. Destination bytes are modeled using an Erlang distribution. The model captures both short-lived and long-lived TCP connections.

4.4.5. Model Validation

The model has been parameterized to generate synthetic workloads that closely match the empirical data collected at the University of Saskatchewan. Close agreement (often within 2%, and nearly always within 10%) has been obtained on all key characteristics of the model.

4.4.6. Summary

Since World Wide Web traffic is the fastest growing component of the aggregate packet and byte traffic on the NSFNET backbone, the ATM-TN TeleSim project has designed and implemented a synthetic workload model for Internet WWW traffic. Modeling the workload characteristics of these World Wide Web sessions is deemed important in any simulation study of the Internet or future high speed networks.

4.5. SUMMARY

This chapter has outlined the design of the network traffic workload models for ATM-TN. Three specific traffic models have been chosen for implementation: an MPEG compressed video traffic model, an Ethernet LAN traffic model, and an Internet World Wide Web traffic model.

Each model is a non-trivial synthetic workload model that is intended to accurately capture the salient characteristics of network traffic workloads. Each model has its own parameters and application-specific workload characteristics. Each model has been designed and implemented using the latest methods and results in traffic modeling and workload characterization. Each model has been parameterized based on empirical measurement data, either from our own network measurements, or from the published literature. Models have been translated into SimKit, validated, and incorporated into the overall ATM-TN simulation model, where they are now used in simulation studies of ATM networks.

Further information about these three traffic models, including C/C++ source code for the models, is available upon request from the author (carey@cs.usask.ca).

A more rigourous treatment of traffic source characterization in ATM networks (and network traffic self-similarity) follows in the next chapter, by Nikolaidis and Akyildiz.

REFERENCES

1. W. LELAND, M. TAQQU, W. WILLINGER, and D. WILSON, "On the Self-Similar Nature of Ethernet Traffic (Extended Version)", IEEE/ACM Transactions on Networking, **2**, 1, pp. 1-15 (February 1994).

    A landmark paper discussing network traffic self-similarity. The authors define self-similarity, present several methods of testing for self-similarity and estimating the Hurst parameter H, and present a rigourous analysis of their voluminous Ethernet LAN traffic data, collected on several Bellcore LANs over a period of four years. A "must read" for the traffic modeler. The original version of this paper appeared at the 1993 ACM SIGCOMM Conference.

2. V. PAXSON and S. FLOYD, "Wide Area Traffic: The Failure of Poisson Modeling", Proceedings of 1994 ACM SIGCOMM Conference (ACM, London, UK, August 1994), pp. 257-268.

> A paper discussing the limitations of Poisson-based traffic models for the modeling of wide area Internet traffic. The authors present a detailed call-level and packet-level model for the `telnet` network application, and present voluminous data indicating the non-Poisson structure of other wide area network traffic. The appendices of this paper (in the extended version only, which is available by anonymous ftp from ee.lbl.gov) present the statistical tests used in their paper, as well as an efficient S program for generation of (synthetic) self-similar time series.

3. M. GARRETT and W. WILLINGER, "Analysis, Modeling and Generation of Self-Similar VBR Video Traffic", in Proceedings of the 1994 SIGCOMM Conference (ACM, London, UK, August 1994), pp. 269-280.

> A detailed study of JPEG-like compressed video traffic generated by the movie *Star Wars*. The authors present a rigourous statistical analysis of the video trace, propose models for self similar video traffic, and then present the results of a simulation study for multiplexed VBR video traffic.

4. V. FROST and B. MELAMED, "Traffic Modeling for Telecommunications Networks", IEEE Communications, **32**, 3, pp. 70-81 (March 1994).

> An excellent discussion of the issues involved in traffic modeling for high speed networks, and a survey of several significant studies on network traffic measurement, workload characterization, and workload modeling, including the TES modeling methodology. A superb starting point for the non-expert.

5. M. ARLITT, Y. CHEN, R. GURSKI, and C. WILLIAMSON, "Traffic Modeling in the ATM-TN TeleSim Project: Design, Implementation, and Performance Evaluation", in the Proceedings of the 1995 Summer Computer Simulation Conference, edited by T. Ören and L. Birta (Society for Computer Simulation, Ottawa, Canada, July 1995), pp. 847-851.

> A description of the TeleSim project, and an overview of the three traffic models written for the ATM-TN network simulator.

6. M. ARLITT and C. WILLIAMSON, "A Synthetic Workload Model for Internet Mosaic Traffic", Proceedings of the 1995 Summer Computer Simulation Conference, edited by T. Ören and L. Birta (Society for Computer Simulation, Ottawa, Canada, July 1995), pp. 831-837.
   A description of the World Wide Web traffic model for ATM-TN, and the Internet WWW network traffic measurement and workload characterization done prior to the model construction.

7. Y. CHEN, Z. DENG and C. WILLIAMSON, "A Model for Self-Similar Ethernet Traffic: Design, Implementation, and Performance Implications", Proceedings of the 1995 Summer Computer Simulation Conference, edited by T. Ören and L. Birta (Society for Computer Simulation, Ottawa, Canada, July 1995), pp. 852-857.
   A description of the Ethernet LAN traffic model developed for ATM-TN, and some simulation experiments conducted with the model to assess the performance implications of self-similar network traffic.

8. B. UNGER, F. GOMES, X. ZHONGE, P. GBURZYNSKI, T. ONO-TESFAYE, S. RAMASWAMY, C. WILLIAMSON and A. COVINGTON, "A High Fidelity ATM Traffic and Network Simulator", in the Proceedings of the 1995 Winter Simulation Conference, (Arlington, VA, December 1995).
   A high-level description of the ATM-TN (Asynchronous Transfer Mode Traffic and Network model) network simulator, including traffic models, switch models, signaling protocols, simulation interface, and parallel simulation executive.

9. B. MELAMED, "TES Modeling of Video Traffic", IEICE Transactions on Communications, E75-B, pp. 1292-1300 (1992).
   A discussion of the Transform-Expand-Sample (TES) modeling methodology, and its application to modeling compressed video traffic.

10. D. GEIST and B. MELAMED, "TEStool: An Environment for Visual Interactive Modeling of Autocorrelated Traffic", Proceedings of the 1992 International Conference on Communications (Chicago, Illinois, June 1992), pp. 1285-1289.
   A description of the `testool` modeling package.

CHAPTER 5

AN OVERVIEW OF
SOURCE CHARACTERIZATION
IN ATM NETWORKS

Ioanis Nikolaidis and Ian F. Akyildiz

5.1. INTRODUCTION

Analytical performance results are used in the proper engineering de-
cisions, such as buffer and link dimensioning, in the deployment of
computer networks including Asynchronous Transfer Mode (ATM) networks. Moreover, such results can also be used by the Call Admission
Control (CAC) of ATM networks in order to provide guarantees for the
Quality of Service (QoS) received by the admitted sources. The only
alternative to analytical results is simulation. However, simulations are
inefficient for checking all possible system parameter scenarios and in-
effective in revealing fundamental relations between system parameters
and performance results.

The analytical approach to the performance evaluation of computer
networks can be loosely decomposed into three tasks. The first, *source
characterization*, is the identification of a suitable and accurate model
that describes the traffic source activity. The second, *node performance*,
is the modeling and analysis of the scheduling discipline at a node given
the specific source model(s). Depending on the scheduling discipline,
it is possible to achieve *statistical multiplexing* of several Variable Bit
Rate (VBR) flows into one logical flow through the sharing of a common bandwidth allocation (and typically, of common buffering). The

123

resulting ability to multiplex together a number of VBR flows using less bandwidth than the sum of bandwidths required by each separate flow is referred to as *multiplexing gain*. The third task, *end–to–end performance*, is the derivation of an analytical model for the end–to–end traffic flow (typically, over a tandem of network nodes) given both the source models and the scheduling disciplines involved. Because of the enormous resulting complexity, the available analytical techniques do not accurately address all three tasks simultaneously.

This chapter is a survey of some of the most important results in the area of source characterization. The related statistical multiplexing results are also presented and, where possible, the related end–to–end models are reviewed. The statistical multiplexing is assumed to be performed by means of servicing a number of traffic flows according to the FCFS discipline. Strictly speaking, statistical multiplexing is not only attainable by plain FCFS, but FCFS dominates the existing literature and also serves as a standard setup where the accuracy of source models is investigated. The issues related to the performance of non–FCFS scheduling disciplines deserve a separate survey altogether and they are not addressed in this chapter.

Two more clarifications are necessary in advance. One is the issue of choosing the proper source model. Ultimately, the decision is left to the engineer to assess which model is properly describing the anticipated traffic and whether it provides adequately accurate results for the statistical multiplexer analysis. Adopting a certain traffic model implies (a) a first approximation to the actual source traffic, (b) restrictions on the type of analytical results available about the statistical multiplexing of such sources and (c) particular tradeoffs between accuracy and computational demands.

The second clarification is in reference to the intuition that a source model with more parameters is necessarily better the one with fewer parameters (thus, "coarser"). The intuition is not necessarily true because the nature of the model plays an important role. For example, even a complicated Markov Modulated Poisson Process (MMPP) with a wealth of parameters to describe its transition rates and per–state arrival intensities can not capture the autocorrelation structure that is present in a Fractional Gaussian Noise defined by only three parameters.

An effort has been made to present a wide set of traffic models. Thus, some of the models that were originally proposed for variable–

length packet networks are presented with the understanding that they can be specialized for the fixed packet length of ATM networks. Additionally, discrete time models are presented alongside continuous time models, with the understanding that any of them can be the basis of a reasonable approximation to the sources under study. Moreover, the terms *packet* and *cell* are used interchangeably in this chapter, where a cell is the fixed size packet as defined in ATM networks. A direct implication of the stated assumptions is that all packet service times are deterministic. The presented models cover data, video and voice sources because this is the traffic in todays high–speed integrated services *multimedia* networks.

The rest of this chapter is organized as follows: In section 5.2, the multiple definitions and quantitative measures of burstiness are introduced as well as the concept of the ON/OFF model. In section 5.3, the phase processes for building Markovian models of bursty traffic are reviewed while in section 5.4 the approximation of the superposition of an arbitrary number of ON/OFF sources by a Markov Modulated Poisson Processes (MMPP) is presented. Another form of approximation, namely fluid–flow approximation, is the topic of section 5.5, while the concept of equivalent bandwidths which is related to the fluid flow models is described in section 5.6. The issue of representing more complex forms of correlation, which is particularly suited for video traffic, is addressed in section 5.7 by Auto–Regressive Models and expanded in section 5.8 to more powerful models. Schemes for deriving quantized rates to enhance the tractability of models related to video traffic are presented in section 5.9. The recent results on Long Range Dependence (LRD) and self–similar models for both data and video traffic are highlighted in section 5.10, along with a brief description of the potential impact of self–similarity on statistical multiplexing. Concluding, section 5.11 presents speculations about new research directions towards the integration of traffic modeling techniques, underlining the potential impact that Short Range Dependence (SRD) may have on the multiplexer performance, even under the presence of LRD.

5.2. CHARACTERIZING THE BURSTINESS

The single common characteristic which dominates all forms of multimedia traffic is *burstiness*. Although there is no common agreement about the quantitative definition of burstiness, the most accepted is that of high traffic variability (squared coefficient of variation (s.c.v.) larger than one), while another frequent definition is the ratio of the peak (or short–term) arrival rate over the mean arrival rate (where bursty are the sources with ratios significantly larger than one). It is worthwhile to note that the above definitions are insufficient in capturing particular autocorrelation structures present in the measured traffic. Thus, it is left up to the particular source model to introduce its own *inherent* autocorrelation which in many circumstances is accepted as a reasonable modeling compromise. The benefit of the compromise is that it opens the possibilities to use a number of available approximate analytical results especially with respect to voice traffic sources. However, such a compromise is hard to defend in the context of video and data traffic where recent studies[1,2] have indicated the strong importance of correctly capturing autocorrelation.

An alternative way to describe the variability, i.e., burstiness, of the traffic is to introduce two functions. Namely, the Index of Dispersion for Intervals (IDI) and the Index of Dispersion for Counts (IDC)[3]. Their purpose is to provide information as to whether the variability of the observed traffic reaches a fixed value in the long run or not. The IDI and the IDC are functions of a lag and a time interval, respectively. In particular, if the observed process is at least weakly stationary, i.e., with time invariant first and second moments, and if the autocovariance depends only on the lag k, then the IDI for a sequence of interarrival times X_i with an s.c.v. of C_J^2, and whose autocorrelation at lag k is ρ_k, is given by:

$$J_n = \frac{\text{var}(X_{i+1} + \cdots + X_{i+n})}{n E^2(X)} = C_J^2 \left[1 + 2 \sum_{k=1}^{n-1} \left(1 - \frac{k}{n} \right) \rho_k \right] \quad (5.1)$$

while the IDC for a sequence of counts of arrivals c_i within an interval of length τ, with the assumption that the process is weakly stationary, and whose autocorrelation at lag k is ξ_k, is given by:

$$I_\tau = \frac{\text{var}\left(\sum_{i=1}^{n} c_i \right)}{E\left(\sum_{i=1}^{n} c_i \right)} = \frac{\text{var}(c_\tau)}{E(c_\tau)} \left[1 + 2 \sum_{k=1}^{n-1} \left(1 - \frac{k}{n} \right) \xi_k \right] \quad (5.2)$$

Note that although the left side equations for J_n and $I\tau$ hold in any case, the right side equations hold only under the assumption that the observed process is weakly stationary. Moreover, for a Poisson process, $J_n = 1$ regardless of n and $I_t = 1$ regardless of t.

In order to introduce both burstiness and, to an extent, correlation in the traffic arrivals, the ON/OFF model has been extensively used. The ON/OFF model is defined as the strict alternation of periods of source activity (ON) and silence (OFF). Packet arrivals occur only during the ON period. The interarrival distribution during the ON period as well as the distributions of the ON and OFF sojourn and any potential dependencies between them are open issues and dependent on the particular modeled traffic. However, the typical case is that of a constant interarrival times in the ON state and exponentially distributed ON and OFF periods. The transition rate from the OFF to the ON state is equal to α and from ON to OFF is equal to β, while the constant arrival rate during the ON state is frequently normalized to be equal to 1 with respect to all other rates in the model. The model introduces short–term autocorrelation by grouping the arrivals together during the active period. The initial interest for the ON/OFF model was due to the success of fitting an ON/OFF model to voice traffic[4] compressed by Speech Activity Detection (SAD) algorithms and for this same reason it remains a popular model for characterizing, at least, voice traffic sources. The basic complication introduced by ON/OFF sources is that their superposition is not a renewal process. Approximating the superposition of ON/OFF sources by a renewal process produces inaccurate results even for the average delay. Hence, a fundamental problem is the construction of a stochastic process describing the superposition of N (possibly heterogeneous) ON/OFF sources feeding the same multiplexer.

5.3. PHASE PROCESSES

Stern[5] first introduced the concept of an underlying Markov Chain (called the *phase process*) which, for a superposition of N homogeneous ON/OFF sources, consists of $N + 1$ states indexed from 0 to N. The state of the MC captures the number of simultaneously active sources at any point in time. Its construction is based on the assumptions of exponentially distributed ON and OFF intervals and it is defined through the following transition rates:

$$r_{i,i+1} = (N - i)\alpha \ \text{ for } \ i = 0, \ldots, N \tag{5.3}$$

$$r_{i,i-1} = i\beta \ \text{ for } \ i = 1, \ldots, (N + 1) \tag{5.4}$$

No other transitions between states are allowed except (5.3) and (5.4). Let the link capacity be equal to C and normalized with respect to the arrival rate in the ON state, then the i-th state corresponds to a rate of change of the queue backlog equal to $(i - C)$. A state i of the MC belongs either to the overload states (if $(i - C) > 0$) or to the underload states (if $(i - C) < 0$). It is obvious that queue built–up can only occur in the overload states. Moreover, the periods that the system is in overload states alternate with the periods that the system is in underload states.

One can define an *overload/underload (OL/UL) cycle* to be the trajectory of the phase process that starts when entering an OL state, it continues throughout its sojourn in OL states, it continues when it enters an UL state and throughout its sojourn in UL states and it ends when it transits back to an OL state. Using the OL/UL cycle definition[5], Stern derived the queue length distribution at the time–points between successive OL/UL underload cycles. Moreover, this model gave a first approximation to the loss ratio by identifying the queue surplus beyond a specified queue limit during the OL stage. Namely, the cell loss ratio is the ratio of the average per–OL surplus over the average arrivals during the complete OL/UL cycle. Nevertheless, the approximation is effective only for small loss ratios since the model does not capture fluctuations of the queue occupancy process due to losses. Therefore, for the exact same arrivals, the queue occupancy according to the model may, at times, be larger than the occupancy in an actual finite buffer multiplexer.

A major improvement for the use use of phase processes came from Daigle and Langford[6] who introduced a two–dimensional state space where each state (i,j) represents the queue length i and the number of active sources j (the phase). The transitions between (i,j) and states $(i,j+1)$ and $(i,j-1)$ are governed by the same logic as in the case of Stern's model and the same classification of states in OL and UL states applies, depending on the value of j. In addition, for all UL states, transitions from (i,j) to $(i-1,j)$ are defined (denoting a queue length decrease) and for all OL states, transition from (i,j) to $(i+1,j)$ are also defined (denoting a queue length increase). Thus, no queue increase in UL states or queue decrease in OL states is captured by the model. The transitions between the states form a Semi–Markov Process (SMP). An underlying MC is subsequently constructed and solved using *matrix geometric techniques*[7] that provide the equilibrium fraction of transitions that enter state (i, j). The ergodic probabilities of the semi–Markov process are then obtained by weighting the equilibrium probabilities of the underlying Markov chain.

The phase transition epochs are renewal epochs of the SMP. This assumption results in two inaccuracies: (a) restarting of service from the beginning for any packet that was being serviced at the time of the phase transition and (b) "forgetting" any residual (partial) arrival underway since the last queue increment or decrement event. The magnitude of these inaccuracies is reduced as the average active time of the sources is increased. At the same time, an inherent limitation of the model is that the rate of queue growth or queue reduction governing the state transitions is defined as the difference between the aggregate arrival rate of the currently active sources and the link capacity C. Thus, the arrival process does not completely capture the cell–level rate fluctuations which, in an actual system, can impact the queue length process. The result is a systematic underestimation that the queue length is zero. Despite its approximate nature, the method is one of the first successful application of a Markovian model to the superposition of ON/OFF sources. Moreover, it produces very good results compared to simulations with respect to the survivor function $(F(x) = \Pr[\text{queue length} > x])$.

5.4. THE MMPP APPROACH

The matrix geometric techniques[7] are essentially successive approximation techniques. The convergence of the approximation deserves special attention since, depending on the parameters, it can be slow. Hence, in general, it is not known in advance what the total computation cost will be. Moreover, in the case of SMP model of Daigle and Langford, the size of the manipulated matrices depends on the number of superposed sources N. An alternative approach, described in the seminal work of Heffes and Lucantoni[8], is to use matrix geometric techniques but to approximate the superposed arrival process by a 2–state Markov Modulated Poisson Process (MMPP) and, thus, to reduce the size of the matrices involved. The contribution of the model lies primarily on the fact that a 2–state MMPP described by four parameters (one Poisson arrival rate λ_i for each state i and one transition rate r_i for each state i towards the other state) is used to model a superposition of an arbitrary number of ON/OFF sources. Thus, by matching the aggregate arrival process characteristics to the 2–state MMPP, it strives to attain reasonable accuracy with respect to the performance quantities of interest without having to introduce the state of each and every individual source into the state vector of the model.

The technique for determining the MMPP parameters proposed by Heffes and Lucantoni[8] has been found to cause inaccuracies with respect to the estimation of even the average waiting times. Consequently, many alternative parameter estimation techniques for MMPPs have been proposed[9] but they all share the common feature of attempting to match the correlation structure of the superposed arrivals. Typically, this is accomplished by observing the variance of the arrival process over both a short–term period as well as asymptotically (as $t \to \infty$) and solving for the four parameter values of the MMPP such that the IDC of the MMPP and the superposed ON/OFF sources match both in the short–term and asymptotically. Finally, the waiting time distribution at the multiplexers is derived[8] through the numerical inversion of a Laplace–Stieljes Transform (LST). The fully general case of the N/G/1 queue with finite buffer (of which MMPP/D/1/K is a special case) is extensively described by Blondia[10] where also the LST of the virtual waiting time can be found and be applied for the derivation of the waiting time distributions while, in addition, the steady state loss probability can be derived as well. Summarizing, the MMPP approach is, fortunately, independent on the number of superposed sources while it can provide all performance quantities of interest.

The MMPP has been refined extensively (e.g. superposition of heterogeneous ON/OFF sources) and its computational needs thoroughly understood. An extensive survey of MMPP and its related analysis is given by Fischer and Meier–Hellstern[11]. Moreover, processes similar to MMPP (or more general, as in the case of Lucantoni's Batch Markovian Arrival Process[12]) in both continuous and discrete time have been proposed. Apart from the computational needs, which depend on the particular extension and/or refinement, the common principle, and the strongest point of the MMPP–based techniques, is the ability to approximate the superposition process with a model which is independent of the number of superposed sources. Moreover, by adopting MMPP processes as an analytical approach to study networks of queues, it was shown by Saito[13] that the covariance present in the arrival MMPP process of an MMPP/D/1/∞ queue may very well be maintained on the aggregate departure traffic from the multiplexer. This phenomenon appears to be independent of the traffic load. At higher traffic loads, a reduction of the total variance is observed but not necessarily a drastic change in the autocovariance. These observations reinforce and summarize the reported cases where the concept of smoothing due to multiplexing of large aggregations of bursty traffic was studied. That is, not only the aggregate arrival process, but the aggregate departure process from the multiplexer as well, are inadequately described by Poisson or renewal processes, even for a relatively large aggregation of individual sources (e.g. a hundred or more voice sources). Thus, for networks carrying bursty traffic, it is important to use a model of correlated traffic arrivals for the end–to–end performance evaluation as well.

5.5.   THE UAS APPROACH

A method which bypasses the need for matrix geometric solutions is the Uniform Arrival and Service (UAS)[14] (and the follow–up extension to finite buffer queues by Tucker[15]) which constitutes a fluid flow approximation. According to this approximation, the rate of the fluid arrival is modulated according to the underlying phase process while the queue occupancy is a continuous function of time. Because of the fluid approximation, the packetization process is not modeled, resulting in inaccuracies when the cell–level dynamics play significant role, e.g., for small buffer sizes. Assuming that $\mathbf{F}(x)$ is the vector with elements $F_i(x)$, where $F_i(x)$ is the equilibrium probability that i sources are active and the queue length is less or equal to x, then the following system of differential equations holds for the multiplexer:

$$\mathbf{D}\frac{d\mathbf{F}(x)}{dx} = \mathbf{M}\mathbf{F}(x), \quad 0 \le x \le \infty \qquad (5.5)$$

where $\mathbf{D}$ is the queue size change rate matrix and $\mathbf{M}$ the transition rate matrix governing the phase process of the number of active sources (both matrices are $(N+1) \times (N+1)$). The system of differential equations possesses an elegant solution which amounts to the spectral decomposition of the queue length process in the following fashion:

$$F_i(x) = \sum_k a_k \{\Phi_k\}_i \exp(z_k x) \qquad (5.6)$$

where the z_k's and the Φ_k's ($\{\Phi_k\}_i$ being the i–th element of the vector) are the eigenvalues and the respective eigenvectors defined by the matrices of the system of differential equations. a_k is a factor associated with the k-th eigenvalue and which (for the case of finite buffer) is the solution of a linear system of equations related to the initial conditions of the differential equation. There exist efficient techniques for the calculation of the particular eigenvectors/eigenvalues which in some cases is even possible in closed form. Thus, the core of the UAS approach is determining eigenvalues of matrices whose size, unfortunately, depends on the number of superposed sources.

Compared to both the MMPP–based solutions (using a proper parameter matching scheme) and the Semi–Markov process solutions, UAS is sufficiently accurate[6,9] with the exception of the small buffer size operating regime. Since the UAS model is a burst–level model it is necessary to introduce a correction for the small buffer sizes which can capture the cell–level dynamics of the multiplexer. To this extent, Kröner et. al.[16] have proposed the use of the stationary queue length distribution of an M/D/1/K queue. Consequently the queue length distribution of the system can be approximated by the convolution of the queue length distribution produced by UAS with the one produced by the M/D/1/K analysis. By comparing the tail of the queue length distribution according to this approximation to simulation results[16] it was shown that the approximation is indeed accurate. It was also observed[16] that sources that are simultaneously in the burst (ON) state at the first queue node will be simultaneously in a burst state at all intermediate nodes. The observation is consistent with the MMPP/D/1 departure process results of Saito[13], in the sense that it supports the statement that the correlation of the traffic is preserved on the departure stream. Consequently, this same observation was used by Kröner et. al. in the construction of an approximate end–to–end model[16]. The underlying technique for constructing the end–to–end model is to derive the conditional probabilities of delay incurred by a single connection at a multiplexer, conditioned on the number of sources that "meet" in their active state at that multiplexer.

Kobayashi[17] has demonstrated that a fluid flow model approximation can be applied even when the assumption of exponential ON and OFF periods is relaxed and, moreover, it can be used to derive the transient behavior of the queue length process of a statistical multiplexers. Indeed, a diffusion approximation of the superposed traffic sources takes the form of an Ornstein–Uhlenbeck diffusion process and it is based only on the mean and variance of the ON and OFF periods[17]. In addition, a formulation of the queue length process can be derived[18] which provides a system of time–dependent differential equations of the form:

$$\frac{d\mathbf{F}(x,t)}{dt} + \mathbf{D}\frac{d\mathbf{F}(x,t)}{dx} = \mathbf{MF}(x,t) \qquad (5.7)$$

where $\mathbf{F}(x,t)$ represents the joint distribution that the queue length is x at time t. Notably, equation (5.5) is nothing more but equation (5.7) taken to its limit as $t \to \infty$, thus representing the steady–state behavior of the multiplexer. The procedure of determining the queue length process is more complicated than in the case of UAS, because it involves the solution of eigenvalue/eigenvector problems but in the LST domain. It nevertheless agrees with UAS in the eventual decomposition of the queue length process to its spectral components and it also provides the transient solution which can find application in the context of call admission.

5.6.   EQUIVALENT BANDWIDTH

One of the major contributions of the fluid flow models, such as the UAS model, is the additional insight that they provide to the asymptotic behavior of the queue length distribution. It can be shown that, asymptotically, the tail of the queue length distribution, $G(x)$, starting from a queue occupancy level x is given by:

$$G(x) \sim Ae^{zx} \quad \text{as} \quad x \to \infty \qquad (5.8)$$

where z is the dominant eigenvalue of the system $(\mathbf{D}, \mathbf{M})$ and A the shorthand of a related constant factor. The exponential tail behavior of the queue length distribution is not a unique feature of the fluid flow models, but it is important in that it reveals the quantitative relationship between the model parameters (through the dominant eigenvalue) and the shape of the tail of the queue length distribution. In addition there exist efficient means to calculate the dominant eigenvalue.

The constant factor A, as well as z, are defined in terms of the link capacity, C, and the source model parameters. Thus, it is possible to invert the asymptotic relationship of the queue length distribution with respect to the link capacity C leading to an expression for C in terms of (a) the source model parameters, (b) a prescribed mass, ϵ, at the tail of the queue length distribution (c) a given buffer size (interpreted as the beginning of the tail of the queue length distribution, x). Such

formulation for C is called an *equivalent bandwidth* and it represents
the smallest bandwidth that, for the given buffer size x, guarantees
that the loss probability will be smaller than a prescribed ϵ (that is,
$G(x) \leq \epsilon$).

The importance of equivalent bandwidth has been enormous in the
definition of call admission schemes[19]. Compared to other methods,
the UAS is the only known method where the relation of the equivalent
bandwidth to the system parameters is straightforward and can be
solved efficiently. At the same time, it inherits the inaccuracies of
UAS with respect to small buffer sizes. It is possible to overcome the
problem of equivalent bandwidth at small buffer sizes by approximating
the losses at the multiplexer with the tail of the binomial distribution
which describes the number of simultaneously active sources. Thus, for
small buffers and N multiplexed sources:

$$\epsilon = \sum_{k=\lfloor C \rfloor + 1}^{N} \binom{N}{k} p^k (1-p)^{N-k} \qquad (5.9)$$

where p is the steady–state probability that a source is in the active
state. The equivalent bandwidth solution, C, results from solving the
above equation with respect to C. Note that the cell losses through
this last approximation are independent of the buffer size since the tail
of the binomial represents a zero–buffer approximation to the losses.

The equivalent bandwidth concept has been extended to a large variety of Markovian processes[20] based primarily on results that provide
a straightforward calculation of the dominant eigenvalue which appears
in equation (5.8). The fact that these techniques can be applied to heterogeneous sources, results in a drastic decrease in the dimensionality
of the problem of finding bounds for the queue length distribution, and
thus, of establishing the equivalent bandwidth of such sources. Nevertheless, tha requirement in order to apply these results is that the source
model is Markovian. Hence, it is first necessary to construct a reasonably accurate Markovian approximation of the source traffic, e.g., one
that adequately approximates the measured autocorrelation, before any
of the existing results on equivalent bandwidths can be applied. Such
construction of a Markovian process is, in general, not trivial, it is frequently approximate, and it may involve higher–dimensional processes
and even several parameters.

An example of traffic sources with particular autocorrelation behavior not captured by the exponential ON/OFF model is video sources.

In addition to exhibiting strong burstiness (e.g., rarely transmitting a burst, but transmitting it with a very high interarrival rate), the occurrence of the ON/OFF cycles is periodic. That is, if the transmissions related to a frame are grouped together in the ON period, the rest of the time until the next frame generation instant is the OFF period. Thus, the ON and OFF intervals are dependent. Despite attempts to characterize the equivalent bandwidth of video sources[21], it remains a fact that the correlation present in the traditional ON/OFF model is not correctly depicting video sources for which the correlation between video frames spans several ON (and hence OFF) periods.

5.7. AUTOREGRESSIVE MODELS

Two factors contribute to the particular autocorrelation structure of video streams. One is the amount of motion in the encoded sequences and the other is the coding techniques used. The coding techniques include inter–frame and intra–frame coding. Inter–frame coding encodes only the differences between subsequent frames on a granularity of a basic element (block) of the picture. One form of inter–frame coding is *conditional replenishment* while another possibility is the use of *motion vectors* to describe the movement in the scene in terms of the blocks of the previous frame. The choice of intra–frame or inter–frame or of a particular inter–frame coding technique, is left up to the coder design. Thus, a coder can select a different technique for each frame or even for each smaller group of data within a frame. The selection of each technique depends on the level of scene activity (in *motion–classified codecs*) and/or based on a *refresh* policy of injecting intra–frame coded frames (whenever the error aggregated by subsequent inter–frame coding becomes unacceptable). Motion–classified codecs are, in fact, quickly becoming the predominant framework for video coding (e.g. H.261, MPEG–1, etc.).

The k-th order autoregressive process $(AR(k))$ is a stochastic process which, to an extent, captures the video traffic's autocorrelation and it can also be described in an elegant form. That is, if an $AR(k)$ is used to describe the amount of data at each frame epoch, then the data (or, equivalently, the per–frame bit–rate) $\lambda(n)$ produced at the

n–th frame is given in the following form:

$$\lambda(n) = a_0 + \sum_{j=1}^{k} a_j \lambda(n-j) + w(n) \qquad (5.10)$$

where the a_i's are constants and $w(n)$ the n–th sample taken from an i.i.d. distribution known as the *distribution of residuals*. Note that, for video sources, the term *bit–rate* is used to describe the size of the data produced for a particular frame divided by frame period. Since the frame period for a particular source is fixed at all times, there exists no difference between studying the statistics of the data produced per frame or of the bit–rate process. A first order ($k = 1$) AR process with Normally distributed residuals that fits observed data from a conditional–replenishment coder was studied in the work of Maglaris et. al.[22]. The fitted AR(1) exhibits a quickly decaying exponential autocorrelation and a symmetric stationary bit rate distribution which is limited to modeling video traffic for low–motion teleconferencing scenes that are produced using conditional replenishment inter–frame coding.

A number of refinements to the AR model have been proposed targeting for a better accuracy with respect to the bit–rate distribution when more complex coding schemes are used, as well as when abrupt scene changes and high levels of motion are possible. In fact, experimental results[23,24,25,26] indicate that the stationary bit–rate distribution of a single video source does not resemble a Normal. Instead, it resembles a skewed long–tailed distribution. One such skewed distribution is the Gamma distribution and it has been observed by Heyman et. al.[23] in actual video coders. Consequently, it was proposed to model the per–frame bit–rate by an AR(2) model which captures the skewed distribution while accurately modeling the measured autocorrelation. The parameters of the AR(2) can be extracted through regression analysis. Although, in principle, one could arbitrarily increase the order of the AR model to gain better accuracy, it was found[23] that extending the AR(2) into an AR(3) model, for the particular coder traffic, did not result in any significant improvement. Another approach is to use multiple AR(1) processes where each one attempts to capture a different component of the autocorrelation. In this spirit, Ramamurthy and Sengupta[27], proposed the superposition of two independent AR(1) processes and, in addition, a third process which adds the occasional traffic spikes in order to model scene changes.

However, none of the above models can capture the operation of the motion–classified codecs because modeling the scene activity becomes indistinguishable from modeling the corresponding coding technique. An approach to this problem was proposed by Yegenoglu et. al.[26] Specifically, three AR(1)s are used. Each one of them represents a different level of motion activity and, corresponding, coding technique. The coding techniques for the particular coder[26] are (a) inter–frame Differential Pulse Code Modulation (DPCM) for low activity, (b) inter–frame motion compensated DPCM for medium–activity and (c) an intra–frame technique for high–activity frames. Thus, it is reasonable to think about the single source process as being in any of three states (one for each coding level selection) at each frame instant. Consequently, the source can be modeled by an underlying probability transition matrix which controls the evolution of the process between these three states from frame to next frame. Each state can then be modeled as an individual AR process that captures the correlation to the previous frame.

The parameters of each AR(1) model at the respective coding level are determined by fitting an AR(1) process to each of the three peaks that are identifiable in the bit rate histogram of the empirical data. Thus, the process for finding the parameters of the model is necessarily complicated and it involves a *statistical discriminant analysis* using the Viterbi algorithm for determining class membership of the empirical per–frame bit–rates. The class membership is also used in order to derive the transition probabilities between the three states of the model from the empirical data. Despite the complications in determining its parameters, the model presented by Yegenoglu et. al.[26] addresses the issue of modeling a motion–classified codec by essentially modeling separately each individual coding technique present in the codec and then combining them through a transition matrix. Such models of "micro" behavior of the coding process are more accurate for motion–classified codecs, than models that treat the entire coder as a "black box".

5.8. CAPTURING THE AUTOCORRELATION

The problem inherent in the proposed auto–regressive models is that they do not provide a systematic approach to accurately approximate both the marginal bit–rate distribution and the particular autocorrelation structure. At the same time, extracting the necessary coefficients may not be a trivial task, especially when complex motion–classified techniques are involved. Auto–Regressive Moving Average (ARMA) models for video traffic have been proposed by Grünenfelder et. al.[28] and they provide a systematic approach to producing a model which accurately captures the autocorrelation of the measured data but at the expense of not capturing accurately the marginal bit–rate distribution. Thus, although it has been shown that ARMA models may be accurate for intra–frame coding[28], their applicability to motion–classified coding is limited due to the non–Normal bit–rate distribution that such coders exhibit. Notably, the proposed ARMA models are structured in a way that it allows them to capture *recorrelation* phenomena.

The recorrelation (also called pseudo–periodicity) is present in the statistical analysis of components of coded video that maintain spatial correlation. That is, by observing the *slices* (horizontal segments) of the same image area between subsequent frames, one can easily determine that they produce correlated traffic loads due to their location in the image area (i.e., spatial correlation). Thus, with respect to the slice statistics, one can observe pseudo–periodic autocorrelation (recorrelation) with period equal to the number of encoded slices per frame. The resulting shape of the slice–level autocorrelation function resembles an exponentially decaying periodic function[24].

The ARMA video source model is a process formed by the tandem of three elementary stages. The first stage is a moving average (MA) process fed by a white noise sequence with zero mean and unit variance. The output of the first stage is fed to an AR process which superposes the sequence over itself, through an attenuation factor a, and with a lag m equal to the desired recorrelation period of the sequence. Finally, the output of the second stage is fed to a zero–mean non–linearity (ZMNL) which scales and translates the random sequence (which up to this point is a colored $N(0,1)$ process) to the desired mean and variance while ensuring that the output sequence is strictly positive in value. Deriving the parameters for the ARMA model involves the mean and the variance of the modeled process as well as the autocorrelation from lag $-m$ and up to $+m$. The mean and the variance of the empirical data are introduced by means of the ZMNL stage. The calculation of the parameters of the MA stage of the model is based on the power density spectrum which is available through application of FFT of the empirical data sequence.

A better answer to the problem of simultaneously fitting a large set of marginal distributions and autocorrelation structures is given by the Transform–Expand–Scale (TES) technique which was proposed by Melamed and subsequently applied to video sources[29,30]. In its simplest form, TES can be described as a pseudo–random uniform variate generation technique that introduces autocorrelation in the uniform variates. The inversion technique is then applied to the uniform variates in order to generate variates conforming to arbitrary marginal distributions (that is, distributions for which the inversion method can be used). Thus, TES greatly simplifies the task of fitting a model to the marginal bit–rate distribution.

The selection of the parameters (two parameters, in the simplest form of TES) that guide the generation of the TES uniform variates must be made such that the autocorrelation of the measured sequence is approximated by the TES sequence with good accuracy. Typically, the starting point, although not sufficient, is to match the lag–1 autocorrelation of the model to the measured lag–1 autocorrelation. Subsequently, a trial–and–error process is followed, based on how accurately the TES model can mimic the desired autocorrelation for given parameter values, until the best parameter setting is found. However, one of the subtle properties of TES is that, with little modification of the basic idea, one can derive TES variants that exhibit particular autocorrelation features, such as recorrelation. For example, Lazar et. al.[30] demonstrated that it is possible, by using a TES variant, to model both the frame level and the slice level statistics (with different parameters for each) for an intra–frame Discrete Cosine Transform (DCT) coder, where the TES model can mimic the recorrelation behavior observed in the slice–level statistics.

5.9. RATE QUANTIZATION

The presented AR, TES and ARMA models are currently used only for the generating *synthetic* traffic but not in the queueing analysis of multiplexers. Moreover, they all constitute frame– or slice–level models and not cell–level models. That is, they describe the total arrivals during a frame or slice but not the individual cell arrivals. Therefore, the subject of transmission *within* a frame (or slice) period is left unresolved despite the fact that the cell–level load fluctuations have impact on the statistical multiplexing performance. Consequently, depending on what constitutes a burst (a slice's or a frame's worth of data), the characteristics of the arrival process can be drastically different. For example, if the bursts are formed on a slice by slice basis, the apparent autocorrelation pseudo–periodicity will be present at the produced traffic while, aggregating the traffic in bursts on a frame by frame basis tends to cancel any such pseudo–periodic behavior[30]. In addition, the lack of a particular model that describes the form of the cell interarrival process within a frame period constraints the number of queueing analysis techniques that can be used. It is therefore not surprising that the most popular approach to analyzing statistical multiplexers of video sources is to use the insensitive to cell–level dynamics fluid flow models. Finally, a conclusive answer to what constitutes an accurate description of the arrivals within a frame period will probably be answered in the near future and it will depend on how the video encoding hardware/software systems will evolve.

Part of the complexity of developing a queueing model from the presented source models is that all these models produce bit–rates that can take any of an infinite set of values. The complexity is avoided by quantizing the bit–rates into multiples of a basic bit–rate λ_q (the *step* of the quantization) and by producing source models that describe the source activity as a quantized process. A quantized continuous time Markov chain model was proposed by Maglaris et. al.[22] and refined by Sen et. al.[31] A similar underlying phase process to Stern's earlier work[5] on ON/OFF sources is constructed where the number of states is $M + 1$, representing bit–rates from 0 to M times the bit–rate quantization step. The same quantization scheme deals with both individual sources and with the superposition of N such sources. Hence, although the resulting MC possesses a binomial stationary distribution that is not representative of the single source's bit–rate distribution, it can be argued that it is asymptotically accurate for the description of the superposition of a large number of homogeneous sources. For example, even for a motion–classified codec[26], the bit–rate distribution of several homogeneous superposed sources tends to a Normal distribution. Nevertheless, the autocovariance of the model is still a fast decaying exponential of the form:

$$C_\lambda(\tau) = C_\lambda^{'}(0)e^{-(\alpha+\beta)\tau} = C_\lambda(0)e^{-\omega\tau} \qquad (5.11)$$

where α and β are derived by matching the mean and the variance of the measured data to the mean and the variance of the model which are given respectively by:

$$E(\lambda) = M\lambda_q p \quad C_\lambda(0) = M\lambda_q^2 p(1-p) \tag{5.12}$$

where M is fixed to a value that results in sufficient accuracy and $p = \frac{\alpha}{\alpha+\beta}$. In fact, it is generally preferable to treat λ_q as an unknown parameter as well and introduce one more equation, namely $\omega = \alpha + \beta$, where ω is the rate of exponential decay of the model autocorrelation and it is matched to the decay rate of the measured autocorrelation. Note that p can be perceived as the probability that an ON/OFF source is in the ON. This observation can then be used to describe the resulting model as the superposition of M ON/OFF *mini–sources* where each mini–process generates arrivals with intensity λ_q when ON. Hence, the statistical multiplexer performance can be treated using the UAS approximation[14], thus providing the survivor function for the multiplexer queue length distribution[22].

The structure of the transition rates in the quantized MC, does not allow the direct transition from a state representing low arrival rate (i.e., low scene activity) to one with very high arrival rate (i.e., high scene activity). An improvement to this model is to consider an alternative, 2–dimensional, MC[31] where transitions on one dimension follow "small steps" and transitions along the other dimension follow "large steps". However, the same drawback as in the case of 1–dimensional MC remains, that is, the fast exponentially decaying autocorrelation. Moreover, it must be noted that the state transitions of the continuous time MC are not driven by any particular events in the video source stream (such as frame epochs etc.) but are simply picked to be exponentially distributed to facilitate in the analytical derivation of the statistical multiplexer performance.

Another alternative of rate quantization and a different construction of an underlying Markov process, is the Discrete AR (DAR) model[23]. The model is able to capture a Negative Binomial (the discrete time equivalent of a Gamma) marginal distribution and also the lag–1 autocorrelation of the frame bit–rates. Thus, the probability of k cell arrivals within a frame period is given by:

$$f_k = \binom{k+r-1}{k} p^r (1-p)^k \tag{5.13}$$

where p and r can be directly derived by matching the mean and variance of the measured data to the mean and the variance of the Negative

Binomial. The basis of the model is an underlying discrete time Markov chain which determines the number of cells produced per frame. Its transition matrix P is constructed as follows:

$$P = \rho I + (1 - \rho)Q \tag{5.14}$$

where ρ is the lag–1 autocorrelation, I is the identity matrix and Q is a transition matrix where each row is of the form $(f_0, f_1, \ldots, f_K, F_K)$ where f_i's are the marginal probability of i cells per frame epoch and F_K corresponds to the tail of the binomial for samples larger than K ($F_K = \sum_{k>K} f_k$). Notice that the information about the measured lag–1 autocorrelation is introduced by ρ. Thus, the DAR(1) model requires only three parameters to be derived from the measured data. Moreover, when K is large, the size of the arrays can be reduced by grouping together the states that fall within a quantization step and accordingly grouping the measurements of the actual traffic. Compared to the quantized rate continuous time MC model[22], the DAR(1) model is more accurate in capturing the marginal bit–rate distribution and the lag–1 autocorrelation. However, due to the particular construction of its transition matrix, the short–term behavior of the DAR(1) model is characterized by a tendency to remain in the same state (same number of arrivals per frame) for a geometrically distributed number of frames with parameter ρ. The impact of this limitation is less pronounced when a number of DAR(1) sources are superposed. Nevertheless, the important result concerning DAR(1), is that it falls in the general category of Markovian processes for which bounds on the tail of the queue length process in statistical multiplexing are known[20] and, hence, its equivalent bandwidth can be calculated as well.

5.10.   LONG RANGE DEPENDENCE

The models presented so far in this chapter are characterized by a decaying autocorrelation which tends to zero for very large lags. The diminishing autocorrelation was for years an acceptable modeling assumption. However, evidence to the contrary from a study of Ethernet LAN traffic[3], seriously challenges such assumptions. Follow–up studies using similar statistical tests to the ones used by Leland et. al.[3] verified the presence of Long Range Dependence (LRD) and even they extended it to the case of video traffic[1]. LRD manifests its existence through the persistence of autocorrelation even for very large lags or, more formally, it exhibits a non–summable autocorrelation (i.e., $\sum_k r(k) = \infty$ for autocorrelation $r(k)$ at lag k). Thus, all models with exponentially decaying autocorrelation can not accurately represent such a process. Additionally, the IDC of the arrivals increases monotonically and does not settle to a fixed value as in the case of Markovian models.

A way to model LRD traffic is by using self–similar processes. Self–similar processes exhibit autocorrelation which decays according to a hyperbolic function, i.e., of the form:

$$r(k) \sim L(k)k^{-\gamma} \tag{5.15}$$

where k is the lag, $L(k)$ is a slowly varying function at infinity (can be perceived as a constant) and $0 < \gamma < 1$. Indeed, the autocorrelation of equation (5.15) is non–summable. Furthermore, in self–similar processes the same autocorrelation structure persists, in the exact or in the asymptotical sense, even if the time series (of arrivals per interval) is aggregated by producing one sample from the mean of every m non–overlapping samples. The convenience that the self–similar models provide is that their behavior at all time scales is governed by a single parameter, H, which is known as the Hurst parameter and it is defined as $H = 1 - \gamma/2$, where $1/2 < H < 1$.

There is still ongoing research in identifying self–similarity for a variety of network setups and traffic sources as well as in isolating cases where the potential non–stationary behavior of the observed process may be perceived falsely as self–similarity. However, the separate task of modeling LRD through self–similar processes has captured the interest of researchers on its own right. For this purpose, a popular model is the Fractional Gaussian Noise (FGN) which is parameterized by the measured mean, variance and H parameter of the traffic. Another (asymptotically) self–similar model is the Fractional Autoregressive Integrated Moving Average (F–ARIMA) process. In fact, it is possible to use a finite differencing technique to construct an ARIMA(0,d,0) process depending on only the value of H ($d = H - 1/2$) and capturing the LRD of the arrival sequence. In order to also capture the particular heavy tailed marginal distribution, a procedure similar to TES has been proposed by Garrett and Willinger[1]. In essence, the arrival process produced by the ARIMA(0,d,0) possesses a zero–mean Normal marginal distribution which is subsequently transformed to a heavy tailed distribution, which can be, for example, a combination of

Gamma and a Pareto distribution[1].

A direct implication of self–similarity is that the results regarding the tail of the queue length distribution of Markovian processes and those concerning the related equivalent bandwidths, cannot be applied. In particular, it is known that the the exponential asymptotic behavior of the queue length tail which is present in Markovian models, is not present in self–similar processes. Indeed, the overwhelming simulation evidence and preliminary analytical results indicate that the buffer dimensioning under the assumption of Markovian traffic is insufficient for LRD traffic. In fact, recent results, e.g, those by Norros[32], show that the tail of the queue length process is asymptotically consistent with a Weibull distribution, that is:

$$G(x) \sim e^{-cx^{2(1-H)}} \qquad (5.16)$$

for a Hurst parameter of H, and c a constant dependent on H. Thus, it is evident that the effectiveness of the buffer size is severely limited since it is raised to the power of $2(1 - H) \leq 1$. For larger values of H the effectiveness of the buffer is practically diminished. Moreover, $G(x)$ is very sensitive to the value of H and since the accurate estimation of H is a research question on its own right, the benefit of the above formula for engineering purposes is limited. It nevertheless provides insight to the problem of loss behavior for multiplexers that were engineered using Markovian models. Such multiplexers, when confronted with self–similar traffic will produce more pronounced losses together with unbounded variance and thus unacceptable jitter for real–time connections.

One would expect that, after the introduction of self–similar traffic models, the interest in ON/OFF models would cease since they do not capture burstiness at multiple time scales. However, in a recent study[33] by Willinger et. al., it was found that the concept of ON/OFF processes can be extended by considering ON and OFF distributions with infinite variance, thus exhibiting the so–called *Noah Effect*. It was demonstrated that the aggregation of such ON/OFF sources results in self–similar traffic. The analytical observations are also found to be in agreement with the experimental results. In the experimental results, the source–to–destination activity can be modeled sufficiently by ON/OFF processes with infinite variance. Deciding on what amounts to a ON and what to an OFF period in data traffic is a problem of selecting a time threshold, t, where arrivals spaced less than t apart are part of an ON burst and arrivals spaced more than t apart define an OFF period between them. The exact same problem for selecting a time threshold was posed originally in the definition of *packet trains* by Jain and Routhier[34]. However, the impressive conclusion in the recent[33] analysis of source–to–destination traffic is that the Noah effect is *robust* with respect to the selection of the t threshold, and hence, one can decide on the division of ON and OFF periods in any of a wide range of time scales (that is, avoiding degenerate cases such as the ones where each packet is an ON period and each interpacket interval an OFF period, or where all the packets form a single ON period).

5.11.   CONCLUSIONS

It is currently an open issue whether self–similar traffic models can be considered "universal" models for all types of traffic sources. Even if the questions pertaining to the stationarity of the measured traffic in LANs and WANs are resolved, it remains a fact that the observed self–similarity includes the effects of the flow control of protocols (mainly TCP). Thus, it represents the aggregate effect of both the source behavior, in terms of traffic generation, and of the protocol behavior, in terms of traffic control and adaptation to congestion. TCP is a clear example where the mechanisms that try to ensure the effective use of the network resources are also subject to time–varying behavior, i.e., through the adaptation of the transmission window sizes. Thus, one must not ignore the fact that the self–similarity in LANs and WANs is behavior observed at the *macro* scale on which the *micro* scale behavior of the individual connections plays an important role. By the same token, it is currently impossible to isolate the impact that one connection can have on the self–similarity of the aggregate traffic (e.g., on the value of H).

Moreover, while self–similar models are motivated by the LRD component of the traffic, they should not be considered as the only important component of the arrival process. Namely, Short Range Dependencies (SRD) still play a role in the multiplexer performance and they can be modeled by the existing Markovian models. It is not clear under which conditions the SRD component is more important than the LRD component and for which performance measures. Thus, even if the LRD component causes occasional losses, the SRD may play a more significant role in the delay distribution. In real–time traffic, where a delayed cell is as good as a lost cell, the SRD behavior can have more important impact than the LRD behavior. In fact, the losses due to effects of the LRD may even go unnoticeable depending on the coding schemes. Therefore, the value of Markovian models, and models that capture SRD in general, is not harmed by the introduction of self–similar models. It is their application that is discouraged unless there exists firm statistical evidence to support their suitability. Thus, an open research area is that of combining the SRD and the LRD components in source models and understanding their compound impact on the performance measures of statistical multiplexers.

It must also be stressed that the self–similarity results pertaining to encoded video are important in the context of multicast distribution of continuous media traffic. If, as the trend seems to be, the volume of multicast coded video increases dramatically, then extra effort must be given to characterizing, and potentially controlling, such video traffic sources. In addition, the proliferation of network services through the World Wide Web (WWW) poses a new trend in the use of computer networks where short–lived TCP connections are becoming the dominating class of traffic and their impact on the transient behavior of multiplexers must be studied and associated with the call admission and bandwidth allocation techniques.

Concluding, it is interesting to observe that almost a decade ago the network performance literature was dominated by Poisson models. The area has regained significant momentum due to the renewed motivation of building networks with sufficient bandwidth capable of supporting multimedia traffic. The interest is not only based on the diversity of traffic sources but also in the variety of performance results that impact the perceived network performance. For example, the need to describe the jitter component in real–time traffic and the very small cell loss ratio in ATM networks resulted in an emphasis, on one hand, on deriving accurate queue length distributions and, on the other, on understanding the asymptotic behavior of losses in multiplexers with large buffers. Consequently, numerous models have been developed, but most of them rely on an underlying ON/OFF source activity structure. The new challenge is to combine the results due to the self–similarity models with the "traditional" models in the context of unified SRD+LRD performance analysis techniques.

REFERENCES

1. M. W. GARRETT and W. WILLINGER, "Analysis, Modeling and Generation of Self–Similar VBR Video Traffic", in Proceedings of the ACM SIGCOMM '94 Conference, (London, UK, August 1994), pp. 269–280.

2. W. E. LELAND, M. S. TAQQU, W. WILLINGER and D. V. WILSON, "On the Self–Similar Nature of Ethernet Traffic (Extended Version)", IEEE/ACM Transactions on Networking, 2, 1, pp. 1–15 (February 1994).

3. R. GUSELLA, "Characterizing the Variability of Arrival Processes with Indexes of Dispersion", IEEE Journal on Selected Areas in Communications, 9, 2, pp. 203-212 (February 1991).

4. P. T. BRADY, "A Model for Generating On–Off Speech Patterns in Two–Way Conversations", Bell System Technical Journal, 48, pp. 2445–2472 (September 1969).

5. T. E. STERN, "A Queueing Analysis of Packet Voice", in Proceedings of the IEEE GLOBECOM '83 Conference, (San Diego, CA, December 1983)), pp. 71–76.

6. J. N. DAIGLE and J. D. LANGFORD, "Models for Analysis of Packet Voice Communications Systems", IEEE Journal on Selected Areas in Communications, 4, 6, pp. 847–855 (September 1986).

7. M. NEUTS, Matrix Geometric Solutions in Stochastic Models: An Algorithmic Approach, (Johns Hopkins University Press, Baltimore, MD, 1981).

8. H. HEFFES and D. LUCANTONI, "A Markov Modulated Characterization of Packetized Voice and Data Traffic and Related Statistical Multiplexer Performance", IEEE Journal on Selected Areas in Communications, SAC–4, 6, pp. 856–868 (September 1986).

9. R. NAGARAJAN, J. F. KUROSE and D. TOWSLEY, "Approximation Techniques for Computing Packet Loss in Finite–Buffered Voice Multiplexers", IEEE Journal on Selected Areas in Communications, 9, 3, pp. 368-377 (April 1991).

10. C. BLONDIA, "The N/G/1 Finite Capacity Queue", Communica-

tions in Statistics – Stochastic Models, **5**, 2, pp. 273–294 (1989).

11. W. FISCHER and K. MEIER–HELLSTERN, "The Markov Modulated Poisson Process (MMPP) Cookbook", Performance Evaluation, **18**, 2, pp. 149–171 (1993).

12. D. M. LUCANTONI, "New Results on the Single Server Queue with a Batch Markovian Arrival Process", Communications in Statistics – Stochastic Models, **7**, 1, pp. 1–46 (1991).

13. H. SAITO, "The Departure Process of an N/G/1 Queue", Performance Evaluation, **11**, 4, pp. 241–251 (1990).

14. D. ANICK, D. MITRA and M. M. SONDHI, "Stochastic Theory of a Data–Handling System with Multiple Sources", Bell System Technical Journal, **61**, 8, pp. 1871–1894 (October 1982).

15. R. C. F. TUCKER, "Accurate Method for Analysis of a Packet Speech Multiplexer with Limited Delay", IEEE Transactions on Communications, **36**, 4, pp. 479–483 (April 1988).

16. H. KRÖNER, M. EBERSPÄCHER, T. H. THEIMER, P. J. KÜHN and U. BRIEM, "Approximate Analysis of the End–to–End Delay in ATM Networks", in Proceedings of the IEEE INFOCOM '92 Conference, (Florence, Italy, May 1992), pp. 978–986.

17. H. KOBAYASHI, "Performance Issues of Broadband ISDN Part I: Traffic Characterization and Statistical Multiplexing", in Proceedings of the ICCC '90 Conference, (New Delhi, India, November 1990), pp. 349–355.

18. Q. REN and H. KOBAYASHI, "Transient Solutions for the Buffer Behavior in Statistical Multiplexing", Performance Evaluation, **23**, 1, pp. 65–87 (1995).

19. R. GUÉRIN, H. AHMADI and M. NAGHSHINEH, "Equivalent Capacity and Its Application to Bandwidth Allocation in High–Speed Networks", IEEE Journal on Selected Areas in Communications, **9**, 7, pp. 968–981 (September 1991).

20. A. I. ELWALID and D. MITRA, "Effective Bandwidth of General Markovian Traffic Sources and Admission Control of High–Speed Networks", IEEE/ACM Transactions on Networking, **1**, 3, pp. 329–343

(June 1993).

21. Z. ZHANG and A. S. ACAMPORA, "Equivalent Bandwidth for Heterogeneous Sources in ATM Networks", in Proceedings of the IEEE ICC '94 (SUPERCOMM/ICC) Conference, (New Orleans, LA, May 1994), pp. 1025–1031.

22. B. MAGLARIS, D. ANASTASSIOU, P. SEN, G. KARLSSON and J. D. ROBBINS, "Performance Models of Statistical Multiplexing in Packet Video Communications", IEEE Transactions on Communications, 36, 7, pp. 834–844 (July 1988).

23. D. P. HEYMAN, A. TABATABAI and T. V. LAKSHMAN, "Statistical Analysis and Simulated Study of Video Teleconference Traffic in ATM Networks", IEEE Transactions on Circuits and Systems for Video Technology, 2, 1, pp. 49–59 (March 1992).

24. P. PANCHA and M. EL ZARKI, "MPEG Coding for Variable Bit Rate Video Transmission", IEEE Communications, 32, 5, pp. 54–66 (May 1994).

25. W. VERBIEST and L. PINNOO, "A Variable Rate Video Codec for Asynchronous Transfer Mode Networks", IEEE Journal on Selected Areas in Communications, 7, 5, pp. 761–770 (June 1989).

26. F. YEGENOGLU, B. JABBARI and Y.-Q. ZHANG, "Motion-Classified Autoregressive Modeling of Variable Bit Rate Video", IEEE Transaction on Circuits and Systems for Video Technology, 3, 1, pp. 42–53 (1993).

27. G. RAMAMURTHY and B. SENGUPTA, "Modeling and Analysis of a Variable Bit Rate Video Multiplexer", in Proceedings of the IEEE INFOCOM '92 Conference, (Florence, Italy, May 1992) pp. 817–823.

28. R. GRÜNENFELDER, J. P. COSMAS, S. MANTHORPE and A. ODINMA-OKAFOR, "Characterization of Video Codecs as Autoregressive Moving Average Processes and Related Queueing System Performance", IEEE Journal on Selected Areas in Communications, 9, 3, pp. 284–293 (April 1991).

29. D. S. LEE, B. MELAMED, A. R. REIBMAN and B. SENGUPTA, "TES Modeling for Analysis of a Video Multiplexer", Performance

Evaluation, **16**, 1–3, pp. 21–34 (November 1992).

30. A. A. LAZAR, G. PACIFICI and D. E. PENDARAKIS, "Modeling Video Sources for Real–Time Scheduling", in Proceedings of the IEEE GLOBECOM '93 Conference, (December 1993), pp. 835–839.

31. P. SEN, B. MAGLARIS, N. RIKLI and D. ANASTASSIOU, "Models for Packet Switching of Variable-Bit-Rate Video Sources", IEEE Journal on Selected Areas in Communications, **7**, 5, pp. 865–869, June 1989.

32. I. NORROS, "A Storage Model with Self–Similar Input", Queueing Systems Theory and Applications, **16**, 3–4, pp. 387–396, 1994.

33. W. WILLINGER, M. S. TAQQU, R. SHERMAN and D. V. WILSON, "Self–Similarity Through High–Variability: Statistical Analysis of Ethernet LAN Traffic at the Source Level", in Proceedings of the ACM SIGCOMM '95 Conference, (Cambridge, MA, August 1995), pp. 100–113.

34. R. JAIN and S. A. ROUTHIER, "Packet Trains: Measurements and a New Model for Computer Network Traffic", IEEE Journal on Selected Areas in Communications, **SAC–4**, 6, pp. 986–995 (September 1986).

CHAPTER 6

PROCEDURES FOR ESTIMATING AND GUARANTEEING DELAYS IN HIGH SPEED COMMUNICATION NETWORKS

Sridhar Seshadri and Vijay Srinivasan

6.1. INTRODUCTION

Emerging high speed broadband networks, such as those based on the Asynchronous Transfer Mode (ATM), will carry a variety of traffic such as video, voice and data. Customers using these networks will expect guarantees on several aspects of the service they receive. The service quality metrics include the average and maximum time to deliver packets, variability in delivery times from packet to packet, and packet loss. Guarantees to customers can be provided in one of two ways: (i) hard guarantees can be given on each of these quality measures, such as the maximum delay will not exceed 200 ms; (ii) soft guarantees can be made in a similar fashion, for example by specifying that the probability that the delay will exceed 200 ms will be less than 10^{-5}. In either case, such guarantees need to be decided and given in real-time every time a customer requests a new connection. Moreover, such service guarantees would have to be built into a pricing scheme that combines other factors (such as the actual usage by the customer and performance delivered by the service provider).

The problem of determining feasible sets of guarantees has attracted a lot of attention. The focus of this paper is on delay guarantees.

Among the many papers that contain results on delay bounds are [8-10,15-20,22,30-32,41-44]. There are many more references cited in this list of papers, and the list is not intended to be complete in any way. Relevant work on single class open queueing networks has been reported in [6,33] and the stability of multiclass open queueing networks in [13,36].

Many approaches to establishing hard delay guarantees follow the seminal work of Cruz[8,9]. We first attempt to motivate the methodology used to obtain bounds without using any technical arguments, and therefore, the following is an intuitive understanding of the issues of stability and delay in multiclass networks. There are two main aspects to determining delay bounds: describing the traffic, and specifying a scheduling rule at each node in the network. The traffic model generally includes a bound on the burstiness, as well as specification of the average and maximum rates at which the source generates traffic. The scheduling rule determines which packet (or connection) receives service next and for how long. These rules also need to be combined with a packet dropping rule when the buffer gets filled. The key insights provided by the many papers cited above, and surprisingly even in the stochastic setting with renewal arrivals as shown in Seshadri and Harche[36] (see Section 6.2), is that the network will remain stable if somehow each connection obtains a fair share of service. Intuitively, the stability under fair sharing of the server can be explained as follows: if the server performs head-of-the-line processor sharing, then using the results from single class open queueing networks, the stability of multiclass networks will follow. What then prevents the fair sharing of servers? Examples of problems in practice include long bursts from a single session blocking up a server, sessions hoarding credits for service and utilizing them to process long bursts, packet lengths growing over time, and the server not accounting for the work done in the past in choosing to serve the next packet. This list does not include the example of misbehaving customers, who deviate from their contracted traffic pattern. Given that the users of the network will conform (at least in the long run) to the average rate claimed in their traffic contract (which can be ensured by a traffic policer such as a leaky bucket), the "fair" sharing of the server(s) can be ensured by: (i) giving a session credit towards obtaining service only when packets from that session are present in the queue, (ii) making sure that the long run average utilization required by each session is met, (iii) using work conservation (i.e., doing work whenever there are packets present in the queue), and (iv) assuming that there is an upper bound to the length of the packets. Several scheduling rules have been proposed in the literature that incorporate some or all these elements, such as a framing strategy[18,19], VirtualClock[43], Weighted Fair Queueing[14,31,32,33], Rate-controlled schedulers[17,44], Fair Processor Sharing[36] (FPS), and recently "rule inference" based upon the unifying notion of service curves as given by Cruz[11].

However, despite these theoretical results, in practice very simple methods for determining network delays are being proposed. These methods either assume that a packet always encounters a full buffer and thus suffers the maximum delay at each hop, or make assumptions regarding the independence of the delay experienced at each hop and convolve (add up) the tails of the delay distributions. In convolving the distributions, the assumption of normality is used in [1]. Two reasons for choosing simple methods are (i) while the delay guarantees can be computed using the schemes proposed in the literature, the information required as well as the computation needed to determine the best value of delay are not quite suitable for real time applications, and (ii) the buffer management system as well as scheduling algorithms required to guarantee the delay are generally too complicated to implement in real-time. A third reason is that the guarantees would, in many cases, have to depend on the traffic parameters of other sessions. These parameters can change over time. The fourth reason is that reliable statistical (or soft guarantees) are difficult to obtain using most of the methods proposed in the literature.

As described by Keshav[27], much of the difficulty in implementing Fair Queueing or a similar algorithm arises from overheads (such as queue maintenance) associated with the large number of virtual connections that can be simultaneously active in a switch. An approach to handling this problem is to treat groups or bundles of connections as one unit for scheduling purposes. Given this aggregation of connections, our objective is to determine delay estimation procedures:

- that can be implemented in real-time using minimal information about the network, and

- that are based on scheduling policies that place minimal burden on buffer management and scheduling of packets.

We describe preliminary investigations based on the assumption that individual connections are grouped (or bundled) into several different classes, and are managed in either several different finite buffers or a common buffer. Services are currently being considered in the standards organizations based on such schemes, and details can be found in the draft specifications[46,47]. We limit our investigation to obtaining statistical delay guarantees. The goal of this research is to propose practical buffer management and scheduling policies that can be implemented in real-time in high speed networks. In the next section, we develop delay bounds for communications networks. In the final section we outline how these bounds can be used in practice.

6.2.   DESCRIPTION AND ANALYSIS OF THE FPS SCHEME

There are several techniques available for approximating the mean delay in a variety of queueing systems. On the other hand, with a few exceptions, such as reversible networks[26], telecommunications networks[8,9], and single-stage queueing systems[41], closed-form expressions for bounds or the exact value for the delay in queueing networks are unavailable. In this section, we first use the classic techniques of Kingman[28] for obtaining upper bounds for the average delay in GI/G/1 queues to provide bounds for the mean delay in a tandem system, under the assumptions of infinite buffer capacities at each switch, i.i.d. inter-arrival times and i.i.d. service times at all switches. These bounds are then specialized to the ATM context in Corollary 6.2.1.

We then define a scheduling rule called Fair Processor Sharing (FPS) that mimics the head of the line Processor Sharing scheduling rule. We construct a sample path inequality for the work done in a multiclass single-stage, single-server system that uses the FPS rule by comparing it with the work done in a single class First Come First Served (FCFS) queue. This inequality is applied to establish bounds for the average delay in ATM networks (see Corollary 6.2.3). We also indicate how the technique can be extended to get the second moment of delay.

Currently available bounds for the mean delay in queueing systems fall into two categories, namely bounds for single-stage systems and for networks. The book by Wolff[41] contains a number of bounds for single-stage systems. For results in the network context, we refer the reader to the excellent surveys given by Harrison and Nguyen[25] and Dai[12].

We briefly discuss only the MONQ results below. There have been several negative results that indicate MONQs need not be stable under given scheduling rules[1,2,13,36,40]. In most of these papers, the arrival and service processes are not stochastic, which makes the phenomenon of instability even more surprising. The recent work of Dai[12] links Harris recurrence to the stability of queueing networks by using fluid limits. In this paper, Dai shows that multiclass feed forward networks (among other systems) are stable. We conjecture that, using the scheduling rule proposed in our paper, the feed forward assumption can be dropped and the MONQ can still be shown to be stable.

Cruz[8,9] shows how to compute the delay in the context of packet-switched networks. The ideas used by Cruz have been seminal to several other works dealing with delays in the context of packet-switched networks[4,5,31,32,33]. In all these papers, the arrival process to the network is assumed to be deterministic. The ideas due to Cruz have not been used, to the best our knowledge, to construct closed form expressions for bounds on delay either for tandem systems or MONQs when the arrival processes to the network are of the renewal type. Recently, Zhang, Towsley and Kurose[45] did obtain bounds on delay under the Generalized Processor Sharing rule (introduced by Parekh[31]) using the Exponentially Bounded Burstiness (E.B.B.) process model introduced in Yaron and Sidi[42]. Another stream of research on the stability of MONQs goes back to the work of Perkins and Kumar[34]. Starting with this paper, several scheduling rules were examined for stability in MONQs[29,30]. In these papers, stability is established using sample path constructions and recursive relations. The methods we use for obtaining the sample path inequality in Section 6.2.3 are similar.

Our proof techniques use ideas found in the literature as follows. Chang and Thomas[6] demonstrated the stability of open Jackson networks using the device of scaling service times. We use the idea in Section 6.2.1 to obtain a bound for the mean delay in a tandem queueing system consisting of single-server queues. Parekh[31] proposed a scheduling rule called Generalized Processor Sharing (GPS) and states that under certain conditions GPS is identical to the Fair Queueing rule proposed in Demers, Keshav and Shenker[15]. Parekh used GPS to compute upper bounds on the mean delay in networks with arbitrary topology assuming deterministic arrival processes[32,33]. The arrival processes in Parekh's work are each characterized by the maximum burst size and the long run average rate of traffic flow, as defined in Cruz[8]. A key aspect of the upper bounds[8,9,31,32,33] is that a pattern of arrivals can be exhibited such that the worst case bound on maximum queue size and delay are actually achieved (also see remark following Corollary 6.2.1 in Section 6.2). Subsequent work that is related to GPS, which provide tight bounds on delay as well as the number of packets in the system include that of Georgiadis et al[16,17]. We define a rule called Fair Processor Sharing (FPS) in Section 6.2.2 , to extend the bounds derived for a single-server queue in Section 6.2.1 to a MONQ. The FPS rule is similar to GPS, but is also different in two ways: FPS is non-anticipative while GPS needs information about the service times of packets in the system, and FPS needs less work to implement when compared to GPS.

6.2.1. Bounds for Delay in Tandem Systems

In this section we establish upper bounds on the mean delay in a tandem system of switches, as well as upper bounds for the first two moments of delay when service times are deterministic and equal for all packets.

We consider K switches in tandem. External arrivals come to the first switch. There is infinite waiting room at all switches. Packets, after being served in First Come First Served (FCFS) order at switch $i, i = 1, 2, ..., K - 1$, proceed at once to the next switch $(i + 1)$. After being served at the Kth switch, packets leave the system. We define the following for the tandem system:

K = Number of switches in the tandem system (using the FCFS scheduling rule)

$\{S_n^k, n = 1, 2, ...\}$ is the sequence of i.i.d. service times at switch k, where S_n^k is the service time for the nth packet to be served at switch k. We assume that, $E[(S_1^k)^2] < \infty, k = 1, 2, ..., K$, and denote the squared coefficient of variation of S_1^k as $c_{S_k}^2, k = 1, 2, ..., K$.

$\{T_n, n = 1, 2, 3, ..\}$ is the sequence of i.i.d. inter-arrival times of packets to the first switch, where T_n is the time between the arrivals of the nth and the $(n + 1)$st packet. $E[T_1] = 1/\lambda$. We assume that $E[(T_1)^2]$ is finite, and write the squared coefficient of variation of the inter-arrival time as c_τ^2 .

$\rho_k = \lambda E[S_1^k], k = 1, 2, ..., K$, is the load offered to switch $k, k = 1, 2, ..., K$. We assume that $\rho_k < 1$, for all k.

W_n^k and D_n^k are the time spent at the kth switch and the delay in queue at the kth switch as experienced by the nth packet, respectively.

Set $W_0^k = D_0^k = 0$ and let

$$TS_n^k = \sum_{i=1}^{n} S_i^k; \quad TS_0^k = 0, n = 1, 2, ...; k = 1, 2, ..., K,$$

$$TT_n = \sum_{i=1}^{n} T_i; \quad TT_0 = 0, n = 1, 2, ...; k = 1, 2, ..., K,$$

$$B_n^k = TS_n^k - TT_n, n = 1, 2, ...; k = 1, 2, ..., K,$$

$$TW_n^k = \sum_{i=1}^{k} W_n^i; \quad TW_0^k = 0, n = 1, 2, ...; k = 1, 2, ..., K, \text{ and}$$

$$TD_n^k = \sum_{i=1}^{k} D_n^i; \quad TD_0^k = 0, n = 1, 2, ...; k = 1, 2, ..., K.$$

In these definitions, TS_n^k is the sum of the first n service times at switch k, TT_n is the sum of the first n inter-arrival times to the first switch, TW_n^k is the total time spent by the nth packet at the first k switches, and TD_n^k is the total delay experienced by the nth packet at the first k switches. We are interested in TD_n^K, the total mean delay in queue in the system. It is shown by Harrison[24] that

$$TW_n^k = \max_{0 \le i_0 \le i_1 \le ... \le i_k = n-1} [(B_{i_k}^k - B_{i_{k-1}}^k) + (B_{i_{k-1}}^{k-1} - B_{i_{k-2}}^{k-1})$$
$$+ ... + (B_{i_1}^1 - B_{i_0}^1)] + S_n^k \tag{1}$$

Further, if the utilization of the switches are strictly less than one, then as $n \to \infty$, the random vector $(TW_n^1, TW_n^2, ..., TW_n^K)$ converges in distribution to a non-defective random vector (see Theorem 1, Harrison[24]) We now address the upper bound on the total delay in the tandem system. The relation in (1) can be rewritten as

$$D_{n+1}^k = \max_{i_{k-1} \le n} \left[TW_{i_{k-1}}^{k-1} - TW_{n+1}^{k-1} + B_n^k - B_{i_{k-1}}^k \right]$$
$$= \left(D_n^k + S_n^k - (TW_{n+1}^{k-1} + T_n - TW_n^{k-1}) \right)^+, \tag{2}$$

where $(TW_{n+1}^{k-1} + T_n - TW_n^{k-1})$ is the inter-arrival time between the nth and the $(n+1)$st packets to the kth switch (to see this, set time to be zero when the nth packet arrives, then the nth packet reaches switch k at time TW_n^{k-1}, and the $(n+1)$st packet reaches switch k at time $TW_{n+1}^{k-1} + T_n$). Rewritten in this form, equation (2) is the standard Lindley recursion for the delay in a single-server queue (for example, see Wolff[41]). The $(n+1)$st packet has to wait for a time at least equal to $(TW_n^{k-1} - T_n)$, i.e., the total time spent by the nth packet at the first $(k-1)$ switches less the inter-arrival time between the nth and the $(n+1)$st packet, before being served at the $(k-1)$st switch. The service time at the $(k-1)$st switch when added to $\left(TW_n^{k-1} - T_n\right)$ gives a lower bound for the flow time TW_{n+1}^{k-1},

$$TW_{n+1}^{k-1} \geq TW_n^{k-1} - T_n + S_{n+1}^{k-1}. \tag{3}$$

We now construct a modified system to obtain an upper bound for the mean delay in the system. We denote all modified quantities in this new system by a bar over the corresponding quantities in the original system. Let $\rho_{\max} = \max_{1 \leq k \leq K} \left[E[S_1^k]/E[T_1]\right]$. In the modified system, retain the sequence of inter-arrival times for the original system, but scale the service times at switch i with constants $a_k, k = 1, 2, ..., K$, such that

$$a_k E[S_1^k]/E[T_1] = \rho_{\max} + \frac{(K-k)}{K}(1 - \rho_{\max}). \tag{4}$$

In other words, the new service times are $\overline{S}_n^k = a_k S_n^k, n = 1, 2, ...; \; k = 1, 2, ..., K$. We see that

$$\rho_{\max} + \frac{(K-1)}{K}(1 - \rho_{\max}) =$$

$$(K-1)/K + \rho_{\max}/K < 1, \text{ if } \rho_{\max} < 1. \tag{5}$$

Identities (4) and (5) show that even with the scaling of the service times, the largest switch utilization in the modified system does not exceed unity if the largest utilization without scaling was less than one. This in turn implies that under the assumption $\rho_{max} < 1$, there exists a limiting distribution for the delay in queue at each switch in this modified system (see Harrison[24]). It can be shown, using a sample path construction as given in Shanthikumar and Yao[38], that the total mean delay in queue in the modified system is larger compared to that in the original system. We observe that by Equation (4), for $k = 2, 3, ..., K$,

$$E[\overline{S}_n^k - \overline{S}_{n+1}^{k-1}]/E[T_1]$$

$$= a_k \rho_k - a_{k-1}\rho_{k-1}$$
$$= \rho_{\max} + \frac{(K-k)}{K}(1 - \rho_{\max}) - (\rho_{\max} + \frac{(K-k+1)}{K}(1 - \rho_{\max}))$$
$$= -(1 - \rho_{\max})/K \tag{6}$$

$$E[\overline{S}_n^1 - T_{n+1}]/E[T_1] = \rho_{\max} + \frac{(K-1)}{K}(1 - \rho_{\max}) - 1$$
$$= -(1 - \rho_{\max})/K. \tag{7}$$

Using relations (2) and (3) for the modified system (and bars as noted before when referring to the modified system), we obtain that

$$\overline{D}_{n+1}^k = \left(\overline{D}_n^k + \overline{TW}_n^{k-1} - \overline{TW}_{n+1}^{k-1} + \overline{S}_n^k - T_n\right)^+$$
$$\leq \left|\overline{D}_n^k + \overline{S}_n^k - \overline{S}_{n+1}^{k-1}\right|$$
$$k = 2, 3, ..., K, \tag{8}$$

$$\overline{D}_{n+1}^1 = \left(\overline{D}_n^1 + \overline{TW}_n^0 - \overline{TW}_{n+1}^0 + \overline{S}_n^1 - T_n\right)^+$$
$$\leq \left|\overline{D}_n^1 + \overline{S}_n^1 - T_{n+1}\right| \tag{9}$$

$$\overline{D}_{n+1}^0 = 0. \tag{10}$$

The delay in queue at the kth switch, $\overline{D}_n^k$, is independent of $\left(\overline{S}_n^k - \overline{S}_{n+1}^{k-1}\right)$, for $k = 2, 3, ...K$. Using this fact, squaring both sides of (8), dividing by $E[T_1]$, using the identities (6) and (7), and rearranging we obtain

$$\left(E[(\overline{D}_{n+1}^k)^2] - E[(\overline{D}_n^k)^2]\right)/E[T_1] + 2E[\overline{D}_n^k](1 - \rho_{\max})/K$$

$$\leq E\left|\overline{S}_n^k - \overline{S}_{n+1}^{k-1}\right|^2 /E[T_1]$$
$$k = 2, 3, ..., K. \tag{11}$$

Similarly, as $\overline{D}_n^1$ is independent of $\left(\overline{S}_n^1 - T_{n+1}\right)$, we obtain

$$\left(E[(\overline{D}_{n+1}^1)^2] - E[(\overline{D}_n^1)^2]\right)/E[T_1] + 2E[\overline{D}_n^1](1 - \rho_{\max})/K$$

$$\leq E\left|\overline{S}_n^1 - T_{n+1}\right|^2 /E[T_1]. \tag{12}$$

Theorem 6.2.1 Given a tandem system having K switches with infinite buffer space, with i.i.d. inter-arrival times to the first switch, i.i.d. service times at each switch, finite second moments of all service and inter-arrival time distributions, switch loads ρ_k, $k = 1, 2, ..., K$ and the maximum utilization, $\rho_{\max} = \max_k\{\rho_k\} < 1$, an upper bound,

$U(\rho_{max})$, for the mean number of packets in this queueing system can be chosen as

$$U(\rho_{\max}) = K(2K + c_a^2 + 2(c_{S_1}^2 + c_{S_2}^2$$
$$+ ... + c_{S_{(K-1)}}^2) + c_{S_K}^2)/(2(1 - \rho_{\max})) + \sum_{k=1}^{K} \rho_k, \quad (13)$$

where c_τ^2 and $c_{s_k}^2$, $k = 1, 2, ..., K$ stand for the squared coefficient of variations (scv) of the inter-arrival time and the service times, and $1/\lambda$ is the mean inter-arrival time.

Proof Denote the stationary total mean delay in queue in the original system as $E[TD^K]$ and the stationary mean delay at the kth switch in the original and the modified system as $E[D^k]$ and $E[\overline{D}^k]$. Combining inequalities (11) and (12), and using the fact that the delays in queue at each switch converge to a stationary distribution, we can write,

$$E[D^k] \leq E[\overline{D}^k]$$
$$\leq \lambda K(E[(\overline{S}_1^k)^2] + E[(\overline{S}_1^{k-1})^2]/(2(1 - \rho_{\max})),$$
$$k = 2, 3, ..., K, \quad (14)$$

$$E[D^1] \leq E[\overline{D}^1] \leq \lambda K(E[(\overline{S}_1^1)^2] + E[(T_1^2)])/(2(1 - \rho_{\max})). (15)$$

From Equation (5),

$$E\left[(\overline{S}_1^k)^2\right] = a_k^2 E\left[(S_1^k)^2\right]$$

$$= ((\rho_{\max} + \frac{(K-k)}{K}(1 - \rho_{\max}))^2 E[(T_1)^2]/E[(S_1^k)^2]) E\left[(S_1^k)^2\right]$$
$$\leq \frac{1}{\lambda^2}(1 + c_{s_k}^2). \quad (16)$$

Using (14), (15) and (16), we obtain

$$E[TD^K] = \sum_{k=1}^{K} E[D^k]$$
$$\leq \frac{K}{\lambda} \left(2K + c_a^2 + 2(\sum_{i=1}^{K-1} c_{S_i}^2) + c_{S_K}^2\right)/2(1 - \rho_{\max}). (17)$$

Using (17) and Little's law

$$E[TN] = \lambda \left(E[TD^K] + \sum_{k=1}^{K} E[S_1^k] \right)$$

$$\leq K \left(2K + c_a^2 + 2(\sum_{i=1}^{K-1} c_{S_i}^2) + c_{S_K}^2 \right) /(2(1 - \rho_{\max}))$$

$$+ \sum_{k=1}^{K} \rho_k.$$

Corollary 6.2.1 If all the service times are deterministic, then the upper bound for the mean number of packets is equal to $U(\rho_{\max})$ $= c_a^2/(2(1 - \rho_{\max})) + \sum_{k=1}^{K} \rho_k$. An upper bound for the second moment of delay $E[(TD^K)^2]$ is given by,

$$\lambda \left(E[TD^K]E[(s - T_1)^2]/(1 - \rho_{\max}) + E[(s - T_1)^3]/(3(1 - \rho_{\max})) \right),$$

where s is the largest service time.

Proof For the upper bound on the mean number of packets, set all service times equal to the largest service time, s. Then it follows by relation (8) that there is no delay in any queue except the first one. The bound now follows from the bound for delay in queue at the first switch as given in Wolff[41]. The bound for the second moment of delay is obtained using similar reasoning and by raising both sides of inequality (9) to the third power, cancelling and rearranging terms.

<u>Remark</u> These bounds can indeed be shown to be tight. For example, if the mean service times are non-increasing for switches $k = 1,,2,...$, and the interarrival time distributions have the DMRL property (see Wolff[41]), then the difference between the upper bound and lower bound for the average number of packets is less than 1. The bounds are tight (regardless of ordering of the service times) when the service times are deterministic and the scv of the arrival process, c_a^2, is not too large.

6.2.2. The Fair Processor Sharing Rule (FPS)

In view of the negative results in MONQs referred to in in the introduction to Section 6.2 , it is necessary to define an appropriate scheduling rule in order to establish bounds for a multiclass open queueing network. For such a scheduling rule to be widely applicable, we wanted the rule to be non-anticipative, non-preemptive and work conserving. To this end, in this section, a scheduling rule called Fair Processor Sharing (FPS) is described. We compare the performance of FPS with that of the FCFS rule in this section. Consider a switch that has C classes of packets arriving. The arrival processes are arbitrary. The service time sequence for each class is given by an i.i.d. sequence of random variables. In addition, the service times are assumed to be uniformly bounded both from below and above. The notation employed and the assumptions used are as follows:

C = number of packet classes. $A_i(t)$ = number of packets of class i that have arrived during time $[0, t]$. $\lambda_i, i = 1, 2, .., C$, are given finite strictly positive constants. In the next section these will be interpreted as arrival rates, but for this section they are arbitrary numbers subject to the constraint given below. $\{S_{i,n}, n = 1, 2, ...\}$ is the i.i.d. sequence of service times, where $S_{i,n}$ is the service time of the nth packet of class $i, i = 1, 2, ..., C$. $\rho_i = \lambda_i E[S_{i,1}], \rho_i > 0, i = 1, 2, ..., C$, and $\sum_{i=1}^{C} \rho_i < 1$. $0 < L_i \leq S_{i,1} \leq U_i < \infty, i = 1, 2, ..., C$ and $U = \max_{i=1,2,...,C}\{U_i\}$. $\theta_i = \rho_i/\rho, i = 1, 2, ..., C$. The fraction θ_i is interpreted as the proportion of time that must be devoted to serving class i packets. $D_i(\sigma, t)$ = number of departures of class i packets from the queue during $[0, t]$ when scheduling rule σ is used to choose which packet to serve next. $N_i(\sigma, t) = A_i(t) - D_i(\sigma, t)$, is the number of class i packets in the system at time t, when the scheduling rule σ is used. Now we define the scheduling rule FPS. Let,

$$
\begin{aligned}
lt_i(t) &= \sup\{s \geq 0 : N_i(FPS, s) = 0\} \\
&\quad if \ N_i(FPS, s) = 0 \ some \ s \in [0, t] \\
&= 0 \ else \ .
\end{aligned} \tag{18}
$$

The value of $lt_i(t)$ is the last instant prior to time t when there were no class i packets under the FPS rule. Also let

$$
Y_i(t) = \theta_i (t - lt_i(t)), i = 1, 2, ..., C. \tag{19}
$$

$Y_i(t)$ may be interpreted as the fraction of time that should have been devoted to serve class i packets using the FPS rule during the time $[lt_i(t), t]$. The processes Y_i's and the θ_i's are quantities similar to those defined in Wein[39]. Define, $W_i(\sigma, a, b)$ = work done during the time interval $[a, b]$ on a class i packet, $i = 1, 2, ..., C$, under scheduling rule σ. $P(t) = \{i : N_i(FPS, t) > 0\}$, the set of packet classes present at time t, when FPS is used. All sample path quantities that are indexed by t are assumed to be right continuous and to have left hand limits.

Definition of the FPS scheduling rule

(i) If a packet service is completed at time t, then the next service is initiated without any delay if there are packets waiting in the queue, and the next packet to be taken up for service will be from the packet class $\arg\max_{i \in P(t)}\{Y_i(t) - W_i(NPS, lt_i(t), t)\}$.

(ii) Packets within a class will be treated on FCFS basis, and once a service is initiated it will not be interrupted until the completion of the service.

The FPS rule is said to be work conserving, i.e., the switch does not idle when there is work to be done, non-anticipative, and non-preemptive, i.e., the service of a packet is not interrupted (Wolff[41]). Having defined the FPS rule, we analyze its performance with respect to departures from the system *for just class 1* packets. In analyzing the performance, we use a second system, called the FCFS system. The original one is referred to as the FPS system. Only class 1 packets arrive to the FCFS system, and their arrival process is given by $A_1(t)$, namely *the same arrival process* of class 1 packets to the FPS system. The service times of the nth packet in the FCFS system will be set to $S_{1,n}/\theta_1, n = 1, 2, ...$ This slows down the FCFS system by a factor of θ_1. Moreover if the ρ_i's were the loads brought in by the various packet classes, the load in the FCFS system will be $\lambda_1 E[S_{1,1}]/\theta_1 = \rho_1(\rho/\rho_1) = \rho$, i.e., the total load on the FPS system.

Theorem 6.2.2 We are given a FPS system, with C arbitrary packet arrival processes $A_i(t), i = 1, 2, ..., C$, i.i.d. service times for class i packets, $\{S_{i,n}, n = 1, 2, ...\}$, that are uniformly bounded above by U and below by $L_i, i = 1, 2, ..., C$, a set of strictly positive numbers $\lambda_i, i = 1, 2, ..., C$; and that the system is operated under the FPS scheduling rule defined above. We are given another system (FCFS), which has only class 1 packets arriving as per $A_1(t)$. The service time sequence in the FCFS system is given by $\{S_{1,n}/\theta_1, n = 1, 2, ...\}$, with $\theta_1 = \lambda_1 E[S_{1,1}] / \left(\sum_{i=1}^{C} \lambda_i E[S_{i,1}]\right)$. Then $[D_1(FCFS, t) - D_1(FPS, t)]^+ \leq CU/L_1, t \geq 0$ where U is the uniform upper bound on all service times and L_1 is the lower bound on class 1 service times.

Proof The proof will be given in two parts. In the first part, we will establish a sample pathwise inequality and conclude the proof using this inequality in the second part. For ease of notation define

$$H_i(t) = Y_i(t) - W_i(FPS, lt_i(t), t), i = 1, 2, ..., C. \qquad (20)$$

The $H_i(t)$'s are to be regarded as the shortfall in work done on class i packets at time t, $i = 1, 2, ..., C$. By the definitions of lt_i, Y_i, and H_i, $H_i(t)$ equals zero (regenerates) every time the FPS system empties of class i packets, $i = 1, 2, ..., C$. We first show that

$$If \quad \sum_{i=1}^{C} H_i(0)^+ \leq CU, \quad then \quad \sum_{i=1}^{C} H_i(t)^+ \leq CU, \forall t \geq 0. \qquad (21)$$

Proof of (21): Fix x such that $0 \leq x \leq S_{j,n}$. Let the nth class j job commence service at time t. In the interval $[t, t+x]$, W_i is nonincreasing for $i \neq j$. By Equation (19), $Y_i(t + x) - Y_i(t)$ is less than or equal to $x\theta_i$. Therefore

$$H_i(t + x) \leq H_i(t) + x\theta_i, \forall i \neq j. \qquad (22)$$

As work is being done on class j in the interval $[t, t + x]$, and by using the same definitions,

$$H_j(t + x) = H_j(t) - x(1 - \theta_j). \qquad (23)$$

If $H_j(t) \geq x(1 - \theta_j)$, then from (22) and (23) we obtain

$$H_i(t + x)^+ \leq H_i(t)^+ + x\theta_i, \forall i \neq j, \qquad (24)$$

$$H_j(t + x)^+ = H_j(t) - x(1 - \theta_j) = H_j(t)^+ - x(1 - \theta_j). \qquad (25)$$

By using (24), (25), and the fact that $\sum_i \theta_i = 1$ we obtain

$$\sum_{i=1}^{C} H_i(t + x)^+ \leq \sum_{i=1}^{C} H_i(t)^+. \qquad (26)$$

Else if $Hj(t) < x(1 - \theta_j)$, as the scheduling rule FPS chose to serve the packet class with the largest value of $H_i(t), i \in P(t)$,

$$x(1 - \theta_j) > H_j \geq H_i, i \in P(t) \qquad (27)$$

and for packet classes not present at time t $lt_i(t + x) > t$, for all $i \notin P(t) \Rightarrow Y_i(t + x) \leq x\theta_i, \forall i \notin P(t)$

$$\Rightarrow H_i(t + x) = Y_i(t + x) - W_i(FPS, lt_i(t + x), t)$$
$$\leq x\theta_i, \forall i \notin P(t). \qquad (28)$$

Using (22), (27) and (28) we obtain

$$\sum_{i \in P(t), i \neq j} H_i(t+x)^+ \leq \sum_{i \in P(t), i \neq j} \left(H_i(t)^+ + x\theta_i \right)$$

$$\leq (|P(t)| - 1)x(1 - \theta_j) + \sum_{i \in P(t), i \neq j} x\theta_i, \quad (29)$$

$$\sum_{i \notin P(t)} H_i(t+x)^+ \leq \sum_{i \notin P(t)} x\theta_i, \quad (30)$$

where $|A|$ is the cardinality of the set A. By the assumption for this case,

$$H_j(t+x)^+ < x(1 - \theta_j). \quad (31)$$

Combining, (29)-(31) we finally have

$$\sum_{i=1}^{C} H_i(t+x)^+ \leq |P(t)| \, x(1 - \theta_j) + \sum_{i \notin P(t)} x\theta_i \leq CU. \quad (32)$$

Inequalities (26) and (32) complete the proof of (21). The steps in the proof can be examined to conclude that the bound in (32) does not depend in any way on the stochastic nature of either the arrival processes or service times. To complete the proof of the theorem, we need to verify that

$$(W_1(FCFS, 0, t) - W_1(FPS, 0, t))^+ \leq CU. \quad (33)$$

Note that the switch is working slower in the FCFS system than in the FPS system. Therefore if the FCFS system works for one unit of time, then the work done will be counted as θ_1 units of work. Proving inequality (33) will complete the proof of the theorem, because (33) states that at any time t, for class 1 packets, the maximum amount by which the total work done during $[0, t]$ in the FCFS system can exceed that done in the FPS system is CU.

Proof of (33): Using the definition of $H_1(t)$, we have

$$H_1(t) = \theta_1(t - lt_1(t)) - W_1(FPS, lt_1(t), t)$$
$$\geq W_1(FCFS, lt_1(t), t) - W_1(FPS, lt_1(t), t), \quad (34)$$

because the FCFS system need not always be busy in $[lt_1(t), t]$, and is slowed down by a factor of θ_1. Inequalities (21), (34) and the definition of $lt_1(t)$, imply that

$$(W_1(FCFS, lt_1(t), t) - W_1(FPS, lt_1(t), t))^+ \leq CU \quad (35)$$
$$N_1(FPS, lt_1(t)) = 0 \quad (36)$$

As $A_1(t)$ is the same for the two systems, (36) implies that

$$W_1(FPS, 0, lt_1(t)) \ \geq \ W_1(FCFS, 0, lt_1(t)). \tag{37}$$

Finally, using (35) and (37),

$$(W_1(FCFS, 0, t) - W_1(FPS, 0, t))^+$$

$$\leq \ (W_1(FCFS, 0, lt_1(t)) - W_1(FPS, 0, lt_1(t)))^+$$
$$+ (W_1(FCFS, lt_1(t), t) - W_1(FPS, lt_1(t), t))^+$$
$$\leq \ 0 + CU = CU. \tag{38}$$

Remarks

(1) It is important to note that the bound in Theorem 6.2.2 does not depend on the stochastic nature of arrivals. The only common elements between the FCFS and the FPS systems are the single common arrival process $A_1(t)$, the common values of $\{S_{1,n}, n = 1, 2, ...\}$ and the value of the parameter θ_1.

(2) Parekh[31] defined a scheduling rule called Generalized Processor Sharing (GPS). The idea behind GPS is to define positive numbers $\varphi_i, i = 1, 2, ..., C$, corresponding to each class. Then if a class i is continuously backlogged during the interval $[t_1, t_2]$ and if the service provided to class i during $[t_1, t_2]$ is denoted as $S_i[t_1, t_2]$, then GPS ensures $\frac{S_i[t_1, t_2]}{S_2[t_1, t_2]} \geq \frac{\varphi_i}{\varphi_j}$. In order to implement GPS without having to share the processor, Parekh then defines a rule called the Packet-by-packet Generalized Processor Sharing, PGPS, scheme. PGPS *tracks* the order in which GPS would have scheduled the packets and implements the GPS schedule in a non-preemptive manner. This implementation of PGPS has properties similar to FPS. PGPS needs information about the service of the packet *before* the service is completed, and therefore does not satisfy our non-anticipative criterion. (This requirement for PGPS is met in ATM networks as the packet length is known on arrival.) Moreover, some simulation is required to track the order in which GPS would have scheduled packets. This computational burden is avoided in FPS.

For the next theorem, we need to relax the assumption that the arrival processes to the two systems are the same. We state a corollary of the theorem that will be used in the sequel.

Corollary 6.2.2 If in Theorem 6.2.2, the arrival processes for the class 1 packets are $A_1^{FCFS}(t)$, and $A_1^{FPS}(t)$; and

$$\left(A_1^{FCFS}(t) - A_1^{FPS}(t) \right)^+ \ \leq \ Q, t \geq 0,$$

then $[D_1(FCFS, t) - D_1(FPS, t)]^+ \leq (Q + CU/L_1), t \leq 0$.

Proof Instead of employing inequality (37) as was done in Theorem 6.2.2, we use the assumption that $\left(A_1^{FCFS}(t) - A_1^{FPS}(t)\right)^+ \leq Q, t \geq 0$, and the fact that there were no class 1 packets at time $lt_1(t)$ to conclude that

$$
\begin{aligned}
D_1(FPS, lt_1(t)) &= A_1^{FPS}(lt_1(t)) - N_1(FPS, lt_1(t)) \\
&= A_1^{FPS}(lt_1(t)) \\
&\geq A_1^{FCFS}(lt_1(t)) - Q \\
&\geq D_1(FCFS, lt_1(t)) - Q.
\end{aligned}
\tag{39}
$$

As inequality (35) still holds, using (39) we obtain

$$
(D_1(FCFS, t) - D_1(FPS, t))^+
$$

$$
\begin{aligned}
&\leq Q + (W_1(FCFS, lt_1(t), t) - W_1(FPS, lt_1(t), t))^+ / L_1 \\
&\leq Q + CU/L_1.
\end{aligned}
\tag{40}
$$

Remark: If the service times are deterministic and equal for all packet classes then $U/L = 1$, and the bound becomes (Q+C).

6.2.3. Bounds for Delay in Networks with Deterministic Service Times

The results from Theorems 6.2.1 and 6.2.2 were used to construct an upper bound for the average delay in the system for a multiclass open network of queues (MONQ), with deterministic routing, uniformly bounded and i.i.d. service times at each step of every packet route, and i.i.d. inter-arrival times for each class of packets in Seshadri and Harche[37]. We will only prove a corollary below. Let $E[TD]$ be the total mean delay along the route followed by a class of sessions with (combined) arrival rate λ and i.i.d. inter-arrival times, switch utilization ρ_i at switch i, along a route of n hops. Let C be the maximum number of packet classes at any switch along the route, $\rho_{\max} = \max_i\{\rho_i\}$, and c_a^2 the scv of the inter-arrival times at the first switch for this class of packets. Each switch along the route uses the FPS scheduling rule assigning the weight of λ to the packets on this route.

Corollary 6.2.3 If the service times are deterministic and equal at all switches for all classes then,

$$E[TD] \le \left(c_a^2 / (2(1 - \rho_{\max})) + \sum_{k=1}^{n} \rho_k \right) / \lambda + nC/\lambda.$$

Proof The second term for the bound follows from the remark after Corollary 6.2.2 and repeated application of the corollary. The first term follows from Corollary 6.2.1.

The delay bound given in Corollary 6.2.3 bears remarkable similarity to the delay bounds found in the literature for "deterministic" traffic models. In particular, the term $c_a^2 / (2(1 - \rho))$ replaces the usual term for the burst (σ). The presence of C (i.e., the number of service classes), in the bounds is not as worrisome as it might seem. In the introduction, we mentioned that in a practical implementation, traffic from several classes would be combined to make fewer number of classes. A similar bound can be constructed for the second moment for delay. These bounds could then can be applied to provide statistical bounds for the total delay. In future work we would like to extend these bounds to the case when there are several priority classes at each switch.

6.3. AN APPLICATION

To apply these results in practice, we need to decide upon acceptable methods for combining parameters of traffic streams to obtain the value of the squared coefficient of variation for the inter-arrival times of the combined traffic. Even more important is the fact that bounds as given in the previous section can be obtained only if the scheduling policies or service curves (Cruz[11]), at different switches, possibly made by different manufacturers, along the route is known in advance. An approximation for the mean and standard deviation of the stationary delay in a GI/G/1 queue can be based on the loss probability (see Borden[1]), as outlined below. Consider a single stage queueing system GI/G/1, mean service time $E[S]$, loss probability ϵ, buffer size B, stationary delay D, and server utilization equal to ρ. Then we may approximate (see Theorem 7.4.1, Ross[35]),

$$E[D] \approx -BE[S]/\log(\epsilon). \tag{41}$$

From the expression for the second moment for the delay in the M/D/1 system, we can further approximate the variance of the delay to be equal to square of the first moment of the delay. The mean and the standard deviation can then be used together to yield a statistical estimate for the total delay. We could instead have used the expression for the bound on the second moment of delay given in Corollary 6.2.1. Further analysis of the bound for the second moment reveals that if the last term, $E[(s - T)^3]/(3(1 - \rho_{\max}))$ is negligible, and the scv of the inter-arrival times large, then the bound for the second moment is approximately twice the bound for the mean delay. Using these observations, and Corollary 6.2.3 we state:

Corollary 6.3.1 In an ATM network, let $\rho_{\max}$ be the maximum switch utilization along a given route of n hops, λ the traffic rate for the session (or all sessions) using the route, B the common buffer size at all switches, ϵ be the acceptable loss fraction, ρ_i the switch utilization along the route, let s be the (common) service time at all switches that use the Fair Processor Scheduling Rule to schedule packets on this route (with weight λ); then the average total delay and its standard deviation for packets using the route may be approximated by

$$E[TD] \leq -B\rho_{\max}/(\lambda \log(\epsilon)) + \left(\sum_{k=1}^{n} \rho_k\right)/\lambda + nC/\lambda,$$

$$\sigma_{TD} \approx -B\rho_{\max}/(\lambda \log(\epsilon)). \tag{42}$$

The important observation about the expression in (42) is that the delay does not grow with the number of hops as a factor of the buffer size (also see the discussion below on queueing delays). A simple bound for the total delay can be obtained from using Corollary 6.2.2 directly. The maximum delay at the first hop will not exceed $B\rho_{max}/\lambda$ in the FCFS queue. So another (but deterministic) bound for total delay using this observation and Corollary 6.2.1 is given by

$$TD \leq B\rho_{\max}/\lambda + \left(\sum_{k=1}^{n_1} \rho_k\right)/\lambda + nC/\lambda. \tag{43}$$

Finally, if the packet is not lost, and the packet scheduling discipline is FCFS, then the delay of the packet surely can not exceed Bns. (The assumption that no packets are lost under FCFS scheduling would also imply that the scv of the arrival processes are smaller compared to the scv which would result in the delay given in Equation (41). Therefore in some sense it is unfair to compare the bounds in Equations (42) and (43) with Bns.) These bounds are compared in Figures 6.1 and 6.2. The values used for the different parameters are, $B = 1,200, s =$

$2.8 \times 10^{-4} sec.$, $n = 10$ and 20, $C = 20, \lambda = 142.9$ packets/sec., and utilization $= 0.8$. In these figures, the "stochastic" bound corresponds to Equation (42), with the bound being set equal to the mean plus six times the standard deviation. The "deterministic" bound corresponds to Equation (43) and the FCFS bound to Bns. From these preliminary results, we may infer that the tightness of the stochastic bound increases with the number of hops and decreasing loss probability.

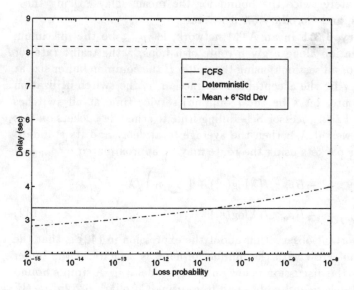

Figure 6.1: B=1200, s=2.7×10^{-4} sec., n=10, C=20, $\lambda = 142.9, \rho = 0.8$

In deriving the bounds in Corollary 6.2.2, we assumed that the packets that are in a class at the first switch continue to be in the same class all along the route, and no other packets get added to the class in the route. This assumption can be weakened by assuming that packets upon leaving a switch, join a class with weight λ. However, this would imply that the queueing delays add up along the route (growing as a factor of the buffer size) – thereby increasing the delay bound. One way of avoiding this problem would be to carefully select the route such that the number of packets (or the number of times packets are) added or dropped is kept minimal. We are currently studying methods that combine route selection and scheduling, in order to reduce the impact of queueing delays at intermediate switches.

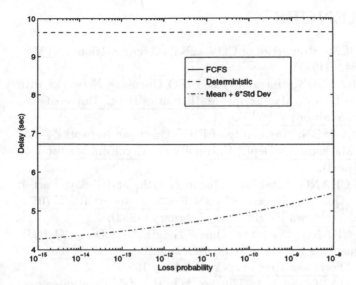

Figure 6.2: B=1200, s=2.7 × 10⁻⁴ sec., n=20, C=20, $\lambda = 142.9, \rho = 0.8$

6.4. CONCLUSIONS

We have provided a method for determining bounds for the moments of delay in broadband networks. Such bounds can be used to provide soft delay guarantees. We plan to extend this approach for computing the moments of delay when packet classes are prioritized. We have also shown that there is a close relationship between the burstiness of data and the squared coefficient of variation of inter-arrival times. They are apparently interchangeable in the formulae for the bound for the worst case delay and mean delay. Our preliminary investigation reveals that in the absence of measured values of the squared coefficient of variation, we could resort to approximations based on the loss probability and compute a "stochastic" bound. Such a bound is tight compared to the "deterministic" bound for small values of the loss probability. Finally, to apply the methods discussed in practice, we pointed out that scheduling and route selection methods need to be combined.

REFERENCES

1. M. BORDEN, "Properties of CDV and its Accumulation", ATM Forum/95-0842, (1995).

2. M. BRAMSON, "Instability of FIFO Queueing Networks with Quick Service Times", Manuscript, Mathematics Dept., University of Wisconsin, Madison, WI 53706, (1993).

3. M. BRAMSON, "Instability of FIFO Queueing Networks", Manuscript, Mathematics Dept., University of Wisconsin, Madison, WI 53706, (1993).

4. C.-S. CHANG, "Stability, Queue Length, and Delay, Part I: Deterministic Queueing Networks" IBM Research Report RC 17708 (No. 77962), Yorktown Heights, NY, February (1992).

5. C.-S. CHANG, "Stability, Queue Length, and Delay, Part II: Stochastic Queueing Networks" IBM Research Report RC 17708 (No. 77963), Yorktown Heights, NY, February 1992).

6. C.-S. CHANG and J. A. Thomas, "On the stability of open networks: a unified approach by stochastic dominance", Queueing Systems, **15**, pp. 239-260, (1994).

7. D. D. CLARK, S. SHENKER and L. ZHANG, "Supporting Real-Time Applications in an Integrated Services Packet Network: Architecture and Mechanism," ACM Computer Communication Review, **22**, (1992).

8. R. L. CRUZ, "A Calculus for Network Delay, Part I: Network Elements in Isolation", IEEE Trans. on Information Theory, **37**, 1, pp. 114-131, (1991).

9. R. L. CRUZ, "A Calculus for Network Delay, Part II: Network Analysis", IEEE Trans. on Information Theory, **37**, 1, pp. 132-141, (1991).

10. R. L. CRUZ and H. LIU, "Single-server Queues with Loss: A Formulation", Proc. Conference on Information Systems and Sciences, Johns Hopkins University, (1993).

11. R. L. CRUZ, "Quality of Service Guarantees in Virtual Switched Networks", IEEE Journal on Selected Areas in Communications, **13**, 6, pp. 1048-1056 (1995).

12. J. G. DAI, "On Positive Harris Recurrence of Multiclass Queueing Networks: A Unified Approach Via Fluid Limit Models", To appear in Annals of Applied Probability, (1994).

13. J. G. DAI and Y. WANG, "Nonexistence of Brownian Models

of Certain Multiclass Queueing Networks," Queueing Systems **13** pp. 41-46, (1993).

14. J. G. DAI, "On Positive Harris Recurrence of Multiclass Queueing Networks: A Unified Approach Via Fluid Limit Models," To appear in Annals of Applied Probability, (1994).

15. A. DEMERS, S. KESHAV and S. SHENKER, "Analysis and Simulation of a Fair Queueing Algorithm," Internetworking: Research i and Experience, **1**, pp. 3-26 (1990).

16. L. GEORGIADIS, R. GUERIN and A. PAREKH, "Optimal Multiplexing on a Single Link: Delay and Buffer Requirements," Proc. INFOCOM, (1994).

17. L. GEORGIADIS, R. GUERIN, V. PERIS and K. SIVARAJAN, "Efficient Network Provisioning Based on per Node Traffic Shaping," Manuscript, IBM T J Watson Research Center, Yorktown Heights, NY 10598, (1995).

18. S. J. GOLESTANI, "A Framing Strategy for Congestion Management," IEEE J. Selected Areas in Communications, **9**, 7, pp. 1064-1077, (1991).

19. S. J. GOLESTANI, "Congestion-Free Communications in High-Speed Packet Networks," IEEE Trans. on Communications, **39**, 12, pp. 1802-1812, (1991).

20. S. J. GOLESTANI, "A Self-Clocked Fair Queueing Scheme for Broadband Applications," Proc. INFOCOM, (1994).

21. S. J. GOLESTANI, "Duration-Limited Statistical Multiplexing of Delay Sensitive Traffic in Packet Networks," Proc. INFOCOM, (1991).

22. S. J. GOLESTANI, "Network Delay Analysis of a Class of Fair Queueing Algorithms," IEEE J. Selected Areas in Communications, **13**, 6, pp. 1057-1070, (1995).

23. A. GREENBERG and N. MADRAS, "How Fair is Fair Queueing?", Journal of the ACM, **39**, 3, pp. 568-598, (1991).

24. J. M. HARRISON, "The Heavy Traffic Approximation for Single-server Queues in Series," Journal of Applied Probability, **10**, pp. 613-629, (1973).

25. J. M. HARRISON and V. NGUYEN, "Brownian Models of Multiclass Queueing Networks: Current Status and Open Problems," Queueing Systems: Theory and Applications, **13**, pp. 5-40, (1993).

26. F. P. KELLY, Reversibility and Stochastic Networks, John Wiley, New York, (1979).

27. S. KESHAV, "On the Efficient Implementation of Fair Queueing", Internetworking: Research and Experience, **2**, pp. 157-173, (1991).

28. J. F. C. KINGMAN, "Some Inequalities for the Queue GI/G/1," Biometrika, **49**, pp. 315-324, (1962).

29. P. R. KUMAR and T. I. SEIDMAN, "Dynamic Instabilities and Stabilization Methods in Distributed Real-Time Scheduling of Manufacturing Systems," IEEE Trans. Aut. Control, **35**, pp. 289-298, (1990).

30. S. H. LU and P. R. KUMAR, "Distributed Scheduling Based on Due Date and Buffer Priorities," IEEE Trans. Aut. Control **36**, pp. 1406-1416, (1991).

31. A. J. PAREKH, "A Generalized Processor Sharing Approach to Flow Control in Integrated Service Networks", Ph.D. Thesis, Dept. of Electrical Engg. and Comp. Sci., MIT, (February 1992).

32. A. J. PAREKH and R. G. GALLAGHER, "A Generalized Processor Sharing Approach to Flow Control in Integrated Service Networks: The Single Node Case", IEEE/ACM Trans. Networking, **1**, 1, pp. 344-357, (June 1993).

33. A. J. PAREKH and R. G. GALLAGHER, "A Generalized Processor Sharing Approach to Flow Control in Integrated Service Networks: The Multiple Node Case", IEEE/ACM Trans. Networking. **2**, 1, pp. 137-150, (April 1994).

34. J. R. PERKINS and P. R. KUMAR, "Stable Distributed Realtime Scheduling of Manufacturing/Assembly/Disassembly Systems," IEEE Trans. Automatic Control, **AC-34**, pp. 139-148, (1989).

35. S. M. ROSS, Stochastic Processes, John Wiley, (1983).

36. T. I. SEIDMAN, "First Come, First Served is Unstable!," Manuscript, Dept. of Mathematics, University of Maryland Baltimore County, (1993).

37. S. SESHADRI and F. HARCHE, "Bounds for the Mean Delay in Some Multiclass Open Queueing Networks," Department of Statistics and Operations Research, New York University, (1995).

38. J. G. SHANTHIKUMAR and D. D. YAO, "Stochastic Monotonicity in General Queueing Networks," J. Appl. Prob. **26**, pp. 413-417, (1989).

39. L. M. WEIN, "Optimal Control of a Two-Station Brownian Network," Math. Operations Research, **15**, 2, pp. 215-242, (1990).

40. W. WHITT, "Large Fluctuations in a Deterministic Multiclass Network of Queues" Management Science, **39**, pp. 1020-1028, (1993).

41. R. W. WOLFF, Stochastic Modeling and the Theory of Queues,

Prentice-Hall, New Jersey, (1989).

42. O. YARON and M. SIDI, "Performance of Stability of Communication Networks via Robust Exponential Bounds," IEEE/ACM Trans. on Networking, 1, 3 372-385, (1993).

43. L. ZHANG, "VirtualClock: A New Traffic Control Algorithm for Packet Switching Networks," Proc. ACM SIGCOMM, (1990).

44. H. ZHANG and D. FERRARI, "Rate-Controlled Service Disciplines," To appear in Journal of High Speed Networks.

45. Z. ZHANG, D. TOWSLEY and J. KUROSE, "Statistical Analysis of Generalized Processor Sharing Scheduling Discipline," Manuscript, Computer Science Department, University of Massachusetts, MA, (1995).

46. Specification of Controlled Delay Quality of Service, Internet Draft, S. Shenker, C. Partridge, Wroclawski (Eds.), (1995),

47. Specification of Predictive Quality of Service, Internet Draft, S. Shenker, C. Partridge (Eds.), (1995).

48. Specification of Guaranteed Quality of Service, Internet Draft, S. Shenker, C. Partridge (Eds.), (1995).

CHAPTER 7

BMAP MODELLING OF A CORRELATED QUEUE

M.B. Combé, O.J. Boxma

7.1. INTRODUCTION

In early queueing models the characteristics of the arrival and service time distributions are constant over time. Hence those queueing models have limited ability to adequately model the typical traffic characteristics of modern communication networks, such as bursty arrival processes and time varying arrival rates.

In the last few decades, analysis concentrating on the typical properties of queueing models for communication networks has led to the development of the theory of the Markov Modulated Queueing System (MMQS). In an MMQS a Markov process describes the time varying behaviour of some of the arrival and service processes. The state of this Markov process contains information about the parameters of the current arrival process and the service time distributions of customers in the system, or it may contain information about current system characteristics, like the speed of the server. For example, the arrival rate of customers generated by an On/Off source may well be described by a Markov process, some states representing On phases of the source, the other states representing the Off phases.

Correspondence to: O.J. Boxma
Note: The first author was supported by NFI

A key aspect of the time varying behaviour of the arrival process and service characteristics in a queueing system is that it reflects a number of *dependence structures* in the sequences of interarrival and service times of customers. In Fendick et al.[11] three types of dependence are mentioned: between consecutive interarrival times, between consecutive service times, and between the interarrival and service time of a customer.

In the past most attention has been paid to describing dependence between consecutive interarrival times and between consecutive service times of customers; dependence between interarrival and service times has been less extensively treated. *The purpose of this chapter is to show how an MMQS can be used to model queueing systems with the latter dependence structure.* In particular we apply the framework of the BMAP (Batch Markovian Arrival Process). A first reason to use the BMAP is that the $BMAP/G/1$ queue, the single server queue with the BMAP as arrival process, has been well analysed and that there exist convenient numerical procedures for most performance measures of interest of the $BMAP/G/1$ queue. A second reason to use the BMAP framework is that it allows a constructional way of modelling dependence between interarrival and service times. In a general MMQS both the interarrival and service time distribution may depend on the state of the directing Markov process, so these distributions can be dependent via this state. However, it appears that a correlation structure between interarrival and service times can be more conveniently modeled with the BMAP than with other MMQS.

Correlation between the interarrival and service time of a customer naturally arises in queueing systems. Kleinrock[14] discusses the traffic characteristics of message flows in a message switching communication network. In the corresponding queueing network the service times of messages at each queue are proportional to the message length. For example, in a tandem configuration successive service times of the same message are correlated, hereby creating a positive correlation between interarrival and service times at the second queue. A second example arises in bridge queues between communication networks. Every now and then, the messages in a network that are destined for other networks are collected and delivered at a bridge queue. In this situation the time between two consecutive arrivals of batches of collected messages at a bridge queue and the number of messages collected is (positively) correlated. This type of correlation structure has been studied by Borst et al.[3, 4] and Bisdikian et al.[2].

Overview of the chapter.
In Section 7.2 we describe how the BMAP can be used to model queueing systems with correlation between the interarrival and service time of a customer. Section 7.3 illustrates the modelling technique with a number of examples. Section 7.4 numerically shows the potential of the modelling technique to obtain performance measures and insights for queueing systems with dependence between interarrival and service times. In Section 7.5 we consider queueing models in which various dependence structures occur simultaneously.
The present chapter extends earlier work on queueing models with dependence between interarrival and service times in several directions; we end this introduction with a discussion of related literature.

Related literature.
Bhat [1] reviews much of the early literature on queueing systems with dependence between successive interarrival times, or between successive service times, or between interarrival and service times. Fendick et al. [11] discuss all these dependencies in the framework of the performance analysis of packet communication networks. In our discussion of the literature, we now restrict ourselves to dependence between interarrival and service times.
Cidon et al. [6] consider a single server queue in which a service time is correlated with the *subsequent* interarrival time. This model can be analysed as an ordinary GI/G/1 queue, as the Lindley equation for that queue allows such dependence. In [7] the same authors study an M/G/1 queue in which the service time τ_n of the nth customer is linearly related to the *preceding* interarrival time σ_n: $\tau_n = \alpha\sigma_n + \tilde{\tau}_n$, with $0 < \alpha < 1$ and $\tilde{\tau}_n$ a service time component that is independent of the interarrival time. Conolly [9] and Conolly and Hadidi [10] had analysed this model without the $\tilde{\tau}_n$ component. Several authors [8, 12, 13, 17] study an M/M/1 queue in which the service time and the preceding interarrival time have a bivariate exponential density, with a positive correlation. Niu [18] observes that the interarrival and service time for this type of dependence are 'associated'. He subsequently proves that the mean waiting time in an M/G/1 queue with associated interarrival and service time is at most equal to the mean waiting time in the corresponding M/G/1 queue with *independent* interarrival and service times.

Borst et al. [3, 4] consider an M/G/1 queue in which the service times depend on the preceding interarrival time in the following way:

$$E[e^{-\omega \tau_n}|\sigma_n = u] = e^{-\lambda(1-\beta(\omega))u}, \quad \omega \geq 0, \tag{1}$$

in which $\beta(\cdot)$ is the Laplace-Stieltjes transform (LST) of the probability distribution of a non-negative random variable b. The covariance of σ_n and τ_n is non-negative: with $Eb = \beta$ and with γ the arrival rate at the queue, it is easily seen that

$$cov(\sigma_n, \tau_n) = \frac{\lambda\beta}{\gamma^2} \geq 0.$$

The correlation structure in (1) contains the linear dependence and bivariate exponential cases mentioned above. It arises in the following framework: individual customers arrive, according to a Poisson process with rate λ, at some collection point; they require service times with transform $\beta(\cdot)$. They are collected according to a Poisson process with intervals σ_n, and the nth collected batch forms one supercustomer with service time τ_n. Borst et al. [3, 4] obtain the distributions of the queue length, waiting and sojourn times of the customers consisting of the collected work, as well as of the individual customers arriving at the collection point.

Boxma and Combé [5] extend the correlation structure of (1) in the following way:

$$E[e^{-\omega \tau_n}|\sigma_n = u] = a(\omega)e^{-\phi(\omega)u}, \quad \omega \geq 0, \tag{2}$$

with $\phi(0) = 0$, and $\phi(\omega)$ having a completely monotone derivative; $a(\omega)$ is the transform of an additional independent component of the service time. The dependent part corresponds to the accumulated work during a collect interval, work arriving at the collection point according to a process with stationary independent increments. The latter process contains the compound Poisson process, that forms the basis of (1), as a special case.

7.2. MODELLING THE DEPENDENCE STRUCTURE WITH THE BMAP

In this section we concentrate on modelling correlation between interarrival and service times of customers with the use of the Batch

Markovian Arrival Process. First we describe the characteristics of the BMAP.

The Batch Markovian Arrival Process.

In the BMAP, the interarrival times of customers are directed by a continuous time Markov process $\{\mathbf{J}(t), t \geq 0\}$ on a finite state space E. A transition from a state i to a state j may induce the arrival of a *batch customer*, the size of the batch depending on i and j. Let the sojourn time in state $i \in E$ be exponentially distributed with parameter $\lambda_i > 0$, and given that a transition takes place, let p_{ij} be the probability of a transition from i to a state $j \in E \backslash \{i\}$, $\sum\limits_{j \in E \backslash \{i\}} p_{ij} = 1$. Defining $p_{ii} = -1$, then the generator of the Markov process $\{\mathbf{J}(t), t \geq 0\}$ is given by the matrix $D = (p_{ij} \lambda_i)$. Next, conditional on a transition from a state i to a state j, the probability of a batch arrival of size k is denoted by q_{ij}^k, $k = 0, 1, \ldots$, where q_{ij}^0 may be interpreted as the probability of having no arrival or of the arrival of an empty batch. With this notation, $p_{ij} q_{ij}^k \lambda_i$ is the transition rate from state i to state j inducing a batch arrival of size k. The BMAP is completely characterized by the sequence of matrices $D_k = \left(p_{ij} q_{ij}^k \lambda_i \right)$, $k = 0, 1, \ldots$, $\sum_k D_k = D$. The BMAP is a special variant of the general Markov modulated arrival process; in the latter case the *service time* distribution may depend on the transitions in $\{\mathbf{J}(t), t \geq 0\}$.

The $BMAP/G/1$ queue is defined as the single server queue with the BMAP describing the arrival process of batch customers, where batches are served in FCFS order, and the service times of single customers are independent and identically distributed with a general distribution function $H(\cdot)$.

The $BMAP/G/1$ has been studied in Lucantoni[15, 16], where one can find results for most of the performance measures of interest, such as the number of customers, waiting times, and the busy period. In the appendix we have collected those results that are of most interest to the present study.

Remark 7.2.1: An important observation is that a batch arrival can be viewed as the arrival of a group of individual customers, or as the arrival of a (super) customer whose service time is distributed as the sum of the service requests of the customers constituting the batch. In this chapter we will consider the BMAP from the latter viewpoint; and this viewpoint will allow us to make service times dependent on interarrival times.   □

Modelling correlation between interarrival and service times.
One of the main observations of the chapter is that dependence between
interarrival and service times can be modeled by viewing $\{\mathbf{J}(t), t \geq 0\}$
as a two-dimensional Markov process, $\{(\mathbf{J}_1(t), \mathbf{J}_2(t)), t \geq 0\}$. $\mathbf{J}_1$ generates the arrivals of batches, and the state of $\mathbf{J}_1$ contains information
about the remaining interarrival time; if the state of $\mathbf{J}_1$ is j_1, this might
for example imply that the remaining interarrival time consists of j_1
exponential phases. The component $\mathbf{J}_2$ contains information about the
batch size distribution; for example, the state of $\mathbf{J}_2$ might stand for
the number of customers in a batch (here and in the remainder of the
chapter we use the convenient notation $\mathbf{J}_i$ for $\{\mathbf{J}_i(t), t \geq 0\}$, i=1,2).

The key idea is to introduce dependence by letting the interarrival
time, the time in $\mathbf{J}_1$ between two batch generating epochs, be the time
parameter in $\mathbf{J}_2$. So, as the time between two arrivals goes by, the
batch size distribution is described by the evolution of $\mathbf{J}_2$. The state
of $\mathbf{J}_2$ just before a batch arrival contains information about the batch
size.

A typical example of this mechanism is given by the Compound
Poisson Process (CPP), which can be viewed as a special batch arrival
process. The interarrival time of a batch is exponentially distributed,
the size of a batch is the number of customers generated by a second Poisson process during that interval. In this example, $\mathbf{J}_1$ is a one
state Markov process, describing the exponentially distributed interarrival times of batch customers, $\mathbf{J}_2$ is a Markov chain with state space
$\{0, 1, \ldots\}$, describing the current size of the batch, i.e., the number of
customers that have arrived in the second Poisson process since the
last batch arrival. In this example, the arrival process of customers in
the second Poisson process represents the process of an incrementing
service time as a function of the interarrival time.

In the next section we show the potential of this construction by elab-
orating on a queueing model with the CPP as the arrival process.

Consider the following model. At a bus stop, customers arrive according to a Poisson process with rate λ. According to a second Poisson
process with rate γ, a bus visits this bus stop, collects the waiting customers, and delivers the customers as a batch at a single server service
facility. With this procedure, the number of customers in a batch is

positively correlated with the interarrival time of batches at the service facility. Indeed, if the interarrival time of the bus is relatively large (small), then also relatively many (few) customers will have arrived at the bus stop, and the service time of the batch customer will be relatively large (small). The arrival process of customers at the bus stop can be viewed as a process of an incrementing service time of the batch customer as a function of the interarrival time.

The queueing model arising from this collecting or reservation mechanism, an $M/G/1$ queue with a typical dependence between interarrival and service times, has been studied in Borst et al.[4]. In [4] results are presented for various performance measures of interest, such as the waiting time, the sojourn time, and the number of customers. Again we remark that we treat the dependence structure from the angle of batch customers whose service times are the sum of the service requests associated to the group of single customers that constitute the batch customer.

7.3. EXPLORING THE MODEL

In this section we use the BMAP for modelling a number of variants (and generalisations) of the collector model that we described in the previous section.

• *Variant 1: Finite bus capacity.*
In Borst et al.[4] the number of customers in the bus can be arbitrarily large. However, the method used in [4] to analyse this case does not seem to be applicable for the natural variant where the number of customers in the bus can not exceed M. With the BMAP, there are two ways of modelling this restriction.

-First approach. If the number of customers at the bus stop has reached M, all future arrivals are rejected until the bus has collected the M customers at the stop. This is an example of the most pure form of the construction; the Markov process J_1 only describes the phase of the interarrival process, the Markov process J_2 only describes the number of customers in the bus, and the interaction of the two chains is limited to the resetting of J_2 to the state corresponding to an empty bus stop, at the moment at which J_1 generates a batch arrival. The Markov chain of J_1 has a single state because the interarrival time is exponentially

distributed, the Markov chain of $\mathbf{J}_2$ has state space $E = \{0, 1, \ldots, M\}$, each state representing the number of customers at the bus stop. In this second Markov chain M is an absorbing state. Note that the arrival process of the busses is still a Poisson process.

In Figure 7.1 the transition rate diagram for $(\mathbf{J}_1, \mathbf{J}_2)$ is presented for the case $M = 3$. The nodes are numbered $0, \ldots, 3$, representing the states of $\mathbf{J}_2$. Figure 7.2 shows the generator matrix D and the matrices $D_0, \ldots, D_3$ it decomposes into.

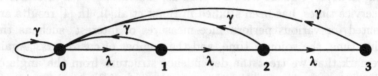

FIGURE 7.1: Transition rate diagram for the collector model with finite bus capacity and blocking of customers. γ is the arrival rate of the bus, λ that of the customers at the bus stop.

$$D = \begin{bmatrix} -\lambda & \lambda & 0 & 0 \\ \gamma & -(\lambda+\gamma) & \lambda & 0 \\ \gamma & 0 & -(\lambda+\gamma) & \lambda \\ \gamma & 0 & 0 & -\gamma \end{bmatrix}, D_0 = \begin{bmatrix} -\lambda & \lambda & 0 \\ 0 & -(\lambda+\gamma) & \lambda \\ 0 & 0 & -(\lambda+\gamma) \\ 0 & 0 & 0 \end{bmatrix}$$

$$D_1 = \begin{bmatrix} 0 & 0 & 0 & 0 \\ \gamma & 0 & 0 & 0 \\ 0 & 0 & 0 & 0 \\ 0 & 0 & 0 & 0 \end{bmatrix}, D_2 = \begin{bmatrix} 0 & 0 & 0 & 0 \\ 0 & 0 & 0 & 0 \\ \gamma & 0 & 0 & 0 \\ 0 & 0 & 0 & 0 \end{bmatrix}, D_3 = \begin{bmatrix} 0 & 0 & 0 & 0 \\ 0 & 0 & 0 & 0 \\ 0 & 0 & 0 & 0 \\ \gamma & 0 & 0 & 0 \end{bmatrix}$$

FIGURE 7.2: Generator matrices for the collector model with finite bus capacity and blocking of customers.

For the $BMAP/G/1$ queue with such generator matrices and a general distribution function $H(\cdot)$ for the service time of a single customer, analytical results and numerical evaluation procedures are presented in Lucantoni[15] for many performance measures of interest, such as the waiting time, the queue length and the busy period; see also the appendix of the present study. For $M \to \infty$ the $BMAP/G/1$ queue reduces to the model studied in Borst et al.[4]. As a particular result of this, we are able to approximate higher moments of the busy period in the latter model as accurately as we wish. In [4] we were only able to obtain the first moment of the busy period.

-Second approach. Here we let $\mathbf{J}_1$ generate batch arrivals, but we also have the bus visit the bus stop when the number of customers at the bus stop reaches M. Hence every time $\mathbf{J}_2$ is in state $M - 1$, the next transition, bus or customer, generates a batch arrival. For this model, for the case $M = 3$, Figures 7.3 and 7.4 show the transition rate diagram for $(\mathbf{J}_1, \mathbf{J}_2)$ and the matrices $D_0, D_1, \ldots, D_3$ respectively.

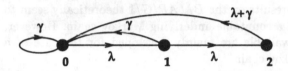

FIGURE 7.3: Transition rate diagram for the collector model with finite bus capacity and no blocking of customers.

$$D = \begin{vmatrix} -\lambda & \lambda & 0 \\ \gamma & -(\lambda + \gamma) & \lambda \\ \lambda + \gamma & 0 & -(\lambda + \gamma) \end{vmatrix}, D_0 = \begin{bmatrix} -\lambda & \lambda & 0 \\ 0 & -(\lambda + \gamma) & \lambda \\ 0 & 0 & -(\lambda + \gamma) \end{bmatrix},$$

$$D_1 = \begin{bmatrix} 0 & 0 & 0 \\ \gamma & 0 & 0 \\ 0 & 0 & 0 \end{bmatrix}, D_2 = \begin{bmatrix} 0 & 0 & 0 \\ 0 & 0 & 0 \\ \gamma & 0 & 0 \end{bmatrix}, D_3 = \begin{bmatrix} 0 & 0 & 0 \\ 0 & 0 & 0 \\ \lambda & 0 & 0 \end{bmatrix}$$

FIGURE 7.4: Generator matrices for the collector model with finite bus capacity and no blocking of customers.

Remark 7.3.1: In the first example, the batch size of an arrival is equal to the state of $\mathbf{J}_2$ at the moment of an arrival. In the second example, a batch arrival may be caused by the arrival of a bus or by the arrival of the $M - th$ customer at the bus stop. Hence, when a batch arrival occurs while $\mathbf{J}_2$ is in state $M-1$, the batch size is with probability $\frac{\gamma}{\lambda+\gamma}$ equal to $M-1$, and with probability $\frac{\lambda}{\lambda+\gamma}$ equal to M. In general, the state of $\mathbf{J}_2$ may describe a batch size *distribution*, rather than just being the number of customers in a batch.   □

• *Variant 2: General arrival processes.*
In the original collector model of Borst et al.[4] the arrival process of
customers at the bus stop and the arrival of busses are both
Poisson. For more general arrival processes it seems hard to extend
the approach of [4] to obtain analytical results. However, when the
interarrival times of busses and customers are of semi-Markov type,
the BMAP modelling can provide approximations for the case of infinite
bus capacity, and exact results for the case of finite bus capacity. Here
we remark that most results on the $BMAP/G/1$ theoretically seem to
extend for the case of a countable underlying Markov chain. However,
numerical methods available are mainly developed for the case of a
finite underlying Markov chain.

As an example of more general arrival processes we present the case
in which the interarrival times of busses are Erlang-2 distributed, the
customers arrive according to a Poisson process at the bus stop, and
customers are rejected once the bus stop is full. Figure 7.5 shows the
corresponding transition rate diagram for the case $M = 3$. The nodes
$(j_1, j_2) \in \{0, 1\} \times \{0, 1, 2, 3\}$ in Figure 7.5 represent the state of $(\mathbf{J}_1, \mathbf{J}_2)$,
$\mathbf{J}_1$ being the state of the bus interarrival process, $\mathbf{J}_2$ representing the
number of customers at the bus stop.

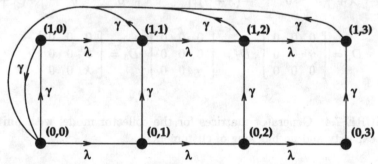

FIGURE 7.5: Transition rate diagram for the collector model with
Erlang-2 distributed interarrival times of batches.

• *Variant 3: Other types of correlation.*
The above mentioned variants of the model with customer collection
all consider a positive correlation between the interarrival and service
time of a batch customer. More specific, the batch size distribution

is stochastically non-decreasing as a function of the interarrival time. In particular, the Markov chain in the first example (cf. Figure 7.1) is related to a birth process. An obvious extension is to construct a negative correlation between interarrival and service times, for example by letting the batch size distribution be stochastically non-increasing as a function of the interarrival time. A second extension is to model customer behaviour at the bus stop; customers may for example leave the bus stop after a while when the bus is 'late'. This queueing model with impatient customers can be adequately modeled with Markov processes J_1 and J_2.

- *An extended BMAP/G/1 queue.*

In the previous examples the service time of a batch consisted of a number of service requests, with the number of requests being dependent on the interarrival time. Boxma & Combé[5] study a dependence structure (cf. (2)) in which the service time of a batch(super) customer consists of two components: a component that is dependent on the interarrival time and a component that is independent of the interarrival time (viz. a set-up time).

We remark that the analysis of the virtual waiting time process of the $BMAP/G/1$ queue (cf. Lucantoni[15]) can be extended to the case where a batch arrival consists of a batch of service requests plus an additional service time component. The batch size is defined in the standard way by the matrices D_i, single service requests have distribution function $H(\cdot)$ with LST $h(\cdot)$. The additional service time component that is added to each batch has a general distribution function, say $A(\cdot)$ with LST $a(\cdot)$. For the single server queue with this work arrival process as input process the expression for the LST of the virtual waiting time can analytically be determined and in fact is quite similar to the expression for the virtual waiting time in the ordinary $BMAP/G/1$ queue.

With this extended BMAP process it is possible to model the dependence structure of [5] for the case where the dependent component can be associated with a compound Poisson process (viz. a customer collecting procedure). A much larger range of correlation structures between interarrival times and service times in queueing models can thus be modelled. And when the actual dependence structure is not known, but the dependence between interarrival and service times has been measured (correlation coefficient, first and second moments of interarrival and service times, etc.), then the (extended) BMAP might also be a useful tool to analyse the model: Parameters of the BMAP may be chosen to fit those measurements.

7.4. NUMERICAL RESULTS

In this section we numerically illustrate the possibilities of our model. We show how infinite collector models might adequately be approximated by a $BMAP/G/1$ queue. We pay attention to the effect of the maximum batch size and we also investigate the influence of the distribution of the intercollecting interval on performance measures of the queueing model. The performance measures considered are the waiting time and the busy period length.

We have restricted ourselves to a few examples, because numerical exploration of $BMAP/G/1$ procedures is not the main purpose of this chapter. Both for batches as well as for individual customers, Lucantoni[15] presents many results and numerical procedures; see also the appendix below.

Approximating infinite bus capacity.

While discussing variant 2 we remarked that most numerical methods for the $BMAP/G/1$ queue are mainly for the case of a finite underlying Markov chain. In Table 7.1 we examine various performance measures as a function of the dimension of this Markov chain for the case of Poisson arrivals of customers and exponentially distributed intercollecting intervals (variant 1). Three service time distributions are considered: exponential, deterministic and hyperexponential H_2. For $M \to \infty$ exact results are adopted from Borst et al.[4]. The terms unforced collect and forced collect which are used in Table 7.1 refer respectively to the first and second approach of variant 1. In the example, the arrival rate λ of customers at the bus stop is 1, the mean service time of a customer is 0.5, and the intercollecting distribution has parameter 1. For the collector model one can distinguish between two types of busy periods: busy periods $\mathbf{B}$ that also include busy periods of length 0, i.e. busy periods started by empty busses, and 'real' busy periods $\mathbf{B'}$, for which only strictly positive busy periods are taken into account. In the table we concentrate on $\mathbf{B'}$.

We notice that for moderate M the values of the mean waiting times $\mathbf{EW}$ and mean busy period length $\mathbf{EB'}$ are already reasonably close to these values for $M = \infty$. The difference for M small is explained by the fact that for unforced collect not all customers arriving at the bus stop will receive service; when $J_2 = M$, newly arriving customers are rejected. In connection with Remark 7.3.1 we note that this might be avoided by having a batch size *distribution* rather than fixing the batch size to M for $J_2 = M$.

	Exponential service				Deterministic service			
	unforced collect		forced collect		unforced collect		forced collect	
M	EW	EB'	EW	EB'	EW	EB'	EW	EB'
5	0.594	1.507	0.630	1.528	0.398	1.454	0.417	1.441
6	0.639	1.554	0.657	1.562	0.436	1.491	0.446	1.487
7	0.666	1.579	0.675	1.582	0.459	1.511	0.464	1.510
8	0.682	1.591	0.686	1.592	0.473	1.522	0.475	1.522
9	0.690	1.597	0.692	1.597	0.481	1.528	0.482	1.528
10	0.695	1.600	0.696	1.600	0.485	1.531	0.486	1.531
20	0.701	1.603	0.701	1.603	0.491	1.533	0.491	1.533
∞	0.701	1.603	0.701	1.603	0.491	1.533	0.491	1.533

	Hyperexponential service			
	unforced collect		forced collect	
M	EW	EB'	EW	EB'
5	0.753	1.528	0.785	1.551
6	0.796	1.576	0.810	1.585
7	0.821	1.600	0.828	1.604
8	0.836	1.612	0.838	1.614
9	0.843	1.618	0.845	1.619
10	0.848	1.618	0.849	1.622
20	0.853	1.625	0.853	1.625
∞	0.853	1.625	0.853	1.625

TABLE 7.1: Mean waiting times and mean busy period lengths as a function of the bus capacity M.

The distribution of the collecting interval.
Figure 7.6 illustrates variant 2, with $M = \infty$. Mean busy period lengths and mean waiting times are presented as functions of the coefficient of variation of Erlang distributed intercollection times. The mean collecting interval is 1, the number of phases in the Erlang intercollection distribution ranges from 1 to 7, and we also examined EW, EB, and EB' for a deterministically distributed collecting interval. For the latter

case we performed a simulation experiment (the reason for taking resort to simulation is that deterministic collect intervals do not fit in the framework of BMAP). Customers arrive according to Poisson processes with rate 1, the mean service time of a customer is 0.5.

Figure 7.6 illustrates the possibility of the BMAP framework to obtain insight in queueing systems with dependence between interarrival and service times, in particular when this dependence is the result of a collection/reservation mechanism. The first observation in Figure 7.6 is that both mean waiting times and busy period lengths are decreasing as the intercollection interval becomes 'more deterministic' - as one would expect. Secondly, and less obviously, the performance measures appear to be almost linear functions of the coefficient of variation of the intercollection interval distribution. Finally, not shown here, we observed that the coefficient of variation of the busy period remains almost constant.

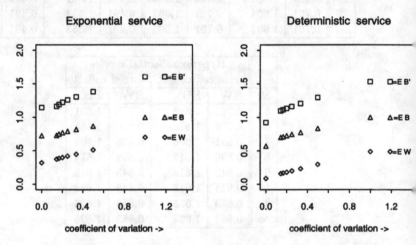

FIGURE 7.6: The effect of the intercollection interval distribution on mean waiting times and mean busy period lengths.

7.5. INTEGRATING VARIOUS DEPENDENCE STRUCTURES

In general one considers three types of dependence in queueing systems: between consecutive interarrival times, between consecutive service times, and between the interarrival and service times of customers. Fendick et al.[11] state that in packet queues with multiple classes of traffic and variable packet lengths all three types of dependence occur *simultaneously*. The BMAP allows us to model this phenomenon. To illustrate this, we present an example in which the arrival process of busses is a two-state Markov Modulated Poisson Process (MMPP), the batch size corresponds to a collecting procedure, and consecutive batch sizes are positively correlated. The example features all three types of dependence.

The dependence between two consecutive batch sizes can be modeled in several ways; for example by letting the arrival process of customers at the bus stop be a Markov Modulated Arrival Process, or by assuming that when the number of customers at the bus stop equals the maximum capacity M of the bus, newly arriving customers will wait for the next bus. The latter can be modeled as follows; at the moments J_1 generates a bus arrival, also allow transitions in J_2 to states other than 0 (this state representing the empty batch).

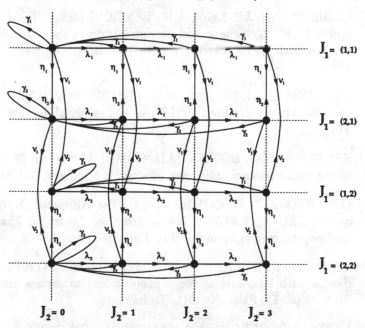

FIGURE 7.7: transition rate diagram for the collector model. Busses and customers arrive according to two-state MMPP's.

For our example we choose to model the dependency of consecutive service times by a two-state MMPP. The two-state MMPP's for the arrivals of busses and customers are as follows: while the underlying Markov process is in state i, the arrival rate for the arrival process of busses (of customers at the bus stop) is γ_i (λ_i), and the sojourn time in state i is exponentially distributed with parameter η_i (ν_i), $i = 1, 2$. For this model it is convenient to describe the evolution of the batch size distribution by a two dimensional Markov chain $\mathbf{J}_2 = (\mathbf{J}_2^1, \mathbf{J}_2^2)$, $\mathbf{J}_2^1$ representing the state of the MMPP for the individual customers, and the state of $\mathbf{J}_2^2$ representing the number of customers at the bus stop. In Figure 7.7 the transition rate diagram is presented for the case $M = 3$.

References

[1] U.N. BHAT (1969). Queueing systems with first-order dependence. Opsearch **6**, 1-24.

[2] C. BISDIKIAN, J.S. LEW, A.N. TANTAWI (1992). The Generalized $D^{[X]}/D/1$ queue and its application in the analysis of bridged high speed token-ring networks. IBM Res. Rep., RC 18387.

[3] S.C. BORST, O.J. BOXMA, M.B. COMBE (1992). Collection of customers: a correlated M/G/1 queue. Perf. Eval. Review **20**, 47-59.

[4] S.C. BORST, O.J. BOXMA, M.B. COMBE (1993). An $M/G/1$ queue with customer collection. Stochastic Models **9**, 341-371.

[5] O.J. BOXMA, M.B. COMBE (1993). The correlated $M/G/1$ queue. AEÜ **47**, 330-335, *Special Issue on Teletraffic Theory and Engineering in memory of F. Pollaczek.*

[6] I. CIDON, R. GUERIN, A. KHAMISY, M. SIDI (1991). On queues with inter-arrival times proportional to service times. Tech. Rept. EE PUB. No. 811, Technion.

[7] I. CIDON, R. GUERIN, A. KHAMISY, M. SIDI (1991). Analysis of a correlated queue in communication systems. Tech. Rept. EE PUB. No. 812, Technion.

[8] B. CONOLLY, Q.H. CHOO (1979). The waiting time process for a generalized correlated queue with exponential demand and service. SIAM J. Appl. Math. **37**, 263-275.

[9] B. CONOLLY (1968). The waiting time for a certain correlated queue. Oper. Res. **15**, 1006-1015.

[10] B. CONOLLY, N. HADIDI (1969). A correlated queue. J. Appl. Probab. **6**, 122-136.

[11] K.W. FENDICK, V.R. SAKSENA, W. WHITT (1989). Dependence in packet queues. IEEE Trans. Comm. **37**, 1173-1183.

[12] N. HADIDI (1981). Queues with partial correlation. SIAM J. Appl. Math. **40**, 467-475.

[13] N. HADIDI (1985). Further results on queues with partial correlation. Oper. Res. **33**, 203-209.

[14] L. KLEINROCK (1964). *Communication Nets.* (McGraw-Hill, New York).

[15] D.M. LUCANTONI (1991). New results on the single server queue with a batch Markovian arrival process. Stochastic Models **7**, 1-46.

[16] D.M. LUCANTONI (1993). The BMAP/G/1 queue: A tutorial. In: *Models and Techniques for Performance Evaluation of Computer and Communication Systems*, eds. L. Donatiello, R. Nelson (Springer, Berlin), pp. 330-358.

[17] C.R. MITCHELL, A.S. PAULSON, C.A. BESWICK (1977). The effect of correlated exponential service times on single server tandem queues. Naval Research Logistics Quarterly **24**, 95-112.

[18] S.-C. NIU (1981). On queues with dependent interarrival and service times. Naval Research Logistics Quarterly **28**, 497-501.

[19] L. TAKACS (1962). *Introduction to the Theory of Queues.* (Oxford University Press, New York).

A   APPENDIX: THE *BMAP/G/*1 QUEUE

In this appendix we present a few of the main results on the single server queue $BMAP/G/1$. The theory presented in this appendix is adapted from Lucantoni[15] and the tutorial paper by the same author[16], to which we also refer for examples of the BMAP and extensive surveys of related literature.

In the Batch Markovian Arrival Process (BMAP), the arrivals of groups of customers are directed by a continuous time Markov process $\{\mathbf{J}(t), t \geq 0\}$ on a finite state space E. The BMAP is fully described by transition rate matrices $\{D_0, D_1, \ldots\}$, with $D = \sum_k D_k$ being the generator matrix of $\{\mathbf{J}(t)\}$. The $ij-th$ element of matrix D_k is the transition rate from state i to state j inducing a batch arrival of size k. Associated with this sequence of matrices is the matrix generating function $D(z) = \sum_{k=0}^{\infty} D_k z^k, \ |z| \leq 1$.

The stationary probability (row) vector of the Markov process is usually denoted by π and satisfies the conditions $\pi D = 0$ and $\pi e = 1$, where e is the $|E|$ dimensional unit (column) vector.

The $BMAP/G/1$ queue is defined as the single server queue with the BMAP describing the arrivals of batches of customers. The customers are served in order of arrival, their service times are independent and identically distributed with distribution function $H(\cdot)$, with LST $h(\cdot)$, and finite first and second moment h_1 and h_2 respectively.

The analysis of the $BMAP/G/1$ queue is close to the analysis of the $M/G/1$ queue; most results for the $BMAP/G/1$ queue are matrix generalizations of $M/G/1$ theory. Below we present results for two main performance measures: the busy period and the (virtual) waiting time.

The busy period
Define

$(G_n(x,y))_{ij} :=$ Pr{ Given that at time 0 the workload consisting of the not completed service requests is y and $\mathbf{J}(0) = i$, the busy period ends at a time $x_1 \leq x$ with $\mathbf{J}(x_1) = j$, and during the busy period exactly n new customers have arrived and have been served }.

The matrices G_n are similar to busy-period expressions as formulated for the ordinary M/G/1 queue, the main difference being the fact that here we also keep track of the changes in the directing Markov process.

Defining $G(z,s) := \int\limits_{y=0}^{\infty} \sum_{n=0}^{\infty} \int\limits_{x=0}^{\infty} e^{-sx} dG_n(x,y) z^n dH(y)$, which describes the number of customers served during a busy period and the length of that busy period, it can be shown that this function satisfies the following functional equation

$$G(z,s) = z \int\limits_{x=0}^{\infty} e^{-sx} e^{D[G(z,s)]x} dH(x), \quad \text{for } |z| \le 1, \ Re \ s \ge 0, \qquad (3)$$

with $D[G(z,s)] := \sum_{k=0}^{\infty} D_k \left(G(z,s)\right)^k$.

Notice that expression (3) can be seen as the matrix equivalent of the busy period equation for the ordinary $M/G/1$ queue: $G(z,s) = zh(s + \lambda - \lambda G(z,s))$ (cf. Takács[19] p.32).

The matrix $G(z,s)$ and the derived matrices $G(s) := G(1,s)$ and $G := G(0)$ are key elements in the analysis of the stationary performance measures of the $BMAP/G/1$; the busy period is related to first-passage times and recurrence times. An important vector is g which satisfies $gG = g$ and $ge = 1$. g can be interpreted as the vector of stationary probabilities $\lim_{t\to\infty}(Pr\{\mathbf{J}(t) = j | \text{server is idle}\})$. The mean arrival rate of the BMAP/G/1 queue is $\lambda' = \pi D'(1)e$, the load ρ is given by $\lambda' h_1$.

The virtual waiting time
Define the vector random variable $\mathbf{V}$ with distribution function $V(\cdot)$

$V_j(x) := Pr\{$ At an arbitrary time the amount of work in the system is at most x and the directing Markov process is in state $j\}$.

Let $v(s)$ denote the LST of $V(\cdot)$, then $v(s)$ satisfies

$$
\begin{aligned}
v(s) &= s(1-\rho)g[sI + D(h(s))]^{-1}, \quad Re \ s \ge 0, \qquad (4)\\
v(0) &= \pi.
\end{aligned}
$$

Again, notice the similarity between expression (4) and the LST $\hat{v}(s)$ of the virtual waiting time in the ordinary M/G/1 queue, which is

$$\hat{v}(s) = \frac{s(1-\rho)}{s - \lambda(1 - h(s))}. \qquad (5)$$

The LST $w(s)$ of the waiting time distribution of an arbitrary batch customer can be obtained from (4) by conditioning on the state of the directing Markov process given that an arrival takes place. Let $q_i = (\sum_{k=1}^{\infty} D_k e)_i / \lambda_i$ denote the probability that a transition from i generates a batch arrival, then

$$w(s) = \frac{v(s)q}{\pi q}, \quad Re \ s \geq 0. \tag{6}$$

For our numerical experiments we calculated the mean virtual waiting time from

$$EV = (EV)e\pi + \pi - ((1 - \lambda' h_1)g + h_1 \pi D'(1))[e\pi + D]^{-1}, \tag{7}$$

in which $(EV)e$ is given by

$$(EV)e = \frac{1}{2(1-\rho)} \Big[2(\rho - ((1-\rho)g + \pi h_1 D'(1)) \ [e\pi + D]^{-1} h_1 D'(1)e)$$
$$+ \pi(h_1^2 D''(1) + h_2 D'(1))e \Big]. \tag{8}$$

Remark on numerical implications

The expressions for the moments of performance measures look complicated; they involve inverses of matrices (e.g. $[e\pi + D]^{-1}$) and solutions of functional equations and linear sets of equations (cf. (3), or $gG = g$). In practice, however, the numerical evaluations can be done quite efficiently. For example, when the LST of the service time distribution is explicitly known, the solution of (3) reduces to an iterative procedure only involving elementary arithmetic operations.

CHAPTER 8

HIERARCHICAL PERFORMANCE MODELING OF COMPUTER COMMUNICATION SYSTEMS

Marco Conti and Raffaela Mirandola

8.1. INTRODUCTION

Performance analysis has a relevant role in network-architecture design, protocol selection and network tuning by providing estimates of network behavior in terms of throughput, response time and network utilization. There are two main approaches in system performance evaluation: the first uses measurement techniques, the second is based on a representation of the behavior of a system via a model.[17,21,22,25,36] The solution to the model gives the performance indices of the model which in turn are an estimate of the indices of the system. The measurement techniques are applied to a real system, considering both real and artificial load configurations, or otherwise to a prototype of the system. The advantage of measurement techniques over using a model is that real system performances are obtained rather than those of a model of that system. Yet, measurement techniques do have their disadvantages. One, for instance, is the need to have a system that is actually functioning (either the real system or a prototype of it), and which can thus be measurable.[17,22,24] Using a model, on the other hand, allows us to study the system in each phase of its life cycle, or rather in each design, development, set-up and modification stage. In this chapter we focus on the use of modeling methods and techniques in computer-networks performance evaluation. Specifically, we concentrate on communication-system models defined by using the queueing formalism (i.e., single server queues,[26,27] polling models,[40] and queueing networks [22,28]). Evaluating system performances via models consists of two steps: *i*) defining the system model, and *ii*) solving the model using various solution techniques to get the model performance indices that make up an estimate of the indices of the system.

There are essentially two classes of model: the first includes analytical models that describe the system and its evolution via a set of mathematical equations; the second includes simulation models that describe the evolution of the state of the system. The solution methods include analytical[21,22,25,30,36,37] and simulative techniques.[24,28,29]

There is a trade-off between analytical and simulative techniques. Analytical models often provide exact results for simple queueing models[6] but approximate results for complex models. They are both efficient and cost-effective.[11,34] However, when analytical models are mathematically intractable, computer simulation is the only alternative. Simulation models are closer to real-systems but they require knowledge of simulation languages (this can be solved by using simulation tools such as RESQ2[38]) and are both expensive and time consuming.[24,28,29]

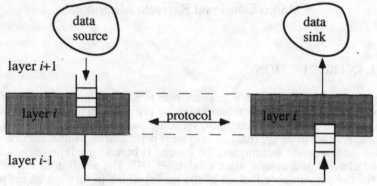

FIGURE 8.1. Network architecture layering.

Computer and communication systems often show a high-structural complexity and large dimensions. The performance evaluation of these systems, based on one level unstructured models and with the direct application of either analytical or simulative technique, may not be sufficiently adequate both in model definition and analysis. Hence, a structured or *Hierarchical Modeling* (*HM*) approach[30,22] can be applied to avoid a single level modeling view of the system and to reduce the size of the model and, consequently, the space and time complexity of model analysis. Specifically, in model analysis, HM, starting from the queueing model which describes the system behavior (*original model*), works in three main steps which can be applied recursively. In the first, *decomposition step,* the model is partitioned into submodels. Submodels are the analyzed in isolation (second step). From this analysis it is possible to define a simpler representation of each submodel. In the third step, *aggregation step*, in the original model each submodel is replaced with a single server queue (with appropriate parameters) which mimics the submodel behavior, and then the reduced model (*aggregate model*) is analyzed by using analytical or simulative techniques. This approach could be very attractive in large models which might otherwise be intractable. In particular, the application of the HM methodology for analyzing computer-communications systems is interesting for several reasons.

1. The architecture of a communication network has a hierarchical structure. The network functionalities are partitioned into layers. As shown in Figure 8.1, each layer i performs a set of functions by exploiting the data-transfer services provided by layer i-1. At the same time, the functionalities performed by layer i provide an enhanced data-transfer service (with respect to the layer i-1 transfer service) to layer i+1. The hierarchical structure of a network architecture makes the use of HM methodology a natural choice. In the HM methodology, first a queueing submodel is constructed for each layer and then the network model is obtained by specifying for each submodel its inputs and outputs. Inputs and outputs define the interactions between submodels.

2. The performance evaluation of communication protocols has been an area of intensive research but most studies have focused on the protocols of a single layer in which lower layers are simply represented with a delay in the information transfer, and the upper layers are the sources and the sink of the information. There is now a growing interest in evaluating the effects of multiple layers of protocols on the end-to-end performance figures (e.g., throughput, delays). However, a multi-layer model shows a high-structural complexity and large dimensions which cannot be handled with an unstructured modeling approach.

3. A computer-network is generally made up of several stations[13,20] (e.g., 100-200 stations). From a performance analysis standpoint, many of these stations exhibit the same statistical behavior, hence, with a hierarchical approach, during the submodel-analysis phase we need to study only one of these stations. We can then use the process which describes its behavior to represent in the aggregate model all the other stations that exhibit the same behavior as the one analyzed. Clearly, this should produce a significant computational gain.

In this chapter we present the Hierarchical Modeling approach both in the definition of a system's model and in the model solution phase. HM has been applied by several authors for the performance analysis of both computer system models[2,8,10] and communications system models.[14,18,19,23,33] However, HM has almost always been presented as an empirical approach, whose effectiveness was related only to the skill of the analyzer. Here the advantages and the drawbacks of the HM methodology are discussed. In addition, we present and analyze the Hybrid Simulation (*HS*) technique which combines analytical and simulative techniques in the solution of hierarchical models. In most cases Hybrid Simulation is the most efficient technique in performing the two solution steps (i.e., submodels analysis, and aggregate model analysis) of the HM methodology.* With the Hybrid Simulation technique each submodel is solved with analytic techniques and then the reduced system model is analyzed with simulative techniques.[35,8] We investigate the conditions under which HS is suitable with respect to simulative analysis of a single level (unstructured) model (*Pure Simulation, PS*).

Throughout this chapter, the use of hierarchical modeling and hybrid simulation is first described in a general setting, and then their use in computer-network analysis is exemplified in a case study. As a case study we consider a simple distributed system: personal computers, file servers, hosts, workstations, printers are interconnected by using a high-speed LAN. The objective of the system analysis is to evaluate the end-to-end response time under a given network configuration and traffic conditions. Various architectural aspects influence the end-to-end performance figures: the flow control techniques, finite buffer strategies, and various priority structures. These aspects make the analytical model of the communication subsystem analytically intractable. Furthermore, a detailed simulation model rapidly becomes time consuming and hence inefficient as the number of network stations increases. We thus show how hierarchical modeling and the HS technique can solve the problem.

8.2. HIERARCHICAL MODELING IN MODEL DEFINITION

HM can be used to define a system model through a top-down stepwise refinement technique. The system is represented by a succession of models, each defined at a different level of detail. Throughout, L will denote the number of levels. By applying this top-down approach, we start from the least detailed model of the system defined at the highest level of abstraction. By specifying with more detail some components of this first model, we define a new more detailed model of the system at a second (lower) level of abstraction. This procedure can be iterated to obtain a model at the appropriate level of detail. The set of models obtained by this top-down approach are hierarchically related in terms of model components. In other words, HM for the model definition consists in the iteration for L times of the specification step.

SPECIFICATION STEP. Starting from a given model, say level i model, this step defines a new model (i.e., a level $i+1$ model) by specifying at a higher

---

* In the literature, the use of simulative and analytical techniques in the first and second step, respectively is also referred to as Hybrid Simulation. Throughout, unless otherwise stated, Hybrid Simulation indicates the use of analytical techniques in the first step, and a simulative solution in the second step.

level of detail some components of the level i model. This is achieved by partitioning a level i component into a set of sub-components and by defining the interactions among them. A typical relation between models for two successive levels of the hierarchy defines the correspondence between a model component at one level, say level i, and a set of subcomponents at a more detailed (lower) level, level $i+1$. Note that each model in the hierarchy is a system representation at a given level of abstraction and can be used to evaluate system performance. Different performance goals can be defined at various levels of the hierarchy. Therefore the number L of the models of the hierarchy depends on the goal of the performance study.

This top-down stepwise hierarchical performance modeling approach can be useful, for example, in the design and development phase of a system. Each specification step corresponds to a design choice, for example the definition of a buffer strategy in a packet switching node.

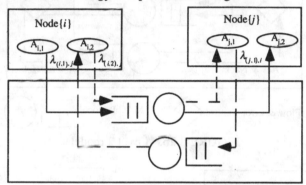

Figure 8.2a.   The highest level model (L=1).

8.2.1. Hierarchical Modeling of a Distributed System

The application of HM for defining the model of our simple LAN-based distributed system, in the case $L = 3$, is given in Figures 8.2a-8.2c. The starting model (model 1) is characterized by a set of application processes $\{ A_{i,1} , A_{i,2} , A_{j,1} , A_{j,2} , ... \}$ and a communication subsystem (see Figure 8.2a). The processes located in different nodes cooperate by exchanging messages. In this model ($L = 1$), the communication subsystem that is in charge of delivering the messages from the sender to the receiver, is simply represented by a single-server queue describing the data-transfer delay. By applying for the first time the specification step, we define a new model ($L=2$ model) in which we make a distinction between the type of service required by applications to perform the data transfer: *connection-oriented* or *connectionless service*.[7,39] Process $A_{i,1}$ requires a connection-oriented service to transfer its data to $A_{j,2}$, while a simple connectionless service is enough for the cooperation between $A_{i,2}$ and $A_{j,1}$. This means that error detection, error recovery and flow control mechanisms[7, 39] are used by the communication system to provide the required service to the connection $A_{i,1}$ - $A_{j,2}$. Specifically, acknowledgements (*Ack*), negative-acknowledgements (*Nack*) and a window-based mechanism are used to provide a connection-oriented service (see Figure 8.2b).

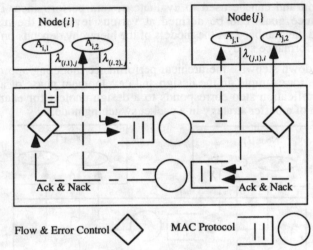

FIGURE 8.2b.   Level 2 model.

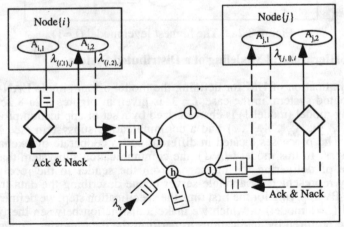

FIGURE 8.2c.   The model with the highest level of detail (*L*=3).

Finally, the model with the highest level of detail ($L=3$) is obtained by representing in the model the features of the LAN on which the distributed system is based on (see Figure 8.2c). Specifically, it is assumed that we have a ring network with a k-limited service discipline[40] which may represent both a Token Ring network,[20] and an FDDI network with synchronous traffic only.[1,13] Furthermore, to model a realistic environment, it is assumed that the buffers, in which packets are queued before their transmissions on the LAN occur, have a finite size. The resulting model of the LAN is therefore a finite-buffer polling system with a k-limited service discipline.[40]

8.3. HM IN MODEL ANALYSIS

HM can be applied to the model analysis. Note that the model to analyze can be obtained through the application of HM in model definition (see Section 8.2) but it can also be defined with a non hierarchical approach.

HM analysis is a bottom-up approach based on a hierarchy of models defined at different levels of detail. Starting from the most detailed model: *i*) we decompose the model into a set of submodels by defining a partition of the set of the model components; *ii*) each submodel is analyzed in isolation from the rest of the system; and *iii*) by exploiting the results of step *ii*), we define for each submodel its aggregate representation at a higher level of abstraction. This procedure can be iteratively applied starting from this second model up to the last detailed model defined at the highest level of abstraction. This final model is analyzed by applying classical non hierarchical techniques. In other words, HM for the model analysis consists in the iteration of these three main steps:

1. *Decomposition step.* A system model (*original model*) is decomposed into a set of submodels. Let us assume that this model corresponds to a given abstraction level L.
2. *Submodel analysis step.* Each submodel is analyzed in isolation.
3. *Aggregation step.* An aggregate representation is defined for each submodel by exploiting results of step 2. Then, an aggregate representation of the original model (corresponding to level $L-1$) is obtained: *i*) by substituting each submodel with its aggregate representation, and *ii*) by defining the interactions among the aggregate submodels.

An example of the application of HM for model analysis, for $L=2$, is given in Figure 8.3. Figure 8.3.a illustrates a generic system model ($L=2$ model) formed by four resources. Step 1 decomposes the model into two submodels A_1 and A_2 as illustrated in Figure 8.3.b. Step 2 analyzes submodel A_2 in isolation (A_1 remains unchanged). Step 3 defines the new aggregate model formed by A_1 (unchanged), by an aggregate component that represents the submodel A_2 and by their interactions, as shown in Figure 8.3.d.

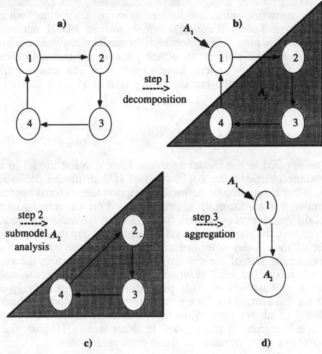

FIGURE 8.3. a) Original model, b) decomposed model c) submodel analysis, d) aggregate model.

Performance indices for each model in the hierarchy, say level L model, can be derived by reversing the hierarchical process and by combining the analysis of each aggregate submodel with the model analysis. The analysis of the final model (L=1) provides performance indices at the highest level of abstraction.

TABLE 8.1. Possible combinations of the solution techniques.

	I	II	III	IV
Submodel analysis	Analytic	Analytic	Simulation	Simulation
Aggregate model analysis	Analytic	Simulation	Analytic	Simulation

At each iteration step various solution techniques can be applied to analyze a model and its submodels. Considering HM for just one level of detail, i.e., $L=2$, Table 8.1 presents the possible combinations of the various solution techniques in the submodels analysis and in the final model solution. In this case, in the two solution steps (i.e., the isolated submodels analysis, and the solution of the whole system) we can use both analytical and simulative techniques in the various combinations outlined in Table 8.1.

The solution of the submodels is a fundamental aspect of HM since it thereby determines the efficiency and exactness. In fact, only if the aggregation step is carried out accurately will the models at the various levels of abstraction be equivalent. Also, the solution cost of the submodels in the aggregation step has a strong influence on the cost of the whole solution. For these reasons the analytical techniques should provide, in the submodel solution step, the best compromise between solution accuracy and computational cost. Balsamo and Mirandola[5] show that combination II (i.e., Hybrid Simulation) is the most promising technique for systems analysis in the HM methodology and identify some criteria which affect the suitability of HS in HM. In particular, the applicability criteria of the Hybrid Simulation, or rather cases where HS is more suitable than pure simulation, depend on the following factors:[5]

a) Type of performance index to estimate: if we are interested in a global index, i.e. for the whole network, then we need to consider the other factors below (i.e., b-g), whereas if we are interested in a performance index that is local to a node (of the non-aggregate network), then we can say a priori that HS is more suitable that PS.
b) A low number (in the original network) of service centres with a service-rate dependent on the load guarantees good HS performance.
c) As the number of aggregate subnetworks increases there is an improvement in the HS performance.
d) HS is effective when the subnetworks to aggregate are equal.
e) HS is effective when the subnetworks to aggregate are of large dimensions.
f) The (near-)decomposability of the network guarantees good HS performance.
g) An ad hoc aggregation procedure may further enhance HS performance.

REMARK ON THE DECOMPOSITION STEP. Several criteria exist to perform the decomposition step (e.g., d, e, f). A special role is played by the decomposability characteristics of the system. Informally, a system is called decomposable if one can partition a system into subsystems such that interactions within each subsystem are much higher than interactions among subsystems. Specifically, a system is said to be *Completely Decomposable (CD)* if it consists of completely independent subsystems that can be analyzed separately. When the interactions among the submodels are (much) weaker with respect to the interactions among the submodels' components the system is said to be *Near Complete Decomposable (NCD)*.

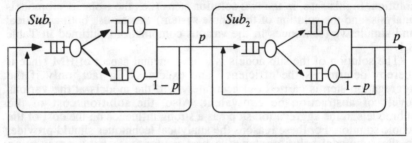

FIGURE 8.4. Example of a decomposable network.

To clarify these concepts let us consider, for example, the queueing model presented in Figure 8.4, where two identical submodels Sub_1 and Sub_2 have been identified. A job, in submodel Sub_1 (Sub_2), reaches submodel Sub_2 (Sub_1) with probability p, while it remains in Sub_1 (Sub_2) with probability $(1 - p)$. By decreasing the p value the interactions between Sub_1 and Sub_2 become looser and thus the network shows the decomposability property. When $p = 0$ the network is completely decomposable, i.e., it is made up of two distinct subnetworks. On the contrary, by increasing the value of p the interactions between Sub_1 and Sub_2 get stronger. For example for $p = 0.9$ the two subnetworks Sub_1 and Sub_2 are strictly connected and the network does not show the decomposability property.

Courtois[15,16] has shown, for generic markovian networks, that an approximate solution based on aggregation and decomposition, has a bounded error ε which depends on the highest level of coupling between the subsystems. A low value of ε thus denotes systems that are *NCD*. Clearly, the choice of the partition of the subsystems is crucial in order to obtain a decomposition with a small ε.

⊠

REMARK ON THE AGGREGATION STEP. The aggregation step consists in defining aggregate components and their interactions. The new model thus obtained is called the aggregate model. The term *exact aggregation* is used when the original and aggregate model have the same behavior, i.e. by analyzing them we get the same results with respect to certain performance indices. In this case the two models are *equivalent*. Exact aggregation techniques have been proposed in the literature for the class of models that includes homogeneous Markov processes [9,15,16] and product form queuing networks.[3,12] In the latter case there is a theorem, known as Norton's theorem or the equivalent flow theorem,[3,12] which allows us to define exactly both the aggregate components and their interactions, thus exploiting the results obtained from the analysis of the model in isolation. In this case the queueing network is decomposed into a set of subnetworks, and each subnetwork is replaced by a so called "flow equivalent" service centre which represents the aggregate behavior of the subnetwork. The service rate of the aggregate service centre depends on the number of customers in the centre and is obtained by evaluating the throughput of the corresponding subnetwork.[3,12]

Exact aggregation techniques can only be applied to limited classes of models. The most commonly used aggregation model is based on the use of the "flow equivalent" principle even when the network of interest does not satisfy the constraints of the product form. In this case we define an aggregate node whose service rate mimics the throughput of the submodel analyzed in isolation. In this case, however, an approximation error is introduced which has to be evaluated.

☒

In the next sections, by exploiting criteria a)-g) we investigate the effectiveness of HM and HS in the analysis of our case study.

8.3.1 HM and HS in the Analysis of a Distributed System Model

In this section we apply the hierarchical methodology to analyze the distributed system models obtained in the decomposition phase (see Figure 8.2c). The aim is to estimate the end-to-end performance figures for the connection-oriented traffic. To perform the steps of the HM method we use the criteria a)-g) outlined in previous section. Specifically, these criteria indicate how to partition the model of the whole system into submodels and how to carry out the aggregation phase efficiently.

DISTRIBUTED SYSTEM DECOMPOSITION. To apply the HM methodology to the solution of the model shown in Figure 8.2c, we need to identify a partition into submodels, aggregate some or all of these submodels, and resolve the aggregate model thus obtained so that we can calculate the network performance indices. First we carry out the partition phase.

The distributed system model is partitioned into two subsystems: one ($S_2^{(1)}$) including the MAC protocol and the connectionless traffic sources, the other ($S_1^{(1)}$) includes the controlled-traffic source together with the flow and error control mechanisms, see Figure 8.5.

$S_2^{(1)}$ has large dimensions and a high level of structural complexity, and thus satisfies the criteria d) and e) in Section 8.3.

To obtain the aggregate model we first solve the submodel $S_2^{(1)}$ in isolation, and then we replace it with a single aggregate node (*aggregate* $S_2^{(1)}$). The final model consists of aggregate $S_2^{(1)}$ and $S_1^{(1)}$ and is solved via simulation to get the system performance indices.

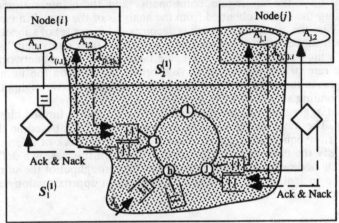

FIGURE 8.5. Model decomposition.

DISTRIBUTED-SYSTEM SUBMODEL ANALYSIS. The submodel-solution step
is carried out with analytical techniques by exploiting the solution methods
known in the literature to determine MAC performance.[13] Specifically, we
use the algorithms for the analysis of polling systems.[40] For the network
model described in the previous section, finite-buffers polling system with
a k-limited service discipline, there are no exact solutions, so in order to
solve it we extend[32] the algorithm proposed by Tran-Gia and Raith[42] for
finite-buffers polling system with 1-limited service discipline.

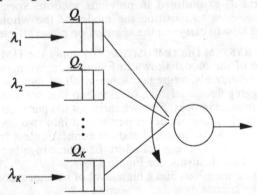

FIGURE 8.6. Polling Model.

Our model of the MAC protocol is shown in Figure 8.6. Specifically, a server (i.e., the token) cyclically serves K queues $\{Q_1, Q_2, ..., Q_K\}$. The time interval, S_i, required to the server to switch from Q_i to Q_{i+1} (*switch-over times*) is constant and depends only on the physical distance between Q_i and Q_{i+1}. We assume a gated k-limited service discipline, i.e., the amount of time the server spends at Q_i during a cycle, Sp_i, depends on the number, $\hat{N}_i$, of packets queued at this station at the beginning of the service period, i.e., the token arrival instant at the station. Specifically, the service period ends after serving $\min\{k, \hat{N}_i\}$ packets. The cycle length, C_i, i.e., the time interval between consecutive arrivals of the server at Q_i, satisfies the following relationship:

$$C_i = \sum_{j=1}^{K} Sp_j + \sum_{j=1}^{K} S_j.$$

Packets arriving at Q_i, according to a Poisson process of rate λ_i, are stored in a finite-buffer queue of size s, and are served in a FIFO order.

By exploiting an iterative algorithm, the steady-state distribution of the number of packets at Q_i at an arbitrary point in time can be derived, i.e., $\{p_i(0), p_i(1), ..., p_i(s)\}$.[41,42] Finally, from $\{p_i(0), p_i(1), ..., p_i(s)\}$ both the packet-loss probability, $P_L(i)$, and the average access delay, $E[R_i]$, can be easily obtained. The packet-loss probability at Q_i is derived by noting that, due to the PASTA property,[26]

$$P_L(i) = p_i(s),$$

while, from Little theorem [26] it follows that

$$E[R_i] = \sum_{k=1}^{s} k \cdot p_i(k) / [\lambda_i \cdot (1 - P_L(i))].$$

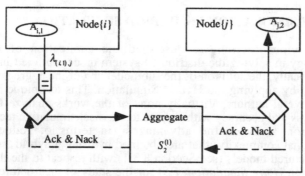

FIGURE 8.7. Aggregate model.

DISTRIBUTED-SYSTEM SUBMODEL AGGREGATION. Once subsystem $S_2^{(1)}$ has been solved, we define its aggregate representation (aggregate $S_2^{(1)}$).

We consider two types of aggregate nodes. The first is defined classically on the basis of the equivalent flow theorem, so that the aggregate node has an exponential service time distribution, Infinite Servers (*IS*) and an average service time equal to the job residence time in

$S_2^{(1)}$, i.e., $E[R_i]$ derived in the previous subsection; this aggregate node will be referred to as *aggregate IS*. In such a way the correlation between the packets with an individual station is not measured. The other way to define the aggregate node is based on observing the MAC behavior. For each station i $(i = 1, ..., K)$, we can observe a period in which the station receives the service (*service period*) and one where the server is waited for (*intervisit period*). During the station service-period its packets are served using a FIFO gated k-limited service discipline. Such a situation can be modeled by a single queue with Poisson arrivals, service times equal to Ts, FIFO gated k-limited service discipline, and server vacation.[42] The duration of the vacation, V, is equal to the station intervisit period, i.e., the sum of the service-periods at the other stations plus the switchover time between one station and another:

$$V = \sum_{j \neq i} Sp_j + \sum_j S_j .$$

We name this second type of aggregate node as *FIFO with vacation*. This representation seems to model a polling system the most realistically. In addition, we can take into account the correlation between the individual queued packets at a station.

By substituting in the original model the aggregate representation of $S_2^{(1)}$, we finally obtain the aggregate model shown in Figure 8.7 which can be solved via a simulative analysis with a reduced computational complexity.

8.4. PURE SIMULATION VS. HYBRID SIMULATION

In the previous section we described the application of the HM methodology in solving the distributed system model outlined in Section 8.2. Specifically, the solution of the submodel and of the aggregate model is obtained by applying the Hybrid Simulation. This technique has been used by several authors. Virtually none of the works analyze the cost-effectiveness and accuracy with respect to classical simulative techniques. This section analyzes the advantages (in terms of reducing the computational complexity) that are obtained by using a hybrid simulation of the structured models (see Section 8.3.1) with respect to the direct use of simulation (*Pure Simulation, PS*) for the study of unstructured model (see Figure 8.2c). The comparison between HS and PS will be based on several experiments, varying the network parameters.

8.4.1 Comparison Criteria

We compare HS and PS in terms of the accuracy of the performance-figures estimates obtained with the same execution time. In other words, for a two level hierarchy of models (see Section 8.3), we apply HS in HM, and PS to the original model.

To define a measure of the accuracy of the estimates obtained via a (hybrid or pure) simulative analysis let us briefly recall the definition of the confidence interval for a given performance index. The estimation of a performance index X (e.g., throughput, mean access delay, server utilization) obtained by simulation can be expressed by the following confidence interval:[28,29]

$$[\ \bar{X} \pm z_{a/2}\ \bar{\sigma}/\sqrt{n}\ ]$$

where $\bar{X}$ denotes the sample mean of X, $\bar{\sigma}$ is the estimated standard deviation of $\bar{X}$, n is the sample dimension, i.e., the number of independent and identical distributed observations of X made in the simulation experiment, and $z_{a/2}$ denotes the $(1-\alpha/2)$ percentile of the standard normal (or the t-student) distribution with $n-1$ degrees of freedom, $\alpha \in [0,1]$. The value $(1-\alpha)$ represents the confidence level. The width of the confidence interval is then a measure of the accuracy of $\bar{X}$ and it is a function of the ratio $\bar{\sigma}/\sqrt{n}$. Since hybrid simulation requires the simulation of the aggregate model, in order to evaluate the HS effectiveness, we have to consider the effects of the aggregation procedure on this ratio $(\bar{\sigma}/\sqrt{n})$. Some preliminary results[4] have shown that, with the same execution time, HS leads to an increase in the number, n, of observations with respect to PS. However, it has also been observed[4] that the standard deviation $\bar{\sigma}$ in the simulation of the aggregate model is approximated and, consequently, the influence of the aggregation in HS on the confidence interval width must be carefully investigated.

In the next subsection, results obtained by the simulations of the unstructured-model and aggregate-model are compared in terms of execution time savings and by measuring the approximation error introduced. Note that HS in HM consists of two steps, and its execution time depends on the analytical aggregation of submodels in the original model and the simulation of the aggregate model.*

8.4.2 Results

The model to analyze is shown in Figure 8.2c. Packet-transmission between two stations is controlled by the MAC protocol and may be subject to flow and error control, and if an error is detected, to retransmission. Access to the transmission medium is regulated by a

---

* The aggregate model (see Figure 8.7) includes the flow control along with error detection and recovery mechanisms, and the aggregate node that represents the MAC. The aggregate-node parameters are obtained by implementing the algorithm for the polling model solution.

polling strategy and the number of stations, K, that share the transmission medium is varied between 4, 10 and 20. The various polling stations have the same parameters (*symmetric system*). We determine these parameters by referring to real situations, for example, to an FDDI network.[1] The service time has a constant distribution and can be obtained by considering the ratio between the length of the message and the capacity of the network. The network under examination has a capacity (C) equal to 100 Mbit. Hence, as the length (L) of the packets is equal to 1000 bit, the service time of an individual station (i.e., the transmission time) is 10 microseconds. The network is 25 km long and the total switchover time is obtained by dividing this distance by the signal propagation time, which is equal to 200000 km a second.[13] The flow control mechanism uses a window W equal to 8 packets.[7,39] As for error control, we assume that there is a probability of detecting an error on a bit (i.e., bit error rate) equal to $10E - 05$,* consequently the probability of finding a packet with an error is $p = 0.01$. The k-limited discipline is characterised by a value of k such that $k > W$, specifically we choose $k = 10$, and the size of the queues, s, is set to satisfy the relationship $s > k$, specifically $s = 12$. The traffic generated by the datagram applications (i.e., the applications which require a connectionless service) normalized with respect to the medium capacity (referred to as offered load, OL) has these values: 0.2, 0.5, 0.8. On the basis of the OL value we calculate the arrival rate, λ_i, of the datagram traffic generated by a node$\{i\}$. In fact, $\lambda_i = (1/K) \cdot (C \cdot OL)/L$. Finally, the traffic arrival rate that undergoes flow control is chosen so as to cause the window to close.[32]

OL = 0.2		% width	OL = 0.8			% width
0.057	0.070	23.2	0.02221	0.0245		9.8
0.059	0.072	19.5			0.029 0.0315	7.2
0.055	0.069	22.6		0.0257	0.0277	7.3

OL = 0.5		% width
0.034	0.0425	20.9
	0.041 0.048	14.5
0.0336	0.0402	18.0

- ——— PS
- ——— HS$_1$
- ·········· HS$_2$

FIGURE 8.8. Comparison between the confidence interval widths for a 20 stations network (200 observations per replication).

---

* The bit error rate on fiber-optics is much lower than this value, but there are less expensive implementations of FDDI based on twisted-pair or copper wires with a higher bit error rate.

We use IBM/RESQ[38] for the simulation solution of the models being examined. We estimate stationary performance indices by applying the independent replications method repeated with 30 replications for each experiment and by varying the number of observations on the packets transmitted successfully from 50 to 100 to 200 per replication. The performance indices are calculated with a 90% confidence level and an initial depolarization which eliminates 10% of the events. For each set of parameters the simulation is carried out varying the seeds of the random-numbers generators.[28,29]

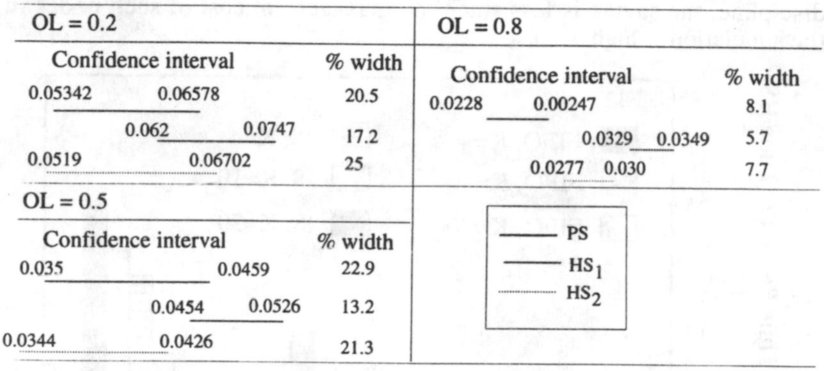

OL = 0.2				OL = 0.8			
Confidence interval			% width	Confidence interval			% width
0.05342	0.06578		20.5	0.0228	0.00247		8.1
	0.062	0.0747	17.2		0.0329	0.0349	5.7
0.0519	0.06702		25		0.0277	0.030	7.7

OL = 0.5			
Confidence interval			% width
0.035		0.0459	22.9
	0.0454	0.0526	13.2
0.0344	0.0426		21.3

——— PS
——— HS$_1$
············ HS$_2$

FIGURE 8.9. Comparison between the confidence interval widths for a 10 stations network (200 observations per replication).

In Figures 8.8-8.10 we show some of the results obtained by comparing PS and HS for the two types of aggregation, both in terms of approximation error (Figures 8.8-8.9) and in terms of CPU time saving (Figure 8.10). The performance index considered is the throughput of the flow-controlled traffic (analogous results are obtained for the access delays). Specifically, Figures 8.8 and 8.9 show a comparison between the widths of the confidence intervals obtained with the PS (continuous line), with the HS where the aggregate node is an IS (HS1, dashed line), and with the HS where the aggregate node is FIFO-k-limited with server vacation (HS2 dotted line). Figures 8.8 and 8.9 show the results for 20 and 10 stations, respectively. The value in the column "% width" indicates the width of the confidence interval normalized with respect to the central value of the interval. Similar results have also been obtained either with a lower number of network stations or with a lower number of observation per replication.[32] Figure 8.10 shows, for the different network configurations considered, the ratio between the PS and HS* execution time. As can be

* For *HS* both types of aggregate node are considered.

seen, both aggregation procedures give a considerable saving in execution times in passing from PS to HS. This saving increases in relation to an increase in the size and use of the aggregate subnetworks. For example, if we consider four stations in the polling, and in the aggregate model the submodel $S_2^{(1)}$ is represented with an IS node, the saving is of a factor 5, 7, 11 for $OL = 0.2, 0.5, 0.8$, respectively; while if, in the original model there are 20 stations the saving is 8, 10, 15 for OL=0.2, 0.5 0.8, respectively. The greatest saving is for the aggregation that uses an IS node, while when there is an aggregate node FIFO with server vacation and k-limited service discipline, the saving is less since the management cost of such nodes in the simulation is high.

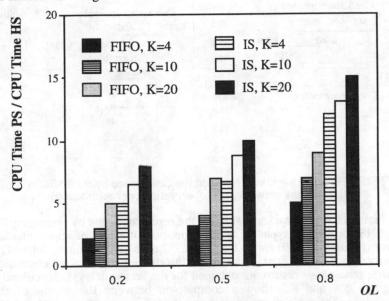

FIGURE 8.10. Comparison of aggregations in terms of CPU time saving.

On the other hand, for the error introduced by the aggregation procedure we observe better performances for the second type of definition of the aggregate node, i.e., HS2, see Figures 8.8-8.9. Also, the approximation error increases as network utilization increases. This error is related to the estimate of the probability of losing the packets due to the finite capacity of the buffers in the station. In the analytical solution this value is always very low, while in the simulation this probability is not negligible and increases as network utilization increases. Thus as network utilization increases so too does the approximation error.

8.5. FINAL REMARKS

Hierarchical Modeling is a standard performance modeling technique based on the decomposition and aggregation method[15] which can be applied both to the model definition and to the model analysis. In model analysis, this technique, starting from the queueing model representing the system, decomposes the model in submodels, where each submodel corresponds to a subset of the model's queues. Then it replaces one (or more) submodel(s) by a single queue with appropriate chosen behavior (i.e., service discipline, service rate, etc.). The resulting model (aggregate model) is solved with a reduced computational complexity. There are several aspects that make HM clearly more favourable than an unstructured approach. First of all, the analysis of a complex system is reduced to solutions of simpler and smaller models. The complexity in space and time of the solution can thus be reduced dramatically using a suitable number of hierarchical levels. The possibility of using several solutions to resolve the submodels in phases 2 (submodels solution) and 3 (aggregate model solution) of the hierarchical methodology is also of fundamental importance. In particular, the Hybrid Simulation technique is the most promising technique to be used in the model analysis. The Hybrid Simulation potential speed-up results from the fact that the submodel needs to be solved once (for each possible customer population) in order to characterize its aggregate representation. Then in the simulation of the entire model, the potentially large number of events that would have occurred when a customer passed through the submodel are replaced by only two events: the arrival and departure of the customer from the composite queue. Finally, another advantage of using HM and HS is that the system structure can be exploited to identify suitable partitions that will help to reduce the number of submodels to solve in the aggregation phase. For example, if the model has a certain number of submodels that are similar or symmetrical, this may reduce the cost of the solution of such submodels. Summarizing, HM analysis yields the following advantages:

- The analysis of a complex model is reduced to the analysis of smaller models with reduced dimension.
- Different performance goals can be defined at various levels of the hierarchy.
- Different solution techniques can be applied at steps 2 and 3 of the HM analysis algorithm (see Section 8.3).
- Model decomposition can be performed by exploiting the structure of the model itself.

HM methodology and HS techniques have sometimes been used in the analysis of computer-network problems. However, the advantage and drawbacks of these techniques have not been analyzed with respect to pure simulation. Here we have shown the advantages of the HM methodology and HS technique, with respect to an unstructured approach, for the evaluation of the performance of a simple distributed system. Results obtained indicate that using combined analytical and simulation techniques to solve the model allows us to study the system at a greater level of detail than that allowed by using models and solution techniques that are purely analytical. Further, there is a lower execution cost than when simulation alone is used. In fact, comparing HS and PS highlights the execution time saving that is tied to the simulation of the aggregate model with respect to the simulation of the global model, and how this saving depends on the size of the aggregate submodel and on the aggregation procedure used. In addition, the aggregation procedure influences the approximation error. Which procedure to use in the aggregation phase thus depends on the aims of the study itself. In the case we have examined, if the aim is maximum reduction of costs, then we should use the procedure that defines the aggregate node with IS; whereas if we want to keep the approximation error low then we should use the procedure that defines the FIFO k-limited server vacation aggregate node.

According to the results presented in this chapter these techniques (i.e., HM and HS) could be successfully exploited to solve some important networking problems such as the analysis of the impact of user mobility on wireless-network architectures.[31] Wireless networks are based on a set of base stations interconnected through the wired network. Each base station controls a cellular radio environment (*cell*), and the wireless terminals inside a cell, via a radio interface, communicate with the base station that cell refers to. Wireless terminals can be either *static* (i.e., terminals of this type always remain inside the same cell), or *dynamic* (i.e., the base station which controls the transmissions of this type of terminals changes in the long run). The analysis of a wireless network, with pure simulative techniques, becomes rapidly intractable with the increase of the number of cells. In this case, the Hierarchical Modeling method and Hybrid Simulation is a suitable and cost-efficient approach to evaluate the quality of service experienced by different types of wireless terminals. There are two main features that make the HM and HS techniques attractive. First, the system is made up of a large number of cells which have the same structure. Second, the interactions among cells (these interactions are caused by dynamic users performing the hand-off operation) are in general weaker with respect to the interactions inside a cell. Hence the model of this system can be decomposed into a large number of submodels which exhibit the same behavior and which have weak interactions (near-decomposability property).

8.6. REFERENCES

1. ANSI, FDDI Token Ring Media Access Control, (ANSI X3.139, New York, 1987).
2. K. BAGCHI, P.DAS AND B.BHAUMIK, Microprocessing and

Microprogramming, **16**, 277 (1985).
3. S. BALSAMO, G. IAZEOLLA, IEEE Trans. Soft. Eng. **8**, 298 (1982).
4. S. BALSAMO, M. CAPPUCCIO, L. DONATIELLO, R. MIRANDOLA, "Some Remarks on Hybrid Simulation Methodology", in Proc. SCS 90, (Calgary, Canada, 1990), 30-37.
5. S. BALSAMO, R. MIRANDOLA, Technical Report RI.95.10, (Laboratory for Computer Science, Universita' di Roma Tor Vergata, July 1995).

The paper presents algorithms both for applying HM both in model definition and in model analysis. The focus is on hybrid simulation. A comparison is presented between hybrid simulation in HM and pure simulation in the solution of extended queueing networks. This comparison between the two methodologies leads to the identification of a set of criteria for HM analysis.

6. F. BASKETT, ,M.K. CHANDY, R.R. MUNTZ, F.G. PALACIOS, J. ACM, **22**, 248 (1975).
7 . D. BERTSEKAS, R. GALLAGER, Data Networks, (Prentice-Hall International, Inc., Englewood Cliffs, New Jersey, 1992).
8   A. BLUM, L. DONATIELLO, P. HEIDELBERGER, S.S. LAVENBERG, E. MAC NAIR, in Proc. International Conference on Modelling Techniques and Tools for Performance Analysis. (INRIA, 1984), 1-18.
9. A. BRANDWAJN, Perf. Eval. **5** 175 (1985).
10. J.C. BROWNE, ET AL., Proc. IEEE **63**, 966 (1975).
11. BUZEN J.P., CACM 16, 527 (1973).
12. K.M. CHANDY, U. HERZOG, L. WOO, IBM Journal of Research and Development **1**, 36 (1975).
13. M. CONTI, E. GREGORI, L. LENZINI, "Metropolitan Area Networks (MANs): Protocols, Modeling and Performance Evaluation", in Lecture Notes in Computer Science, edited by L. Donatiello and R. Nelson (Springer Verlag, Berlin, 1993), **729**, 81.
14. A.E. CONWAY, IEEE JSAC, **9**, 1 (1991).

This paper defines a methodology for a hierarchical analysis of network architectures defined according to the OSI[39] reference model.

15. P.J. COURTOIS, CACM **18**, 337 (1975).
16. P.J. COURTOIS, Decomposability: Queueing and Computer System Applications (Academic Press, New York, 1977)

Courtois presents the application of decomposition and aggregation techniques to solve a generic markovian network and, more specifically, an exponential queueing network. A bound on the approximation error, and a sufficient condition for decomposability are given in terms of network parameters.

17. D. FERRARI, G. SERAZZI, A. ZEIGNER, Measurement and Tuning of Computer Systems (Prentice Hall, Englewood Cliffs, NJ, 1983).
18. V.S. FROST, W.W. LARUE, K.S. SHANMUGAN, IEEE JSAC, **6**, 146 (1988).

A review of efficient solution techniques for the prediction of performance indices of communication systems. The focus is on hybrid modeling and the use of variance reduction technique.

19. O. GIHR, P. KUEHN, "Modelling of new services in computer and communication networks" in Computer Networking and Performance Evaluation edited by T. Hasegawa, H. Takagi, Y. Takahashi (Elsevier 1985).
20. J.L. HAMMOND, P.J.P. O'REILLY, Performance Analysis of Local Computer Networks (Addison-Wedsley, 1988).
21. P.G. HARRISON, N.M. PATEL, Performance Modelling of Communication Networks and Computer Architectures (Addison-Wesley Publishing Company, 1993).
22. P. HEIDELBERG, S.S. LAVENBERG, IEEE Trans. Comput., 33, 1195 (1984).
23. H. INAI, T. NISHIDA, T. YOKOHIRA, H. MIYAHARA, Proc. IEEE 78, 442 (1990).
24. R. JAIN, The Art of Computer Systems Performance Evaluation (Wiley, New York, 1991).
25. K. KANT, Introduction to Computer System Performance Evaluation (McGraw Hill Int. Editions 1992).
26. L. KLEINROCK, Queueing Systems, 1 (Wiley, New York, 1975).
27. L. KLEINROCK, Queueing Systems, 2 (Wiley, New York, 1976).
28. S.S. LAVENBERG, Computer Performance Handbook (Academic Press, New York, 1983).
29. A.M. LAW, W.D. KELTON, Simulation Modeling and Analysis (McGraw Hill, New York, 1982).
30. E.D. LAZOWSKA, J.L. ZAHORJIAN, G.S. GRAHAM, K.C. SEVCICK, Quantitative System Performance (Prentice Hall, NJ, 1984).
31. V.O.K. Li, X. Qiu, Proc. IEEE, 83, 1210 (1995).
32. R. MIRANDOLA, I Modelli gerarchici per la Valutazione delle Prestazioni di Sistemi di Elaborazione e di Comunicazione, (Ph.D Thesis, Laboratory for Computer Science, Universita' di Roma Tor Vergata, Januray 1994).
33. M. MURATA, H. TAKAGI, IEEE Trans. Commun., 36, 1022 (1988).
34. M. REISER, S.S. LAVENBERG, J ACM, 27, 313 (1980).
35. J.G. SHANTHIKUMAR, R.G. SARGENT, Oper. Res. 31, 6, 1030 (1983).
36. C.H. SAUER, K.M. CHANDY, Computer Systems Performance Modeling (Prentice Hall, 1981).
37. K.W. ROSS, Multiservice Loss Models for Broadband Telecommunication Networks, (Springer Verlag, TNCS series, London, 1995).
38. C.H. SAUER, E. MACNAIR, Simulation of Computer Communication Systems (Prentice-Hall, Inc., Englewood Cliffs, NJ, 1983).
39. M. SCHWARTZ, Telecommunication Networks (Addison Wesley 1987).
40. H. TAKAGI, ACM Comp Surveys 20, 5 (1988).
41. M. TANGEMANN, AND K. SAUER, IEEE JSAC, 9, 271 (1991).
42. P. TRAN-GIA, T. RAITH, Perf. Eval. 9, 1 (1988).

CHAPTER 9

A FRAMEWORK FOR MEASURING THE PERFORMANCE OF ALTERNATIVE PROCESS ARCHITECTURES FOR PARALLELIZING COMMUNICATION SUBSYSTEMS

Douglas C. Schmidt and Tatsuya Suda

9.1. INTRODUCTION

Advances in VLSI and fiber optic technology are shifting performance bottlenecks from the underlying networks to the communication subsystem. A communication subsystem consists of *protocol tasks* and *operating system mechanisms*. Protocol tasks include connection establishment and termination, end-to-end flow control, remote context management, segmentation/reassembly, demultiplexing, error protection, session control, and presentation conversions. Operating system mechanisms include process management, timer-based and I/O-based event invocation, message buffering, and layer-to-layer flow control. Together, protocol tasks and operating system mechanisms support the implementation and execution of communication protocol stacks composed of protocol tasks[1].

Executing protocol stacks in parallel on multiprocessor platforms is a promising technique for increasing protocol processing performance. Significant increases in performance are possible, however, only if the speed-up obtained from parallelism outweights the context switching and synchronization overhead associated with parallel processing. A context switch is triggered when an executing process relinquishes its associated processing element (PE) voluntarily or involuntarily. Depending on the underlying OS and hardware platform, a context switch

219

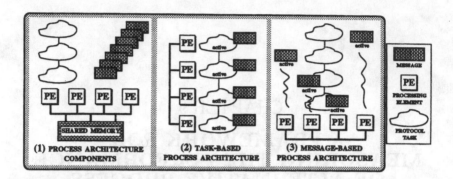

Figure 9.1: Process Architecture Components and Interrelationships

may require dozens to hundreds of instructions to flush register windows, memory caches, instruction pipelines, and translation look-aside buffers. Synchronization overhead arises from locking mechanisms that serialize access to shared objects (such as message buffers, message queues, protocol connection records, and demultiplexing maps) used during protocol processing[2].

A number of *process architectures* have been proposed as the basis for parallelizing communication subsystems[2,3,4]. There are two fundamental types of process architectures: *task-based* and *message-based*. Task-based process architectures are formed by binding one or more PEs to units of protocol functionality (such as presentation layer formatting, transport layer end-to-end flow control, and network layer fragmentation and reassembly). In this architecture, parallelism is achieved by executing protocol tasks in separate PEs, and passing data messages and control messages between the tasks/PEs. In contrast, message-based process architectures are formed by binding the PEs to data messages and control messages received from applications and network interfaces. In this architecture, parallelism is achieved by simultaneously escorting multiple data messages and control messages on separate PEs through a stack of protocol tasks.

Protocol stacks (such as the TCP/IP protocol stack and the ISO OSI 7 layer protocol stack) may be implemented using either task-based or message-based process architectures. However, these two types of process architectures exhibit significantly different performance characteristics that vary across operating system and hardware platforms. For instance, on shared memory multiprocessor platforms, task-based process architectures exhibit high context switching and data movement overhead due to scheduling and caching properties of the OS and hardware[5]. In contrast, in a message-passing multiprocessor environment, message-based process architectures exhibit high levels of synchronization overhead due to high latency access to global resources such as shared memory, synchronization objects, or connection context information[3].

Existing studies have generally selected a single task-based or message-based process architecture and studied it in isolation. Moreover, these studies have been conducted on different OS and hardware platforms, using different protocol stacks and implementation techniques, which makes it difficult to meaningfully compare results. In this paper, we describe the design and implementation of an object-oriented framework that supports controlled experiments with several alternative parallel process architectures. The framework controls a number of relevant confounding factors (such as protocol functionality, concurrency control strategies, application traffic characteristics, and network interfaces), which enables precise measurement of the performance impact of using different process architectures to parallelize communication protocol stacks. This paper reports the results of systematic, empirical comparisons of the performance of several message-based and task-based process architectures implemented on a widely-available shared memory multiprocessor platform.

The paper is organized as follows: Section 9.2 outlines the two fundamental types of process architectures and classifies related work accordingly; Section 9.3 describes the key components in our object-oriented framework; Section 9.4 examines empirical results from experiments performed using the framework; and Section 9.5 presents concluding remarks.

9.2. ALTERNATIVE PROCESS ARCHITECTURES

Figure 9.1 (1) illustrates the following basic elements of a process architecture:

- *Data messages and control messages* – which are sent and received from one or more applications and network devices
- *Protocol tasks* – which are the units of protocol functionality that process the control messages and data messages
- *Processing elements* (PEs) – which execute protocol tasks

There are two fundamental types of process architectures that structure these basic elements in different ways:

- *Task-based process architectures* – which bind one or more PEs to protocol processing tasks (shown in Figure 9.1 (2)). In this architecture, tasks are the active elements, whereas messages processed by the tasks are the passive elements.
- *Message-based process architectures* – which bind the PEs to the control messages and the data messages received from applications and network interfaces (shown in Figure 9.1 (3)). In this architecture, messages are the active elements, whereas tasks that process the messages are the passive elements.

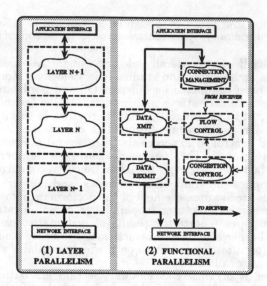

Figure 9.2: Task-based Process Architecture Examples

The remainder of this section briefly examines several alternative process architectures in each category.

9.2.1. Examples of Task-based Process Architectures

Task-based process architectures associate processes* with clusters of one or more protocol tasks. Two common examples of task-based process architectures are *Layer Parallelism* and *Functional Parallelism*. The primary difference between these two process architectures involves the granularity of the protocol processing tasks. Protocol layers are generally more coarse-grained than protocol tasks since they cluster multiple tasks together to form a composite service (such as the end-to-end transport service provided by the ISO OSI transport layer).

As shown in Figure 9.2 (1), Layer Parallelism associates a separate process with each layer (*e.g.,* the presentation, transport, and network layers) in a protocol stack. Certain protocol header and data fields in the messages may be processed in parallel as they flow through a pipeline of layers in a protocol stack. Buffering and flow control may be necessary within a protocol stack if processing activities in each layer

---

*In this paper, the term "process" is used to refer to a series of instructions executing within an address space; this address space may be shared with other processes. Different terminology (such as lightweight processes or threads) has also been used to denote the same basic concepts.

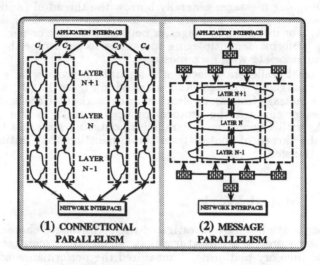

Figure 9.3: Message-based Process Architecture Examples

execute at different rates.

Functional Parallelism associates a separate process with various protocol tasks (such as header composition, acknowledgement, retransmission, segmentation, reassembly, and routing). As shown in Figure 9.2 (2), these protocol tasks execute in parallel and communicate by passing control messages and data messages to each other to coordinate parallel protocol processing.

9.2.2. Examples of Message-based Process Architectures

Message-based process architectures associate processes with messages, rather than with protocol layers or protocol tasks. Two common examples of message-based process architectures are *Connectional Parallelism* and *Message Parallelism*. The primary difference between these process architectures involves the point at which messages are demultiplexed onto a process. Connectional Parallelism demultiplexes all messages bound for the same connection onto the same process, whereas Message Parallelism demultiplexes messages onto any available process.

Connectional Parallelism uses a separate process to handle the messages associated with each open connection. As shown in Figure 9.3 (1), connections C_1, C_2, C_3, and C_4 reside in separate processes that execute a stack of protocol tasks on all messages associated with their respective connection. Within a connection, multiple protocol tasks are invoked sequentially on each message flowing through the protocol stack. Outgoing messages generally borrow the thread of control from the application process and use it to escort messages down a protocol stack. For incoming messages, a network interface or packet filter typically performs demultiplexing operations to determine the correct process to associate with each message.

Message Parallelism associates a separate process with every incoming or outgoing message. As illustrated in Figure 9.3 (2), a process receives a message from an application or network interface and escorts that message through the protocol processing tasks in the protocol stack. As with Connectional Parallelism, outgoing messages typically borrow the thread of control from the application that initiated the message transfer.

9.2.3. Related Work

A number of studies have investigated the performance characteristics of task-based process architectures that ran on either message passing or shared memory platforms. [5] measured the performance of several implementations of the transport and session layers in the ISO OSI reference model using an ADA-like rendezvous-style of Layer Parallelism in a nonuniform access shared memory multiprocessor platform. [6] measured the performance of Functional Parallelism for presentation layer and transport layer functionality on a shared memory multiprocessor platform. [7] measured the performance of a de-layered, function-oriented transport system using Functional Parallelism on a message passing transputer multiprocessor platform.

Other studies have investigated the performance characteristics of message-based process architectures. All these studies utilized shared memory platforms. [8] measured the performance of the TCP, UDP, and IP protocols using Message Parallelism on a uniprocessor platform running the x-kernel. [9] examined performance issues in parallelizing TCP-based and UDP-based protocol stacks using a multiprocessor version of the x-kernel. [4] measured the performance of the ISO OSI protocol stack, focusing primarily on the presentation and transport layers using Message Parallelism. [10] measured the performance of the TCP/IP protocol stack using Connectional Parallelism in a multiprocessor version of System V STREAMS.

This paper extends existing work by measuring the performance of several representative task-based and message-based process architectures in a controlled environment. Furthermore, our experiments report the impact of both context switching and synchronization overhead on communication subsystem performance. In addition to measuring data link, network, and transport layer performance, our experiments also measure presentation layer performance. The presentation layer is widely considered to be a major bottleneck in high-performance communication subsystems[11].

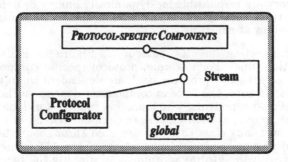

Figure 9.4: Class Categories in the ASX Framework

9.3. AN OBJECT-ORIENTED FRAMEWORK FOR PROCESS ARCHITECTURE EXPERIMENTATION

To facilitate controlled experiments with alternative process architectures, we have developed an object-oriented communication framework called the "ADAPTIVE Service eXecutive" (ASX). This framework is an integrated collection of components that provide an infrastructure for developing and testing protocol stacks within communication subsystems.

The term "component" is used in this paper to refer to a precisely defined abstraction in a communication subsystem. Components in the ASX framework are described below and include classes, class inheritance hierarchies, class categories, and objects related to communication protocol stacks.

After prototyping a number of alternative designs, we identified and implemented the class categories illustrated in Figure 9.4. A class category is a collection of components that collaborate to provide a set of related services. A protocol stack may be configured by combining components in each of the following Stream, Concurrency, and Protocol Configurator class categories via C++ language features such as inheritance, object composition, and template instantiation:

- Stream class category – Components in this category are responsible for coordinating the installation-time and run-time configuration of *Streams*, which are collections of hierarchically-related protocol tasks that are composed to form communication protocol stacks.
- Concurrency class category – Components in this category are responsible for spawning, executing, synchronizing, and gracefully terminating protocol tasks that execute concurrently using one or more threads of control.
- Protocol Configurator class category – Components in this

category are responsible for dynamically linking or unlinking protocol tasks into or out of the address space of a communication subsystem at run-time.

The lines connecting the class category in Figure 9.4 indicate dependency relationships. For example, protocol-specific components that implement a particular protocol stack are dependent upon the Stream components. In turn, the Stream components depend on the Protocol Configurator components, which provide support for dynamic configuration and reconfiguration of Stream components. Since components in the Concurrency class category are used throughout the protocol-specific and protocol-independent portions of the ASX framework, they are marked with the **global** adornment to simplify the figure.

The ASX framework helps control for several confounding factors such as protocol functionality, concurrency control strategies, application traffic characteristics, and network interfaces. In the experiments described in Section 9.4, the ASX framework is used to hold protocol functionality constant, while allowing the process architecture to be systematically altered in a controlled manner.

The ASX framework incorporates concepts from several existing communication frameworks such as System V STREAMS[12], the x-kernel [8], and the Conduit [13]. These frameworks contain tools that support the flexible configuration of communication subsystems. These tools support the interconnection of building-block protocol components (such as message managers, timer-based event dispatchers, and connection demultiplexers[8] and other reusable protocol mechanisms[14]) to form protocol stacks. In addition to supplying building-block protocol components, the ASX framework also extends the features provided by existing communication frameworks. In particular, ASX provides components that decouple protocol-specific functionality from the following structural and behavioral characteristics of a communication subsystem:

- The type of locking mechanisms used to synchronize access to shared objects
- The use of message-based and task-based process architectures
- The use of kernel-level vs. user-level execution agents

These ASX framework components simplify development of and experimentation with protocol stacks that are functionally equivalent, but possess significantly different process architectures.

The remainder of this section describes the main components in each of the ASX framework's class categories. Throughout the paper, components in the ASX framework are illustrated with Booch notation. Solid clouds indicate objects; nesting indicates composition relationships between objects; and undirected edges indicate a link exists between two objects. Dashed clouds indicate classes; directed edges indicate inheritance relationships between classes; and an undirected edge with a small circle at one end indicates either a composition or a uses relation between two classes. Solid rectangles indicate class categories, which combine a number of related classes into a common name space.

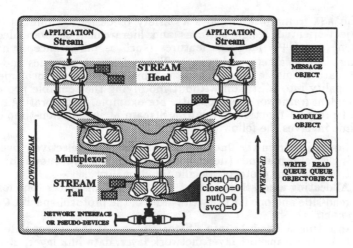

Figure 9.5: Components in the Stream Class Category

9.3.1. The Stream Class Category

Components in the Stream class category are responsible for coordinating the installation-time and/or run-time configuration of one or more Streams. A Stream is an object that applications communicate with at run-time to configure and execute protocol stacks in the ASX framework. As illustrated in Figure 9.5, a Stream contains a series of interconnected Module objects. Module objects are used to decompose a protocol stack into a functionally distinct levels. Each level implements a cluster of related protocol tasks (such as an end-to-end transport service or a presentation layer formatting service).

Any level that requires multiplexing and/or demultiplexing of messages between one or more related Streams may be developed using a Multiplexor object. A Multiplexor is a container object that provides mechanisms that route messages between Modules in a collection of related Streams. Both Module and Multiplexor objects may be flexibly configured into a Stream by developers at installation-time, as well as by applications at run-time.

Every Module contains a pair of Queue objects that partition a level into the read-side and write-side functionality required to implement a particular protocol task. A Queue provides an abstract domain class that may be specialized to target a specific domain (such as the domain of communication protocol stacks or the domain of network management applications[15]). Each Queue contains a Message_List, which is a reusable ASX framework component that queues a sequence of data messages and control messages for subsequent processing. Protocol tasks in adjacent Modules communicate by exchanging typed messages via a uniform message passing interface defined by the Queue class.

The ASX framework employs a variety of design techniques (such as object-oriented design patterns and hierarchical software decomposition) and C++ language features (such as inheritance, dynamic binding, and parameterized types). These design techniques and language features enable developers to flexibly configure protocol-specific functionality into a Stream without modifying the reusable protocol-independent framework components. For example, incorporating a new level of protocol functionality into a Stream at installation-time or at run-time involves the following steps:

1. Inheriting from the Queue class interface and selectively overriding several methods (described below) in the new Queue subclass to implement protocol-specific functionality
2. Allocating a new Module that contains two instances (one for the read-side and one for the write-side) of the protocol-specific Queue subclass
3. Inserting the Module into a Stream object at the appropriate level (*e.g.*, the transport layer, network layer, data-link layer, etc.)

To avoid reinventing terminology, many component names in the Stream class category correspond to similar componentry in the System V STREAMS framework[12]. However, the techniques used to support extensibility and concurrency in the two frameworks differ significantly. As describe above, incorporating new protocol-specific functionality to an ASX Stream is performed by inheriting interfaces and implementations from existing ASX framework components. Using inheritance to add protocol-specific functionality provides greater type-safety compared with the pointer-to-function techniques used in System V STREAMS. In addition, the ASX Stream classes redesign and reimplement the co-routine-based, "weightless"[†] service processing mechanisms used in System V STREAMS. These ASX changes enable more effective use of multiple PEs on a shared memory multi-processing platform by reducing the opportunities for deadlock and simplifying flow control between Queues in a Stream. The remainder of this section discusses the primary components of the ASX Stream class category: the Stream class, the Module class, the Queue class, and the Multiplexor class.

9.3.1.1. The STREAM Class

The STREAM class defines the application interface to a Stream. A STREAM object provides a bi-directional get/put-style interface that allows applications to access a protocol stack containing a series of interconnected Modules. Applications send and receive data and control messages through the stack of Modules that comprise a STREAM object. In addition, the STREAM class implements a push/pop-style interface

---

[†]A weightless process executes on a run-time stack that is also used by other processes. This complicates programming and increases the potential for deadlock since a weightless process may not suspend execution to wait for resources to become available or for events to occur[10].

that enables applications to configure a Stream at run-time by inserting and removing protocol-specific `Module` class objects.

9.3.1.2. The Module Class

The `Module` class defines a distinct level of protocol functionality in a protocol stack. A Stream is formed incrementally by connecting each `Module` object in the Stream with two adjacent `Module` objects (one "upstream" and one "downstream"). Each `Module` contains a pair of objects that inherit from the `Queue` class described in Section 9.3.1.3. A `Module` uses its two `Queue` subclass objects to implement its bi-directional, protocol-specific functionality. A `Module` communicates with its neighboring `Module` objects by passing typed messages. Message passing overhead is minimized by passing a pointer to a message between two `Modules`, rather than by copying the data.

The `Stream_Head` and `Stream_Tail` `Module` objects shown in Figure 9.5 are installed automatically when a Stream is first opened. These two `Modules` interpret pre-defined `ASX` framework control messages and data messages that pass through a Stream at run-time. In addition, the `Stream_Head` `Module` provides a synchronous message queueing interface between an application and a Stream. The read-side of a `Stream_Tail` `Module` transforms incoming messages from a network interface (or from a pseudo-interface such as a loop-back device) into a canonical internal Stream message format. These messages are subsequently processed by higher-level components in a Stream and subsequently delivered to an application. The write-side of a `Stream_Tail` `Module` transforms outgoing messages from their internal Stream format into the appropriate network message format and passes the message to a network interface.

9.3.1.3. The Queue Abstract Class

The `Queue` abstract class[‡] defines an interface that subclasses inherit and selectively override to provide the read-side and write-side protocol functionality in a `Module`. The `Queue` class is an abstract class since its interface defines the four pure virtual methods (`open`, `close`, `put`, and `svc`) described below. By defining `Queue` as an abstract class, the protocol-independent components (such as message objects, message lists, and message demultiplexing mechanisms) provided by the `Stream` class category are decoupled from the protocol-specific subclasses (such as those implementing the data-link, IP, TCP, UDP, and XDR protocols) that inherit and use these components. This decoupling enhances

---

[‡]An abstract class in C++ provides an interface that contains at least one *pure virtual method*. A pure virtual method provides only an interface declaration, without supplying any accompanying definition for the method. Subclasses of an abstract class must provide definitions for all its pure virtual methods before any objects of the subclass may be instantiated.

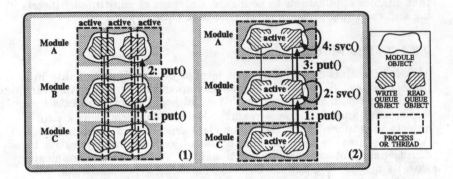

Figure 9.6: Alternative Methods for Invoking put and svc Methods

component reuse and simplifies protocol stack development and configuration.

The open and close methods in the Queue class may be specialized
via inheritance to perform activities that are necessary to initialize
and terminate a protocol-specific object, respectively. These activities
allocate and deallocate resources such as connection control blocks, I/O
descriptors, and synchronization locks. When a Module is inserted or
removed from a Stream, the ASX framework automatically invokes the
open or close method of the Module's write-side and read-side Queue
subclass objects.

The put method in a Queue is invoked by a Queue in an adjacent
Module passing it a message. The put method runs *synchronously* with
respect to its caller by borrowing the thread of control from the Queue
that invoked its put method. This thread of control typically originates
either upstream from an application, downstream from process(es) that
handle network interface device interrupts, or internal to a Stream from
an event dispatching mechanism (such as a timer-driven callout queue
used to trigger retransmissions in a connection-oriented transport protocol).

The svc method in a Queue may be specialized to perform protocol-
specific processing *asynchronously* with respect to other Queues in its
Stream. A svc method is not directly invoked from an adjacent Queue.
Instead, it is invoked by a separate process associated with the Queue.
This process provides a separate thread of control that executes the
Queue's svc method. This method runs an event loop that waits continuously for messages to be inserted into the Queue's Message_List.
A Message_List is a standard component in a Queue. Protocol-specific
code may reuse the Message_List to queue data messages and control
messages for subsequent protocol processing. When messages are inserted into a Message_List, the svc method dequeues the messages and

performs the protocol-specific processing tasks defined by the Queue subclass.

Within the implementation of a put or svc method, a message may be forwarded to an adjacent Queue in a Stream via the Queue::put_next method. Put_next calls the put method of the next Queue residing in an adjacent Module. This invocation of put may borrow the thread of control from its caller and process the message immediately (*i.e.,* the synchronous processing approach illustrated in Figure 9.6 (1)). Conversely, the put method may enqueue the message and defer processing to its svc method, which executes in a separate thread of control (*i.e.,* the asynchronous processing approach illustrated in Figure 9.6 (2)).

In general, message-based process architectures perform their protocol-specific processing *synchronously* within the put methods of their Queues. For instance, in the ASX-based implementation of the Message Parallelism process architecture, a message arriving at a network interface is associated with a separate thread of control. This thread of control is obtained from a pool of pre-initialized processes (which are labeled as the active objects in Figure 9.6 (1)). The incoming message is escorted through a series of interconnected Queues in a Stream. A synchronous upcall to the put method in an adjacent Queue is performed to pass a message to each higher level in a protocol stack.

In contrast, task-based process architectures perform their processing *asynchronously* in the svc methods of their Queues, which execute in separate threads of control. For instance, each protocol layer in the ASX-based Layer Parallelism process architecture is implemented in a separate Module object, which is associated with a separate process. Messages arriving from a network interface are passed between Queues running in the separate processes (which are labeled as the active objects in Figure 9.6 (2)). Each Queue in a Stream asynchronously executes its protocol-specific tasks within its svc method. Section 9.4 illustrates the performance impact of using synchronous vs. asynchronous processing to parallelize communication protocol stacks on a shared memory multiprocessor platform.

9.3.1.4. The Multiplexor Class

A Multiplexor routes messages between different Streams that implement layered protocol stacks. Although layered multiplexing and demultiplexing is generally disparaged for high-performance communication subsystems, most conventional communication models (such as the Internet model or the ISO/OSI reference model) require some form of multiplexing. Thus, the ASX framework provides mechanisms that support it.

A Multiplexor is implemented via a C++ template class called Map_Manager. The Map_Manager class is parameterized by an external identifier type (which serves as the search key into a map) and an internal identifier type (which contains the information associated with each search key). Protocol-specific Multiplexors may be formed by instantiating particular external and internal identifier type parameters into the Map_Manager template class. This instantiation produces specialized objects that perform efficient intra-Stream message routing. Common external identifiers used in protocol stacks include network addresses, port numbers, or type-of-service fields. Likewise, common internal identifiers include pointers to Modules or pointers to protocol connection records.

9.3.2. The Concurrency Class Category

Components in the Concurrency class category are responsible for spawning, executing, synchronizing, and gracefully terminating services via one or more threads of control at run-time. These threads of control execute protocol tasks and pass messages between Modules in a protocol stack. The following section outlines the classes in the Concurrency class category.

9.3.2.1. The Synch Classes

The Synch classes provide type-safe C++ interfaces for two basic types of synchronization mechanisms: Mutex and Condition objects. A Mutex object is used to ensure the integrity of a shared resource that may be accessed concurrently by multiple processes. A Condition object allows one or more cooperating processes to suspend their execution until a condition expression involving shared data attains a particular state.

A Mutex object serializes the execution of multiple processes by defining a critical section where only one thread of control may execute its code at a time. To enter a critical section, a process invokes the Mutex::acquire method. When a process leaves its critical section, it invokes the Mutex::release method. These two methods are implemented via adaptive spin-locks that ensure mutual exclusion by using an atomic hardware instruction. An adaptive spin-lock polls a designated memory location using the atomic hardware instruction until one of the following conditions occur:

- The value at this location is changed by the process that currently owns the lock. This signifies that the lock has been released and may now be acquired by the spinning process.
- The process that is holding the lock goes to sleep. At this point, the spinning process also goes to sleep to avoid unnecessary polling[16]

On a multiprocessor, the overhead incurred by a spin-lock is relatively minor. Hardware-based polling does not cause contention on the system bus since it only affects the local PE caches of processes that are spinning on a Mutex object.

A Condition object provides a different type of synchronization mechanism. Unlike the adaptive spin-lock Mutex objects, a Condition object enables a process to suspend itself indefinitely (via the

Condition::wait method) until a condition expression involving shared data attains a particular state. When another cooperating process indicates that the state of the shared data has changed (by invoking the Condition::signal method), the associated Condition object wakes up a process that is suspended on that Condition object. The newly awakened process then re-evaluate its condition expression and potentially resumes processing if the shared data has attained an appropriate state.

Condition object synchronization is not implemented using spin-locks. Spin-locks consume excessive resources if a process must wait an indefinite amount of time for a particular condition to become signaled. Therefore, Condition objects are implemented via sleep-locks that trigger a context switch to allow another process to execute. Section 9.4 illustrates the consequences of context switching and synchronization on process architecture performance.

Components in the Stream class category described in Section 9.3.1 contain minimal internal locking mechanisms. By default, synchronization mechanisms provided by the Synch classes protect only those ASX framework components (such as enqueueing messages onto a Queue's Message_List, demultiplexing messages onto internal Module addresses stored in a Multiplexor object, or registering an Event_Handler object with the Reactor) that would not function correctly in a preemptive, multi-threaded parallel processing environment. This minimalist synchronization strategy avoids over-constraining the granularity of a process architecture's concurrency control policies.

The ASX framework enables the concurrency control strategies used by different process architectures to be selected by instrumenting protocol tasks with various combinations of Mutex and Condition synchronization objects. When used in conjunction with C++ language features such as parameterized types, these synchronization objects help to decouple protocol processing functionality from the concurrency control strategy used by a particular process architecture. An example to illustrate how ASX framework synchronization objects are transparently parameterized into communication protocol code is presented in [14].

9.3.2.2. The Process_Manager Class

The Process_Manager class contains a set of mechanisms that manipulate multiple threads of control atomically. Typically, these threads of control collaborate to implement collective actions (such as rendering different portions of a large image in parallel). The Process_Manager class also shields applications from non-portable incompatibilities between different flavors of multi-threading mechanisms (such as POSIX threads, MACH cthreads, Solaris threads, and Windows NT threads).

The Process_Manager class provides methods (such as suspend_all and resume_all) that suspend and resume a set of collaborating threads of control atomically. This feature is useful for protocol stacks that execute multiple tasks or process multiple messages in parallel. For

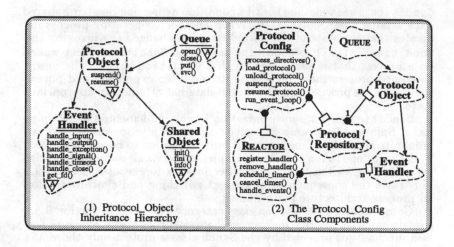

Figure 9.7: Components in the `Protocol Configurator` Class Category

example, a Stream implemented using the Layer Parallelism process architecture is composed of `Modules` that execute in separate threads of control. It is crucial that all `Modules` in the Stream are completely interconnected before allowing messages to be passed between `Queues` in the Stream. The mechanisms in the `Process_Manager` class allow these initialization activities to execute atomically.

9.3.3. The Protocol Configurator Class Category

Components in the `Protocol Configurator` class category are responsible for dynamically linking or unlinking protocol tasks into or out of the address space of a communication subsystem at run-time. Dynamic linking enables the configuration and reconfiguration of protocol-specific services *without* requiring the modification, recompilation, relinking, or restarting of an executing system. The `Protocol Configurator` components discussed below include the `Protocol_Object` inheritance hierarchy (Figure 9.7 (1)) and the `Protocol_Config` class (Figure 9.7 (2)). This discussion focuses on using the `Protocol Configurator` class category in the context of configuring application-tailored protocol stacks. However, these components are also useful in other domains such as network management[15] and configurable distributed systems[17].

9.3.3.1. The Protocol_Object Inheritance Hierarchy

The Protocol_Object class is the focal point of a multi-level hierarchy of types related by inheritance. The interfaces provided by the abstract classes in this type hierarchy may be selectively implemented by protocol-specific subclasses in order to access various Protocol Configurator features. These features provide transparent dynamic linking, registration of protocol-specific Modules, event demultiplexing, event-driven dispatching, and run-time control of protocol stacks (such as suspending and resuming a Stream temporarily during run-time reconfiguration).

The Protocol_Object inheritance hierarchy decouples the protocol-specific portion of a task from the underlying protocol-independent Protocol Configurator mechanisms. This decoupling reduces the effort necessary to insert and remove protocol stacks and protocol tasks from a communication subsystem at run-time. Likewise, by using pure virtual methods, the Protocol Configurator ensures that a Protocol _Object handler honors its obligation to provide certain configuration-related information. This information is subsequently used by the Protocol Configurator to automatically link, initialize, identify, and unlink the Modules in a protocol stack at run-time.

The Protocol_Object inheritance hierarchy consists of the Event _Handler and Shared_Object abstract base classes, as well as the Protocol_Object abstract derived class. The functionality of these classes is outlined below.

- The Event_Handler Abstract Base Class – this base class provides an abstract interface for defining and registering protocol-specific handlers whose methods are invoked automatically in response to events. Typical events include (1) I/O-based events received on communication ports, (2) time-based events generated by a callout queue, and (3) signal-based events. The Protocol Configurator class category automatically detects these events and dispatches the associated methods of pre-registered handlers. Each handler is implemented as a subclass that defines protocol-specific methods to override the Event_Handler base class interface.
- The Shared_Object Abstract Base Class – this abstract base class specifies an interface for dynamically linking and unlinking Modules into and out of the address space of a communication subsystem. The Shared_Object class specifies virtual methods that impose a contract between the reusable components provided by the Protocol Configurator and protocol-specific Modules that utilize these components.
- The Protocol_Object Abstract Derived Class – the Protocol _Object class combines the interfaces inherited from both the Event_Handler and the Shared_Object abstract base classes. In addition, this class defines methods that perform actions necessary to suspend a protocol task without unlinking it, as well as

to resume a previously suspended protocol task. The `Queue` class (from the `Stream` class category described in Section 9.3.1) inherits from the `Protocol_Object` class (illustrated in Figure 9.7 (1)). This enables hierarchically-related, protocol-specific `Queues` (which are grouped together to form `Modules`) to be linked and unlinked into and out of a Stream at run-time.

9.3.3.2. The Protocol_Config Class

As illustrated in Figure 9.7 (2), the `Protocol_Config` class integrates other ASX framework components such as the `Protocol_Repository` and the `Reactor`. The `Protocol_Repository`[17] is an object manager that simplifies the run-time configuration and administration of the `Modules` used to implement protocol stacks in a Stream. The `Reactor`[14] is an extensible event demultiplexer and event handler dispatcher that portably encapsulates and enhances the functionality of various OS event demultiplexing mechanisms (such as the Windows NT `WaitForMultipleObjects` and the UNIX `select` and `poll` system calls). Together, the `Protocol_Repository` and the `Reactor` collaborate to decouple the protocol-independent mechanisms that configure, demultiplex, and dispatch pre-registered `Protocol_Objects` from the protocol-specific functionality performed by methods in these objects.

A `Protocol_Config` object may be used at run-time to orchestrate the static and/or dynamic configuration of a communication subsystem that contains one or more Streams. A configuration script guides the initial configuration and subsequent reconfiguration(s) of a `Protocol_Config` object. A communication subsystem is composed using a configuration script. This script characterizes the essential attributes of one or more protocol stack. These attributes specify the location of a shared object library for each dynamically linked `Module`, as well as the parameters required to initialize a protocol stack at run-time. By consolidating attributes and installation parameters into a single configuration script, the administration of Streams within a communication subsystem is simplified significantly. In addition, subsystem composition is simplified by decoupling the configuration and reconfiguration mechanisms provided by the framework from the protocol-specific attributes and parameters specified in the configuration script.

9.4. COMMUNICATION SUBSYSTEM PERFORMANCE EXPERIMENTS

This section presents performance results obtained by measuring the data reception portion of protocol stacks implemented using several different process architectures. Two different types of protocol stacks were implemented: *connection-oriented* and *connectionless*. Three different variants of task-based and message-based process architectures were used to parallelize the protocol stacks: *Layer Parallelism* (which is a task-based process architecture), as well as *Message-Parallelism* and *Connectional Parallelism* (which are message-based process architectures).

9.4.1. multiprocessor Platform

All experiments were conducted on an otherwise idle Sun SPARCcenter 2000 shared memory symmetric multiprocessor. This SPARCcenter platform contained 640 Mbytes of RAM and 20 superscalar SPARC 40 MHz processing elements (PEs), each at approximately 135 MIPs. The operating system used for the experiments was SunOS release 5.3. SunOS 5.3 provides a multi-threaded kernel that allows multiple system calls and device interrupts to execute in parallel on the SPARCcenter platform[16]. All the process architectures in the experiments execute protocol tasks using separate SunOS unbound threads. These unbound threads are multiplexed over $1, 2, \ldots 20$ SunOS lightweight processes (LWPs) within an OS process. The SunOS scheduler maps each LWP directly onto a separate kernel thread. Since kernel threads are the units of PE scheduling and execution in SunOS, multiple LWPs run protocol tasks in parallel on the SPARCcenter 20 PEs.

The memory bandwidth of the SPARCcenter platform is approximately 750 Mbits/sec. In addition to memory bandwidth, communication subsystem throughput is significantly affected by the context switching and synchronization overhead of the multiprocessor platform. Scheduling and synchronizing a SunOS LWP requires a kernel-level context switch. This context switch flushes register windows and updates instruction and data caches, instruction pipelines, and translation lookaside buffers. These activities take approximately 50 μsecs to perform between LWPs running in the same process. During this time, the PE incurring the context switch does not execute any protocol tasks.

ASX `Mutex` and `Condition` objects were both used in the experiments. `Mutex` objects were implemented using SunOS adaptive spinlocks and `Condition` objects were implemented using SunOS sleeplocks[16]. Synchronization methods invoked on `Condition` objects were approximately two orders of magnitude more expensive compared with methods on `Mutex` objects. For instance, measurements showed that approximately 4 μsecs were required to acquire or release a `Mutex` object when no other PEs contended for the lock. In contrast, when all 20 PEs contended for a `Mutex` object, the time required to perform the locking methods increased to approximately 55 μsecs.

Approximately 300 μsecs were required to synchronize LWPs using `Condition` objects when no other PEs contended for the lock. Conversely, when all 20 PEs contended for a `Condition` object, the time required to perform the locking methods increased to approximately 520 μsecs. The two orders of magnitude difference in performance between `Mutex` and `Condition` objects was caused by the more complex algorithms used to implement `Condition` object methods. In addition, performing the `wait` method on a `Condition` object incurred a context switch, which further increased the synchronization overhead. In contrast, performing an `acquire` method on a `Mutex` object implemented with an adaptive spin-lock rarely triggered a context switch.

9.4.2. Functionality of the Communication Protocol Stacks

Two types of protocol stacks were investigated in the experiments. One was based on the connectionless UDP transport protocol; the other was based on the connection-oriented TCP transport protocol. Both protocol stacks contained data-link, network, transport, and presentation layers. The presentation layer was included in the experiments since it represents a major bottleneck in high-performance communication subsystems[4,11].

Both the connectionless and connection-oriented protocol stacks were developed by specializing reusable components in the `ASX` framework via inheritance and parameterized types. As discussed in Section 9.3.2.1, inheritance and parameterized types were used to hold protocol stack functionality constant, while the process architecture was systematically varied. Each layer in a protocol stack was implemented as a `Module`, whose read-side and write-side inherit interfaces and implementations from the `Queue` abstract class. The synchronization and demultiplexing mechanisms required to implement different process architectures were parameterized using C++ template class arguments. As illustrated in Section 9.3.2.1, these templates were instantiated based upon the type of process architecture being tested.

Data-link layer processing in each protocol stack was performed by the `DLP Module`. This `Module` transformed network packets received from a network interface into the canonical message format used internally by the interconnected `Queue` components in a Stream. Preliminary tests conducted with the widely-available `ttcp` benchmarking tool indicated that the SPARCcenter multiprocessor platform processed messages through a protocol stack much faster than our 10 Mbps Ethernet network interface was capable of handling. Therefore, the network interface in our process architecture experiments was simulated with a single-copy pseudo-device driver operating in loop-back mode. This approach is consistent with those used in[2,4,9].

The network and transport layers of the protocol stacks were based on the IP, UDP, and TCP implementations in the BSD 4.3 Reno release. The 4.3 Reno TCP implementation contains the TCP header prediction enhancements, as well as the TCP slow start algorithm and congestion avoidance features. The UDP and TCP transport protocols were configured into the `ASX` framework via the `UDP` and `TCP Modules`. Network layer processing was performed by the `IP Module`. This `Module` handled routing and segmentation/reassembly of Internet Protocol (IP) packets.

Presentation layer functionality was implemented in the `XDR Module` using marshaling routines produced by the ONC eXternal Data Rep-

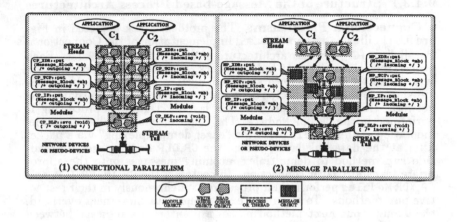

Figure 9.8: Message-based Process Architectures

resentation (XDR) stub generator. The ONC XDR stub generator
translates type specifications into marshaling routines. These marshaling routines encode/decode implicitly-typed messages before/after exchanging them among hosts that may possess heterogeneous processor
byte-orders. The ONC presentation layer conversion mechanisms consist of a type specification language (XDR) and a set of library routines
that implement the appropriate encoding and decoding rules for built-
in integral types (*e.g.*, char, short, int, and long), as well as real types
(*e.g.*, float and double). These library routines may be combined to produce marshaling routines for arbitrarily complex user-defined composite
types (such as record/structures, unions, arrays, and pointers). Messages exchanged via XDR are implicitly-typed, which improves marshaling performance at the expense of run-time flexibility.

The XDR routines generated for the connectionless and connection-
oriented protocol stacks converted incoming and outgoing messages into
and from variable-sized arrays of structures containing a set of integral
and real values. The XDR processing involved byte-order conversions,
as well as dynamic memory allocation and deallocation.

9.4.3. Structure of the Process Architectures

The remainder of this section outlines the structure of the message-
based and task-based process architectures used to parallelize the connectionless and connection-oriented protocol stacks described above.

9.4.3.1. Structure of the Message-based Process Architectures

• **Connectional Parallelism:** The protocol stack depicted in Figure 9.8 (1) illustrates an ASX-based implementation of the Connectional Parallelism (CP) process architecture outlined in Section 9.2.2. Each process performs the data-link, network, transport, and presentation layer tasks sequentially for a single connection. Protocol tasks are divided into four interconnected Modules, corresponding to the data-link, network, transport, and presentation layers. Data-link processing is performed in the CP_DLP Module. The Connectional Parallelism implementation of this Module performs "eager demultiplexing" via a packet filter at the data-link layer. Thus, the CP_DLP Module uses its read-side svc method to demultiplex incoming messages onto the appropriate transport layer connection. In contrast, the CP_IP, CP_TCP, and CP_XDR Modules perform their processing synchronously in their respective put methods. To eliminate extraneous data movement overhead, the Queue::put_next method passes a pointer to a message between protocol layers.

• **Message Parallelism:** Figure 9.8 (2) depicts the Message Parallelism (MP) process architecture used for the TCP-based connection-oriented protocol stack. When an incoming message arrives, it is handled by the MP_DLP::svc method. This method manages a pool of pre-spawned SunOS unbound threads. Each message is associated with an unbound thread that escorts the message synchronously through a series of interconnected Queues that form a protocol stack. Each layer of the protocol stack performs the protocol tasks defined by its Queue. When these tasks are complete, an upcall may be used to pass the message to the next adjacent layer in the protocol stack. The upcall is performed by invoking the put method in the adjacent layer's Queue. This put method borrows the thread of control from its caller and executes the protocol tasks associated with its layer.

The Message Parallelism process architecture for the connectionless protocol stack is similar to the one used to implement the connection-oriented protocol stack. The primary difference between the two protocol stacks is that the connectionless stack performs UDP transport functionality, which is less complex than TCP. For example, UDP does not generate acknowledgements, keep track of round-trip time estimates, or manage congestion windows. In addition, the connectionless MP_UDP::put method handles each message concurrently and independently, without explicitly preserving inter-message ordering. In contrast, the connection-oriented MP_TCP::put method utilizes several Mutex synchronization objects. As separate messages from the same connection ascend the protocol stack in parallel, these Mutex objects serialize access to per-connection control blocks. Serialization is required to protect shared resources (such as message queues, protocol connection records, TCP segment reassembly, and demultiplexing tables) against race conditions.

Both Connectional Parallelism and Message Parallelism optimize

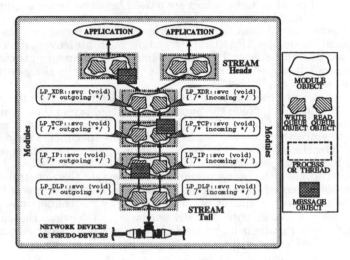

Figure 9.9: Layer Parallelism

message management by using SunOS thread-specific storage[16] to buffer messages as they flow through a protocol stack. This optimization leverages off the cache affinity properties of the SunOS shared memory multiprocessor. In addition, it minimizes the cost of synchronization operations used to manage the global dynamic memory heap.

9.4.3.2. Structure of the Task-based Process Architecture

● **Layer Parallelism:** Figure 9.9 illustrates the ASX framework components that implement a Layer Parallelism (LP) process architecture for the TCP-based connection-oriented protocol stack. The connectionless UDP-based protocol stack for Layer Parallelism was designed in a similar manner. The primary difference between them was that the read-side and write-side Queues in the connectionless transport layer Module (LP_UDP) implement the simpler UDP functionality.

Protocol-specific processing at each protocol layer shown in Figure 9.9 is performed in the Queue::svc method. Each svc method is executed in a separate process associated with the Module that implements the corresponding protocol layer (*e.g.,* LP_XDR, LP_TCP, LP_IP, and LP_DLP). These processes cooperate in a producer/consumer manner, operating in parallel on message header and data fields corresponding to their particular protocol layer. Every svc method performs its protocol layer tasks before passing a message to an adjacent Module running in a separate process.

All processes share a common address space, which eliminates the need to copy messages that are passed between adjacent Modules. However, even if pointers to messages are passed between processes, per-PE data caches may be invalidated by hardware cache consistency protocols. Cache invalidation degrades performance by increasing the level of contention on the SPARCcenter system bus. Moreover, since messages are passed between PEs, the memory management optimization techniques (described in Section 9.4.3.1) that used the thread-specific storage are not applicable.

A strict implementation of Layer Parallelism would limit parallel processing to only include the number of protocol layers that could run on separate PEs. On a platform with 2 to 4 PEs this is not a serious problem since the protocol stacks used in the experiments only had 4 layers. On the 20 PE SPARCcenter platform, however, this approach would have greatly constrained the ability of Layer Parallelism to utilize the available processing resources. To alleviate this constraint, the connection-oriented Layer Parallelism process architecture was implemented to handle a cluster of connections (*i.e.,* 5 connections per 4 layer protocol stack, with one PE per-layer). Likewise, the connectionless Layer Parallelism process architecture was partitioned across 5 network interfaces to utilize the available parallelism.

9.4.4. Measurement Results

This section presents results obtained by measuring the data reception portion of the protocol stacks developed using the process architectures described in Section 9.4.3. Three types of measurements were obtained for each combination of process architecture and protocol stack: *average throughput, context switching overhead,* and *synchronization overhead.* Average throughput measured the impact of parallelism on protocol stack performance. Context switching and synchronization measurements were obtained to help explain the variation in the average throughput measurements.

Average throughput was measured by holding the protocol functionality, application traffic, and network interfaces constant, while systematically varying the process architecture in order to determine the impact on performance. Each benchmarking run measured the amount of time required to process 20,000 4 kbyte messages. In addition, 10,000 4 kbyte messages were transmitted through the protocol stacks at the start of each run to ensure that all the PE caches were fully initialized (the time required to process these initial 10,000 messages was not used to calculate the throughput performance). Each test was run using $1, 2, 3, \ldots 20$ PEs, with each test replicated a dozen times and the results averaged. The purpose of replicating the tests was to insure that the amount of interference from internal OS process management tasks did not perturb the results.

Various statistics were collected using an extended version of the widely available `ttcp` protocol benchmarking tool. The `ttcp` tool measures the amount of OS processing resources, user-time, and system-time required to transfer data between a transmitter process and a receiver process. The flow of data is uni-directional, with the transmitter flooding the receiver with a user-specified number of data buffers. Various sender and receiver parameters (such as the number of data buffers transmitted and the size of data buffers and protocol windows) may be selected at run-time.

The version of ttcp used in our experiments was modified to use ASX-based connection-oriented and connectionless protocol stacks. These protocol stacks were configured in accordance with the process architectures described in Section 9.4.3. The ttcp tool was also enhanced to allow a user-specified number of connections to be active simultaneously. This extension enabled us to measure the impact of multiple connections on the performance of the connection-oriented protocol stacks using message-based and task-based process architectures.

9.4.4.1. Throughput Measurements

Figures 9.10, 9.11, and 9.12 depict the average throughput for the message-based process architectures (Connectional Parallelism (CP) and Message Parallelism (MP)) and the task-based process architecture (Layer Parallelism (LP)) used to implement the connection-oriented protocol stacks. Each test run for these connection-oriented process architectures used 20 connections. These figures report the average throughput (in Mbits/sec), measured both with and without presentation layer processing. The figures illustrate how throughput is affected as the number of PEs increase from 1 to 20.

The results from Figures 9.10 and 9.11 indicate that increasing the number of PEs generally improves the average throughput in the message-based process architectures. Connection-oriented Connectional Parallelism exhibited the highest performance, in average throughput. As shown in Figure 9.10, the average throughput of Connectional parallelism with presentation layer processing peaks at approximately 100 Mbits/sec. The average throughput without presentation layer processing peaks at just under 370 Mbits/sec. These results indicate that the presentation layer represents a significant portion of the overall protocol stack overhead. The average throughput of Connectional Parallelism with presentation layer processing increases steadily from 1 to 12 PEs, at which point it begins to level off. This is due to the additional overhead from data movement and synchronization performed in the presentation layer.

As shown in Figure 9.11, the average throughput achieved by connection-oriented Message Parallelism without presentation layer processing peaks at just under 130 Mbits/sec. When presentation layer processing is performed, the average throughput is 1.5 to 3 times lower, peaking at approximately 90 Mbits/sec. Note, however, that the average throughput without presentation layer processing flattens out after 8 CPUs. This occurs when presentation layer processing is omitted due to increased contention for shared synchronization objects at the transport layer. This synchronization overhead is discussed further in Section 9.4.4.3.

In contrast, the average throughput of connection-oriented Message Parallelism with presentation layer processing grows steadily from 1 to 20 PEs. This behavior suggests that connection-oriented Message Parallelism benefits more from parallelism when the protocol stack contains presentation layer processing. This finding is consistent with those reported in[9].

In contrast to Connectional Parallelism and Message Parallelism, the performance of the connection-oriented Layer Parallelism (in Figure 9.12) did not scale up as the number of PEs increased. The average throughput with presentation layer processing peaks at approximately 36 Mbits/sec. This amount is much less than half the throughput achieved by Connectional Parallelism and Message Parallelism. The throughput exhibited by Layer Parallelism peaks at 40 Mbits/sec when presentation layer processing is omitted. This is over 3 times lower than Message Parallelism and approximately 9 times lower than Connectional Parallelism. The average throughput both with and without presentation layer processing increases until after 10 and 7 PEs, respectively. After peaking, average throughput levels off and gradually begins to decrease. This decrease in Layer Parallelism performance occurs from the high levels of context switching (discussed in Section 9.4.4.2), as well as the high levels of Condition object synchronization overhead (discussed in Section 9.4.4.3).

A limitation with Connectional Parallelism is that each individual connection executes sequentially. Therefore, Connectional Parallelism becomes most effective as the number of connections approaches the number of PEs. In contrast, Message Parallelism utilizes multiple PEs more effectively when the number of connections is much less than the number of PEs. Figure 9.13 illustrates this point by graphing average throughput as a function of the number of connections. This test held the number of PEs constant at 20, while increasing the number of connections from 1 to 20. Connectional Parallelism consistently outperforms Message Parallelism as the number of connections becomes greater than 10.

Figures 9.14 and 9.15 depict the average throughput for the message-based and task-based process architectures used to implement the connectionless protocol stacks (note that Connectional Parallelism is not applicable for a connectionless protocol stack). These figures report the throughput measured both with and without presentation layer processing.

The connectionless message-based process architecture (Figure 9.14) significantly outperforms the task-based process architecture (Figure 9.15). This behavior is consistent with the results from the connection-oriented tests shown in Figure 9.10 through Figure 9.12. With presentation layer processing, the throughput of connectionless Message Parallelism is slightly higher than the connection-oriented version shown in Figure 9.11. However, without presentation layer processing, the throughput of connectionless Message Parallelism is substantially higher (500 Mbits/sec vs. 130 Mbits/sec).

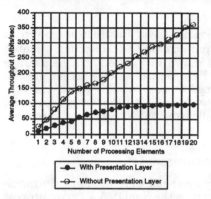

Figure 9.10: Connection-oriented Connectional Parallelism Throughput

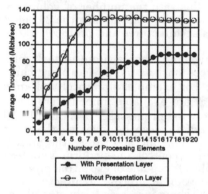

Figure 9.11: Connection-oriented Message Parallelism Throughput

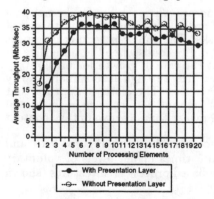

Figure 9.12: Connection-oriented Layer Parallelism Throughput

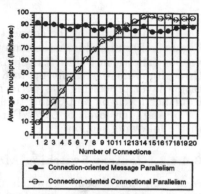

Figure 9.13: Comparison of Connectional and Message Parallelisms

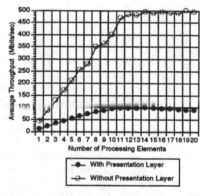

Figure 9.14: Connectionless Message Parallelism Throughput

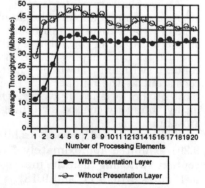

Figure 9.15: Connectionless Layer Parallelism Throughput

The throughput of the connectionless Layer Parallelism (shown in Figure 9.15) suffered from the same problems as the connection-oriented version (shown in Figure 9.12). As shown in Figure 9.12, the average throughput increases only up to 6 PEs, regardless of whether presentation layer processing was performed or not. At this point, the performance levels off and begins to decrease. This behavior is accounted for by the high levels of Layer Parallelism context switching discussed in the following section.

9.4.4.2. Context Switching Measurements

Measurements of context switching overhead were obtained by modifying the ttcp benchmarking tool to use the SunOS 5.3 /proc process file system. The /proc file system provides access to the executing image of each process in the system. It reports the number of voluntary and involuntary context switches incurred by SunOS LWPs within a process. Figures 9.16 through 9.20 illustrate the number of voluntary and involuntary context switches incurred by transmitting the 20,000 4 kbyte messages through the process architectures and protocol stacks measured in this study.

A voluntary context switch is triggered when a protocol task puts itself to sleep awaiting certain resources (such as I/O devices or synchronization locks) to become available. For example, a protocol task may attempt to acquire a resource that is not available immediately (such as obtaining a message from an empty list of messages in a Queue). In this case, the protocol task puts itself to sleep by invoking the wait method of an ASX Condition object. This method causes the SunOS kernel to preempt the current thread of control and perform a context switch to another thread of control that is capable of executing protocol tasks immediately. For each combination of process architecture and protocol stack, voluntary context switching increases fairly steadily as the number of PEs increase from 1 through 20 (shown in Figures 9.16 through 9.20).

An involuntary context switch occurs when the SunOS kernel preempts a running unbound thread in order to schedule another thread of control to execute other protocol tasks. The SunOS scheduler preempts an active thread of control every 10 milliseconds when the time-slice alloted to its LWP expires. Note that the rate of growth for involuntary context switching shown in Figures 9.16 through 9.20 remains fairly consistent as the number of PEs increase. Therefore, it appears that most of the variance in average throughput performance is accounted for by voluntary context switching, rather than by involuntary context switching.

The task-based process architectures (shown in Figures 9.19 and 9.20) exhibited approximately 4 to 5 times higher levels of voluntary context switching than the message-based process architectures (shown in Figures 9.16, 9.17, and 9.18).

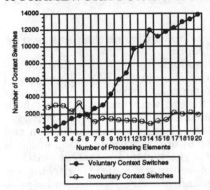

Figure 9.16: Connection-oriented Connectional Parallelism Context Switching

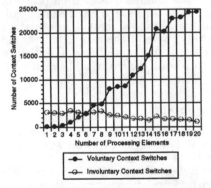

Figure 9.17: Connection-oriented Message Parallelism Context Switching

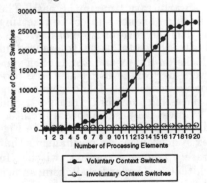

Figure 9.18: Connectionless Message Parallelism Context Switching

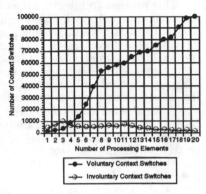

Figure 9.19: Connection-oriented Layer Parallelism Context Switching

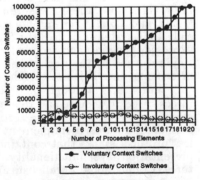

Figure 9.20: Connectionless Layer Parallelism Context Switching

This difference stems from the synchronization mechanisms used for the Layer Parallelism process architecture.

This process architecture uses sleep-locks to implement flow control between protocol stack layers running in separate PEs. This type of flow control is necessary since processing activities in each layer may execute at different rates. In SunOS, the `wait` and `signal` methods on `Condition` objects are implemented using sleep-locks, which trigger voluntary context switches. In contrast, Connectional Parallelism and Message Parallelism use adaptive spin-lock synchronization, which is less costly since it typically does *not* trigger voluntary context switches.

The substantially lower-levels of voluntary context switching exhibited by Connectional Parallelism and Message Parallelism helps to account for their consistently higher overall throughput and greater relative speedup discussed in Section 9.4.4.1.

As shown in Figure 9.16, Connectional Parallelism incurred the lowest levels of context switching for the connection-oriented protocol stacks. In this process architecture, after a message has been demultiplexed onto a connection, all that connection's context information is directly accessible within the address space of the associated thread of control. In general, a thread of control in Connectional Parallelism processes its connection's messages without incurring additional context switching overhead.

9.4.4.3. Synchronization Measurements

Measurements of synchronization overhead were collected to determine the amount of time spent acquiring and releasing locks on ASX `Mutex` and `Condition` objects during protocol processing on the 20,000 4 kbyte messages. Unlike context switches, the SunOS 5.3 `/proc` file system does not maintain accurate metrics on synchronization overhead. Therefore, these measurements were obtained by bracketing the `Mutex` and `Condition` methods with calls to the `gethrtime` system call. This system call uses the SunOS 5.3 high-resolution timer, which expresses time in nanoseconds from an arbitrary time in the past. The time returned by the `gethrtime` system call is not subject to resetting or drifting since it is not correlated with the current time of day.

Figures 9.21 through 9.25 indicate the total time (measured in msecs) used to acquire and release locks on `Mutex` and `Condition` synchronization objects. These tests were performed using all three process architectures to implement connection-oriented and connectionless protocol stacks that contained data-link, network, transport, and presentation layer functionality. The message-based process architectures (Connectional Parallelism and Message Parallelism, shown in Figures 9.21, 9.22, and 9.24) used `Mutex` synchronization mechanisms that utilize adaptive spin-locks (which rarely trigger a context switch). In contrast, the task-based process architecture (Layer Parallelism, shown in Figures 9.23 and 9.25) utilized both `Mutex` and `Condition` objects (`Condition` objects *do* trigger context switches).

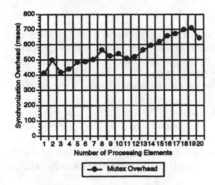

Figure 9.21: Connection-oriented Connectional Parallelism Synchronization Overhead

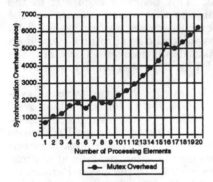

Figure 9.22: Connection-oriented Message Parallelism Synchronization Overhead

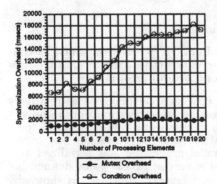

Figure 9.23: Connection-oriented Layer Parallelism Synchronization Overhead

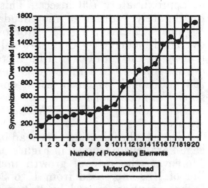

Figure 9.24: Connectionless Message Parallelism Synchronization Overhead

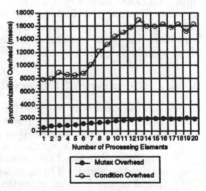

Figure 9.25: Connectionless Layer Parallelism Synchronization Overhead

Connection-oriented Connectional Parallelism (shown in Figure 9.21) exhibited the lowest levels of synchronization overhead, which peaked at approximately 700 msecs. This synchronization overhead was approximately 1 order of magnitude lower than the results shown in Figures 9.22 through 9.25. Moreover, the amount of synchronization overhead incurred by Connectional Parallelism did not increase significantly as the number of PEs increased from 1 to 20. This behavior occurs since after a message is demultiplexed onto a PE/connection, few additional synchronization operations are required. In addition, since Connectional Parallelism processes messages within a single PE cache, it leverages off of SPARCcenter 2000 multiprocessor cache affinity properties.

The synchronization overhead incurred by connection-oriented Message Parallelism (shown in Figure 9.22) peaked at just over 6,000 msecs. Moreover, the rate of growth increased fairly steadily as the number of PEs increased from 1 to 20. This behavior occurs from the lock contention caused by **Mutex** objects that serialize access to the **Map_Manager** connection demultiplexer (discussed in Section 9.3.2.1). In contrast, the connectionless Message Parallelism protocol stack does not require the use of this connection demultiplexer. Therefore, the amount of synchronization overhead it incurred was much lower, peaking at under 1,800 msecs.

Connection-oriented Layer Parallelism exhibited two types of synchronization overhead (shown in Figure 9.23). The amount of overhead resulting from **Mutex** objects peaked at just over 2,000 msecs, which was lower than that of connection-oriented Message Parallelism (shown in Figure 9.22). However, the amount of synchronization overhead from the **Condition** objects was much higher, peaking at approximately 18,000 msecs (shown in Figure 9.23). In the Layer Parallelism implementation, the **Condition** objects implemented flow control between separate layers executing on different PEs in a protocol stack. The connectionless version of Layer Parallelism also exhibited high levels of synchronization overhead (shown in Figure 9.25).

9.4.4.4. Summary of Observations

The following observations resulted from our experience gained by conducting performance experiments on alternative process architectures for connectionless and connection-oriented protocol stacks:

- Implementing the task-based process architectures was relatively straightforward. These process architectures map onto conventional layered communication models using well-structured "producer/consumer" designs. Minimal synchronization was necessary *within* a layer since parallel processing was serialized at a service access point (such as the service access point defined between the network and transport layers). However, as shown by the performance experiments, the task-based Layer Parallelism process architecture exhibited high levels of context switching and synchronization overhead on the SunOS shared memory multiprocessor platform.

- Implementing the message-based process architectures was challenging since the concurrency control mechanisms were more complex. However, the message-based process architectures used parallelism more effectively than the task-based process architectures. This is due in part to the fact that message-based process architecture parallelism was based upon dynamic characteristics (such as messages or connections). This dynamism enables the message-based process architectures to use a larger number of PEs effectively. As described in Section 9.4.4.1, the relative speedups gained from parallel message-based process architectures scaled up to use a relatively high number of PEs. In contrast, the parallelism used by the task-based process architectures depended on relatively static characteristics (such as the number of layers or protocol tasks), which did not scale up. In addition, the higher rate of growth for context switching and synchronization (discussed in Sections 4.4.2 and 4.4.3) hampered the ability of Layer Parallelism to effectively utilize a large number of PEs.

- Connectional Parallelism becomes more suitable than Message Parallelism as the number of connections approaches the number of PEs. Message Parallelism, on the other hand, is more suitable when the number of active connections is significantly less than the number of available PEs. In addition, unlike Connectional Parallelism, Message Parallelism is suitable for connectionless applications.

- It appears that connection-oriented Message Parallelism benefits more from parallelism when the protocol stack contains presentation layer processing. As shown in Figure 9.11, the average throughput curve for connection-oriented Message Parallelism without presentation layer processing flattens out after 8 PEs. In contrast, when presentation layer processing is performed, the average throughput continues to increase up to 16 PEs. This behavior results from the relatively low amount of synchronization overhead associated with parallel processing at the presentation layer. In contrast, the average throughput for Connectional Parallelism without presentation layer processing continues to increase steadily up to 20 PEs (shown in Figure 9.10). Connectional Parallelism performs well in this case due to its low levels of synchronization and context switching overhead.

- It appears that the relative cost of synchronization operations has a substantial impact on process architecture performance. On the SPARCcenter 2000 shared memory multiprocessor running SunOS 5.3, the message-based process architectures benefit from their use of inexpensive adaptive spin-locks. In contrast, the task-based process architectures were penalized by the much higher (*i.e.*, two orders of magnitude) cost of sleep-lock synchronization. We conjecture that a multiprocessor platform possessing different synchronization properties would produce significantly different results. For example, if the experiments reported in this paper were replicated on a non-shared memory, message-passing transputer platform[3], it is likely that the performance of the task-based process architectures would improve relative to the message-based process architectures.

9.5. CONCLUDING REMARKS

This paper describes communication protocol stack performance measurements obtained using the ASX framework. This framework provides an integrated set of object-oriented components that facilitate experimentation with message-based and task-based process architectures on multiprocessor platforms.

Components in the ASX framework are freely available via anonymous ftp from ics.uci.edu in the file gnu/C++_wrappers.tar.Z. This distribution contains complete source code, documentation, and example test drivers for the ASX C++ components. Components in the ASX framework have been ported to both UNIX and Windows NT. The ASX framework is currently being used in a number of commercial products including the AT&T Q.port ATM signaling software product [14], as well as the network management subsystems in the Ericsson EOS project [17] and the Motorola Iridium global personal communications system.

BIBLIOGRAPHY

1. D. C. SCHMIDT and T. SUDA, "Transport System Architecture Services for High-Performance Communications Systems," IEEE Journal on Selected Areas in Communication, 11, pp. 489–506 (May 1993).

2. M. BJORKMAN and P. GUNNINGBERG, "Locking Strategies in Multiprocessor Implementations of Protocols," in Proceedings of the ACM SIGCOMM Symposium on Communications Architectures and Protocols (1993).

3. M. ZITTERBART, "High-Speed Transport Components," IEEE Network Magazine, pp. 54–63 (January 1991).

4. M. GOLDBERT, G. NEUFELD, and M. ITO, "A Parallel Approach to OSI Connection-Oriented Protocols," in Proceedings of the 3rd IFIP Workshop on Protocols for High-Speed Networks (May 1992).

5. C. M. WOODSIDE and R. G. FRANKS, "Alternative Software Architectures for Parallel Protocol Execution with Synchronous IPC," IEEE/ACM Transactions on Networking, 1 (April 1993).

6. B. LINDGREN, B. KRUPCZAK, M. AMMAR, and K. SCHWAN, "Parallelism and Configurability in High Performance Protocol Architectures," in IEEE Proceedings of the Second Workshop on the

Architecture and Implementation of High Performance Communication Subsystems (September 1993).

7. T. BRAUN and M. ZITTERBART, "Parallel Transport System Design," in Proceedings of the 4th IFIP Conference on High Performance Networking (1993).

8. N. C. HUTCHINSON and L. L. PETERSON, "The x-kernel: An Architecture for Implementing Network Protocols," in IEEE Transactions on Software Engineering, **17**, pp. 64–76 (January 1991).

9. E. M. NAHUM, D. J. YATES, J. F. KUROSE, and D. TOWSLEY, "Performance Issues in Parallelized Network Protocols," in Submission to the Operating Systems Design and Implementation Conference, USENIX Association (November 1994).

10. S. SSXENA, J. K. PEACOCK, F. YANG, V. VERMA, and M. KRISHNAN, "Pitfalls in Multithreading SVR4 STREAMS and other Weightless Processes," in Proceedings of the Winter USENIX Conference, pp. 85–106 (January 1993).

11. D. D. CLARK and D. L. TENNENHOUSE, "Architectural Considerations for a New Generation of Protocols," in Proceedings of the ACM SIGCOMM Symposium on Communications Architectures and Protocols, pp. 200–208 (September 1990).

12. D. RITCHIE, "A Stream Input–Output System," AT&T Bell Labs Technical Journal, **63**, pp. 311–324 (October 1984).

13. J. M. ZWEIG, "The Conduit: a Communication Abstraction in C++," in Proceedings of the 2nd USENIX C++ Conference, pp. 191–203, USENIX Association (April 1990).

14. D. C. SCHMIDT and T. SUDA, "A Framework for Evaluating Process Architectures for Parallelizing Communication Subsytems," Technical Report, University of California, Irvine (1996).

15. D. C. SCHMIDT and T. SUDA, "Experiences with an Object-Oriented Architecture for Developing Extensible Distributed System Management Software," in IEEE Proceedings of the Conference on Global Communications (GLOBECOM) (November/December 1994).

16. J. EYKHOLT, S. KLEIMAN, S. BARTON, R. FAULKNER, A. SHIVALINGIAH, M. SMITH, D. STEIN, J. VOLL, M. WEEKS, and D. WILLIAMS, "Beyond Multiprocessing... Multithreading the SunOS Kernel," in Proceedings of the Summer USENIX Conference (June 1992).

17. D. C. SCHMIDT and T. SUDA, "An Object-Oriented Framework for Dynamically Configuring Extensible Distributed Communication Systems," IEE/BCS Distributed Systems Engineering Journal (Special Issue on Configurable Distributed Systems), **2**, pp. 280–293 (December 1994).

CHAPTER 10

SMURPH: A PROTOTYPING AND MODELING TOOL FOR COMMUNICATION NETWORKS AND PROTOCOLS

Wlodek Dobosiewicz and Pawel Gburzynski

10.1. INTRODUCTION

We introduce SMURPH—an object-oriented programming environment based on C++ for specifying communication protocols and modeling communication networks. By a communication network we understand a configuration of *stations* interconnected via *channels*, running a collection of *processes*. The distributed algorithm realized by those processes is called the communication protocol.

Unlike other protocol specification systems, e.g., ESTELLE (Budkowski and Dembinski[1]), LOTOS (Bolognesi and Brinksma,[2] Logrippo et al.[3]), or PROMELA (Holzmann[4]), SMURPH has a built-in notion of time. Thus, it can express protocol operations and physical phenomena occurring at the boundary of data-link and physical layers, e.g., at the medium access control (MAC) level.

Besides the specification language, the system provides a virtual environment for executing protocols. This environment is based on an event-driven, discrete-time simulator. The user has an impression of running the protocol in a realistic environment, which reflects all relevant physical phenomena occurring in a real network, e.g., limited accuracy of independent clocks, race conditions, faulty channels. From this end, SMURPH can be viewed as a network simulator. Compared to other network simulators and evaluators, e.g, COMNET (Mills and Skinner[5]), GILDA (Palmer, Naghshineh, Chen[6]), NETSIM (Jump and Lakshmanamurthy[7]), SMURPH has a number of distinct features:

- Protocols in SMURPH are fully specified. In principle, a SMURPH specification can be made completely functional in a mechanical way.

- In SMURPH, networks and protocols are *emulated* rather than simulated. Thus it makes sense to use SMURPH for protocol verification, e.g., conformance testing.

- SMURPH doesn't purport to be a no-programming system. Intentionally, SMURPH is a protocol prototyping environment, and with the current state of the art in program synthesis, it is extremely difficult to produce novel protocols by moving icons on the screen. On the other hand, owing to the object-oriented nature of SMURPH specifications, it is easy to build libraries of networks, protocols, and their components.

SMURPH and its predecessor LANSF (Gburzynski and Rudnicki[8]) have been used to investigate the performance and correctness of a number of protocols for local and metropolitan area networks (LANs and MANs), e.g., Bertan,[9] Gburzynski and Rudnicki,[10,11] including ATM networks (Gburzynski and Shankar[12]). In some cases, modeling in SMURPH revealed hidden implementation problems with apparently simple protocols (e.g., Gburzynski and Rudnicki[13]).

The package (runnable on a variety of popular platforms) is freely available to the research community via *anonymous ftp* from ftp.cs.ualberta.ca (129.128.4.241). A book (Gburzynski[14]) on protocols for LANs and MANs with numerous examples in SMURPH has been published recently.

10.2. THE STRUCTURE OF SMURPH

The structure of the package is presented in figure 10.1. A SMURPH program consisting of the protocol source code, network description, and traffic specification is translated by SMPP into a program in C++. The code in C++ is then compiled and linked with the SMURPH library. This way a stand-alone executable module is built, which can be viewed as a simulator for the system described by the user program.

The standard linkable SMURPH library is augmented by a source library of types (the "include" library), which is extensible by the user. This library typically contains predefined network topologies (i.e., parametrizable network configurations) and traffic patterns.

When run, the simulator produces results which may be related to the observed performance of the modeled system or to some logical

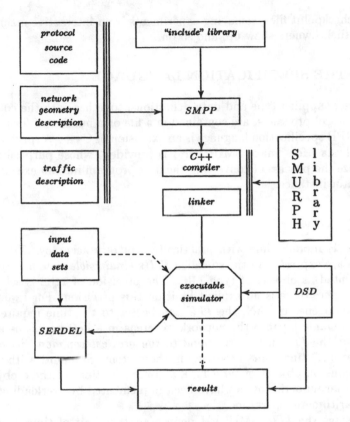

Figure 10.1: The structure of SMURPH.

aspects of its behavior. It is also possible to monitor the execution of the modeled system on-line. This is done by DSD—a separate display program which communicates with the simulator and displays selected information in a collection of windows. DSD and the simulator don't have to run on the same machine.

Instead of running the simulator directly, the user may choose to execute it under control of SERDEL, which provides support for coordinating multiple simulation experiments executed in the environment of a local network of computers. SERDEL takes care of migrating the experiments from busy machines to idle ones, starting new experiments when more machines become available, periodic checkpointing, detecting machine/system failures and restarting the affected experiments from checkpoint files, removing experiments from interactive machines when their owners show up, and so on.

10.3. THE SPECIFICATION LANGUAGE

The user-supplied type and data definitions, together with the code of the protocol processes, are contained in a file or a number of files. The SMURPH specification language is an extension of C++. A special tool (called mks—for "make SMURPH") is provided, whose purpose is to organize the process of converting the user program into an executable simulator instance.

10.3.1. Time

SMURPH models time with practically arbitrary accuracy. Time intervals are expressed in the so-called *ITU*s (*indivisible time units*) and represented as objects of type TIME. The precision of TIME is selected by the user; there is no explicit limit on this precision. For example, in a homogeneous LAN, the *ITU* can be set to the time required to insert a single bit into the network, whereas in a heterogeneous environment the *ITU* may correspond to the *greatest common divisor* of all "natural" time units occurring in the system. Standard arithmetic operations on objects of type TIME and combinations of these objects with other numeric entities have been implemented by overloading the usual arithmetic operators.

Besides the *ITU*, SMURPH defines another unit of time, the so-called *ETU*, which stands for the *experimenter time unit*. This unit is used for presenting simulation results.

10.3.2. Hierarchy of built-in SMURPH classes

All user-visible compound types (TIME is viewed as a simple type) are organized into a hierarchy presented in figure 10.2. This hierarchy reflects the inclusion of types in terms of the C++ subclass concept. We assume that a (nonexistent) type *class* is the root of this hierarchy.

All objects exhibiting dynamic behavior belong to type *Object* which is not directly visible to the user. Most of the standard subtypes of *Object* can (and sometimes must) be extended by the user. For example, type Station defines a skeleton for creating *stations*, i.e., the network nodes. Typically, this skeleton has to be augmented by some protocol-specific elements before it can be used to build actual stations.

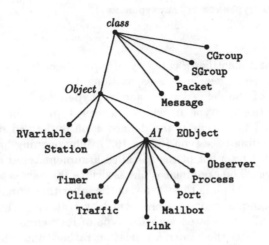

Figure 10.2: SMURPH hierarchy of built-in compound types.

All *Objects* are *exposable*, i.e., there is a standard way of visualizing information associated with them. In particular, this information can be displayed in a window (by DSD) and updated automatically while the experiment is in progress. Type EObject provides a base class for defining non-standard dynamic and exposable object types.

There is a special category of dynamic objects called *activity interpreters* (*AIs*). These objects define the protocol's interface with the outer world. An *AI* can be viewed as a *daemon* that absorbs protocol *activities* and turns them into future events. These events in turn can be perceived by the protocol and influence its behavior. By timing future events, *AIs* advance the modeled time. They also cover the internal event-processing mechanism with a higher-level interface, which is perceived by the protocol processes as a realistic reactive environment.

Types of objects that do not act on their own, but instead are subjects of activities of other objects, are straightforward classes. An example of such a type is Packet describing a packet skeleton.

10.3.3. Type declaration

SMURPH offers more than a C++ class library: it actually extends the syntax of C++. For example, the syntax of a SMURPH type declaration is as follows:

```
keyword typename :  suptypename {
   ...
};
```

where **keyword** identifies a category of types describing a common superclass of objects, e.g.: processes, stations, traffic patterns; **typename** is the name of the defined type; and **suptypename** is the identifier of the immediate supertype in which the new type is contained. This last part need not occur if the defined type is derived directly from the corresponding base type (figure 10.2). The opening brace is sometimes preceded by a list of the so-called argument types encapsulated in parentheses. The argument types associate the new type with other types, without including those types in the inheritance prefix of the new type. For example, processes are owned by stations. Thus, a process type is typically associated with the type of its owning stations. This association reflects the *ownership* relation rather than inheritance.

It is also possible to define new types as combinations of already defined types, taking advantage of the *multiple inheritance* apparatus of C++. In such a case, **suptypename** is a list of type names. This mechanism has been adopted and modified in SMURPH.

The declaration body (the text between the braces) contains declarations of new attributes and methods. If the type extension declares a method called **setup**, this method will be automatically called when an object of the extended type is created. The **setup** methods play the role of object *constructors* and they supplement the standard C++ constructors.

SMURPH provides its private tool for generating objects. The syntax of this operation, in its two flavors, is as follows:

```
ptr = create typename (...);
ptr = create (s) typename (...);
```

where **typename** is the type of the created object and **s** is an optional station identifier. Operation **create** can be viewed as a function returning a pointer to the created object. The optional text enclosed in the parentheses following the type name is passed as a list of arguments to the object's setup method.

All *Objects*, built by **create** or declared statically, are assigned identifiers. There are several classes of such identifiers; most of them are used by DSD to identify the objects for the purpose of *exposing* them on the terminal screen. One simple identifier type is the object's serial number, which typically reflects the order in which objects have been created.

Some objects, e.g., mailboxes, ports, processes, are owned by stations. An object belonging to one of these types is always created *in the context of some station*. This context can be implicit (e.g., a port created by the station's setup method is automatically assigned to the station), or explicit, i.e., specified directly at the moment of creation. One way to indicate that an object is to be assigned to a specific station is to use the second variant of `create`, where s is either a pointer to a station object or the station's serial number. Deallocation of SMURPH objects is performed by the standard C++ operation `delete`.

10.3.4. Describing network topology

The topology of the modeled network is defined as an interconnection of *stations*, *ports*, and *links*. Stations are objects belonging to type `Station`; subtypes of this type can be defined to describe stations with specific characteristics. Stations represent dynamic elements of the network: they are computers capable of executing protocol processes, possibly several such processes in parallel.

A station is typically attached to a link (or a number of links) via ports. A port (an object of type `Port`) represents a connection of one station to one link. A link (an object of type `Link`) models a communication medium, e.g.: an optical fiber, a coaxial cable, or a radio channel (see Gburzynski and Rudnicki[15]).

The network configuration is described in a dynamic way, i.e., by a program that explicitly assigns ports to stations and connects them to specific links in specific places. The geometry of a link is determined by a *distance matrix*, which determines distances between all pairs of ports connected to the link. There are a number of ways to specify a link distance matrix; the most natural way is to explicitly assign a distance to each combination of two ports connected to the link. The distance between a pair of ports can be assigned by calling the port method `setDTo`—in the following way: `p1->setDTo (p2, d)`, where p1 and p2 are port pointers and d is the assigned distance between p1 and p2. SMURPH facilitates creating libraries of network configurations. The package comes with a library of standard topologies, including buses, rings, stars, and meshes (e.g., tori, hypercubes).

10.3.5. Defining traffic conditions

Traffic in the modeled system consists of *messages* arriving to the network to be processed by stations. Messages are turned into *packets*, which can be transmitted and received by stations on their ports. The traffic distribution is described by a collection of the so-called *traffic patterns*, which are objects of type `Traffic`. Each traffic pattern is associated with specific message and packet types. Messages and packets belonging to different traffic patterns may have different, protocol-dependent structures. The behavior of a traffic pattern is described by a set of virtual functions and processes that can be redefined in user-created subtypes of `Traffic`. Libraries of traffic patterns can be built in a natural way.

10.3.6. Processes

A process consists of its private data area and a possibly shared code. Besides accessing its private data, a process can reference the attributes of the station owning the process, and some other variables constituting the so-called *process environment*. Processes can communicate in several ways, even if they do not belong to the same station.

A process type usually defines a number of attributes (they can be viewed as the local data area of the process), an optional setup method, and one special method defining the process code. A process type declaration has the following syntax:

```
process ptype :  supptype (fptype, stype) {
... attributes and methods ...
setup (...) {
   ...
};
states {s0, s1, ... , sk};
perform {
   ...
};
};
```

where `ptype` is the name of the declared process type, `supptype` is a previously defined process type, `fptype` is the type of the process' *parent*, and `stype` is the type of the station owning the process. As for the other SMURPH types, `supptype` can be omitted if the new process type is derived directly from `Process`. The two arguments in parentheses are also optional: they can be skipped if they are not useful to the process.

A process is always created by another process which is considered its parent. Initially, before any user-defined process is created, there exists a built-in system process called `Kernel`. This process creates one instance of a user-supplied process named `Root`. The role of `Root` can be compared to the role of function `main` in a C (or C++) program.

A process code method resembles the description of a finite state machine. The `states` declaration assigns symbolic names to the states of this machine. The first state on the list is the initial state: the process gets into this state immediately after it is created.

The operation of a process consists in responding to events. The occurrence of an event awaited by a process wakes the process up and forces it into a specific state. Then the process (its code method) performs some operations and suspends itself. Among these operations are indications of future events that the process wants to perceive. A typical code method has the following structure:

```
perform {
    state s0:
        ...
    state s1:
        ...
    ...
    state sk:
        ...
};
```

Two standard pointers (whose declarations are implicit and invisible) are available to the code method. They are: F (of type `fptype`) pointing to the process' parent, and S (of type `stype`) pointing to the station owning the process. This way, besides having natural access to its private objects, a process can reference public attributes of its parent and its station.

10.3.7. Activity interpreters

Events that drive processes are generated by *activity interpreters* (*AI*s). One common element of the interface between an *AI* and a process is the *AI*'s wait method callable as `ai->wait (ev, st)`. The first argument of `wait` identifies an event; its type and range are *AI*-specific. The second argument is a process state identifier: upon the nearest occurrence of the indicated event the process will be awakened in the specified state.

An awakened process usually performs a sequence of protocol-related operations and issues a number of `wait` requests describing its future waking conditions. Eventually, the process suspends itself, either by exhausting the list of statements associated with its current state or by executing `sleep`. All the `wait` requests issued by a process at one state are combined into an *alternative* of waking conditions: as soon as one of these conditions is fulfilled, the process will be restarted in the state indicated by the second argument of the corresponding wait request. The other pending wait requests are then canceled. The simulated time does not flow while a process is active. This way multiple processes can be active *simultaneously* within the same *ITU*.

The collection of standard *activity interpreters* consists of the Timer (used to implement alarm clocks), Traffic objects (responsible for traffic generation), the Client, which can be viewed as a combination of all Traffic *AI*s, Port objects (triggering communication events that originate in links), Mailbox objects (providing means for inter-process communication), and Process objects (which are also *activity interpreters*).

Processes running at the same station communicate by exchanging signals via Mailbox *AI*s. A process may suspend itself awaiting the occurrence of a signal on a Mailbox. Then some other process may supply this signal and restart the waiting process. Depending on the complexity of a Mailbox, multiple pending signals can be queued; they can also carry some information. Another (direct) way to synchronize processes is to take advantage of the fact that each process is itself an activity interpreter. For example, it is possible for a process *A* to issue a wait request to another process *B*, to be awakened when *B* gets into some specific state (in particular terminates itself).

10.3.8. User interface

Typically, the protocol modeling program reads some input data and produces some output. SMURPH offers private operations for reading input data and private structural tools for producing output results. Most of the output results are generated by *exposing* objects, i.e., calling special high-level output methods associated with objects.

Another part of the SMURPH-user interface is DSD—a separate program which communicates with the simulator via IPC tools. It is possible to run the simulator on one machine, e.g., a CPU server, and monitor its execution on another computer, e.g., a graphic workstation.

DSD can be used to trace the protocol execution "on-line" and is also very useful for debugging. Windows displayed by DSD can be "stepped." In this mode, the simulator halts after every event that "has something to do" with the contents of the selected windows. An explicit user action is required to advance the simulator to the next "step." This way the user can trace the protocol, e.g., to find a reason for its misbehavior or just to understand its operation.

10.3.9. Performance measures

Some standard performance measures are computed automatically while the protocol program is running. SMURPH offers tools for collecting non-standard statistics. Objects of type RVariable can be created by the user and processed by a collection of standard methods implementing typical operations on random variables, e.g., adding a new sample, combining two random variables into one, and exposing (i.e., printing out or displaying) the parameters of a random variable.

10.3.10. Observers

Besides conventional tools for program debugging, such as local assertions and protocol tracing functions, SMURPH offers means for verifying compound dynamic conditions that can be viewed as an alternative specification of the modeled protocol.

Observers are process-like objects that can be used for expressing global assertions involving the combined behavior of more than one regular process. They are somewhat reminiscent of the tools with the same name described by Groz.[16]

A regular process specifies its waking conditions (by calling wait) in terms of events triggered by *AI*s. An observer specifies its waking conditions by invoking a sequence of inspect requests identifying classes of waking scenarios for regular protocol processes. By calling inspect (s, p, ps, os), the observer indicates that it wants to be restarted in state os when a process of type p owned by station s is awakened in state ps. The symbol ANY used in place of any of the first three arguments is a wildcard—it stands for an arbitrary value. In such a case, the observer is restarted by any event that matches the other parameters of inspect.

Configurations of inspect requests describe the observer's transition function, which can be viewed as a description of state transitions in the entire collection of protocol processes. As regular assertions verify some Boolean properties of a program, observers verify state transitions in a distributed system and make sure that these transitions conform to a set of specifications. In this sense, observers are conformance testing tools.

10.4. ATM SWITCH MODEL IN SMURPH

To demonstrate how our package can be used to model realistic networking solutions, we will discuss a SMURPH prototype of an ATM switch. The limited size of this chapter makes it impossible to discuss the full implementation of a realistic ATM switch; however, we can have a look at a generic model of the common part of all ATM switches. Real ATM switches may exist in different flavors, depending on the organization of their switching fabric, buffer space, and call admission and traffic policing schemes (e.g., see Roojolamini, Cherkasky, and Garver[17]). In our generic model, we encapsulate the common properties of all ATM switches into one base type that can be used to derive specific switch models.

10.4.1. Generic switch architecture

The base ATM switch type can be defined as follows:

```
station Switch {
  Port **IPorts, **OPorts; int NPorts;
  Mailbox **Ready;
  virtual int vciSwitch (Cell*, int) { };
  virtual void callCell (Cell*, int) { };
  virtual void dataCell (Cell*, int) { };
  virtual CBuf *outCell (int) { return NULL; };
  void setup (int np) {
    NPorts = np; IPorts = new Port* [np];
    OPorts = new Port* [np]; Ready = new Mailbox* [np];
    for (i = 0; i < np; i++) Ready [i] = create Mailbox;
  };
};
```

An ATM switch must be equipped with a number of input ports and the same number of output ports (ATM links are bidirectional). These elements are represented by the arrays of port pointers (IPorts and OPorts). Note that the arrays are created by the switch setup method, but the ports themselves are not. This end will be taken care of by a separate "geometry" module that will configure the switch into a network. The number of port pairs is specified when the switch is created (the argument of setup) and stored in NPorts.

At this level of description, the functionality of our switch is described by four virtual methods acting as placeholders for the switch's functional modules that will have to be provided for each specific switch type. Method callCell is called upon the arrival of a signaling cell; its role is to carry out the connection setup protocol. The first argument points to the cell itself and the second gives the index of the input port on which the cell has arrived. Method dataCell is used to deposit outgoing cells in the switch's buffer storage. The first argument

identifies the cell to be deposited and the second gives the index of the
output port on which the cell should be retransmitted. Another virtual method, outCell, removes from the switch's cell storage the buffer
containing the next cell to be transmitted on the output port specified
by the argument. The role of the mailboxes (array Ready) is to indicate
the availability of outgoing cells (per output port) by triggering events
when such cells become available.

VCI switching is implemented by method vciSwitch, which takes
an incoming cell together with the index of the port of its arrival and
produces the index of the output port on which the cell should be
retransmitted. As a side effect, the function also replaces the VCI
number in the cell header with a new value.

Although our switch is far from being fully specified, its object-
oriented organization makes it possible to program the generic part
of its behavior without having to worry about implementation details.
Below we list the complete specification of the *input process* responsible
for accepting cells arriving at the switch. A separate instance of this
process is run for every input port.

```
#define TheCell ((Cell*) ThePacket)

process Input (Switch) {
  Port *IPort; int PIndx;
  void setup (int pn) { IPort = S->IPorts [PIndx = pn]; };
  states {WaitCell, Enter};
  perform {
   int op;
   state WaitCell:
    IPort->wait (BOT, Enter);
   state Enter:
    if (TheCell->Type != DATA)
      S->callCell (TheCell, PIndx);
    else
      if ((op = S->vciSwitch (TheCell, PIndx)) != NONE)
        S->dataCell (TheCell, op);
    skipto WaitCell;
  };
};
```

When the process is created, its setup method assigns the index of
the input port to be serviced by the process to its local attribute PIndx
and the pointer to the actual port to IPort (S is a standard attribute
pointing to the station at which the process is running). The execution
starts in the first state (WaitCell) in which the process waits for a cell

arrival on the input port (event BOT). When this happens, the process
transits to state Enter, where it examines the cell type.

The cell whose arrival has triggered the standard BOT (beginning
of transmission) event is available to the process via TheCell, which
is an alias for the standard pointer ThePacket belonging to the process environment. For any event caused by a packet, this pointer is
automatically set to point to the packet responsible for the event.

If the cell is not a data cell (i.e., it is a signaling cell), the process
calls the callCell method of the switch. Otherwise, based on the
VCI attribute of the cell, the cell is entered to the buffer storage (by
dataCell) and tagged with the index of the output port. Data cells
with incorrect VCIs (indicated by value NONE returned by vciSwitch)
are ignored. Having completed the processing of one incoming cell,
the process moves back to state WaitCell (operation skipto) to await
another cell arrival.

The output end of the switch is serviced by a collection of *output
processes*, one output process associated with one output port.

```
process Output (Switch) {
  Port *OPort; int PIndx; CBuf *SBuf; Mailbox *Ready;
  void setup (int pn) {
    OPort = S->OPorts [PIndx = pn]; Ready = S->Ready [pn];
  };
  states {Acquire, XDone};
  perform {
    state Acquire:
     if ((SBuf = S->outCell (PIndx)) == NULL)
       Ready->wait (NEWITEM, Acquire);
     else
       OPort->transmit (SBuf->cell (), XDone);
    state XDone:
     OPort->stop (); SBuf->free ();
     proceed Acquire;
  };
};
```

The process starts in state Acquire, where it calls outCell trying
to get a ready cell directed to the output port. If this operation fails,
the process awaits a mailbox event indicating the availability of an
outgoing cell and then tries again. Note that outCell returns a pointer
to the cell buffer. To get hold of the cell, the process executes the cell
method of the buffer (see the next section). The cell is transmitted
on the output port (operation transmit) and, when this operation is
complete, the process transits to state XDone. In that state, the process

terminates the cell transmission, frees the buffer,* and proceeds back
to state `Acquire` to take care of another outgoing cell.

10.4.2. Messages, cells, and buffers

A SMURPH message (section 10.3.5) represents a logical unit of information exchanged between a pair of communicating hosts, e.g., a
transmitted file, a video scene, or a voice packet. In our ATM model,
such units have the following structure:

```
message ATMMessage {
  int VCI, Type, SeqNum;
  FLAGS Attributes;
};
```

The `VCI` attribute identifies the session to which the message belongs. At a host's end, an ATM session is identified by the VCI returned to the host by its interfacing ATM switch when the session was
set up. Attribute `Type` indicates the message type and is used to identify various kinds of signaling messages and also to tell data messages
from signaling messages. `SeqNum` is the serial number of the message;
its role is to enable the recipient to detect lost messages. `Attributes`
is a collection of binary flags that describe some properties of the message. For example, within the class of "data" messages, some messages
may actually carry the data while some others may represent acknowl-
edgments.

Some attributes of messages are implicit and their automatic declarations are invisible. Examples of such attributes are `Length` (message length in bits) and `Receiver` (the identifier of the host station to
which the message is addressed). Global properties of messages and
their general characteristics (e.g., length distribution, arrival process,
delay sensitivity) are described in *traffic patterns* (section 10.3.5).

Individual ATM cells are described by the following data type:

```
packet Cell {
  int VCI, Type, SeqNum; FLAGS Attributes;
  void setup (ATMMessage *m) {
    VCI = m -> VCI; Type = m -> Type;
    SeqNum = m -> SeqNum ++; Attributes = m -> Attributes;
  };
};
```

---

*The reason why we have to distinguish between cells and cell buffers at this level
is the need to be able to implement correctly the operation of freeing the storage
occupied by an outgoing cell.

All attributes are inherited from `ATMMessage`. Every cell is assumed to have been derived from some message. As a byproduct of the standard SMURPH operation of acquiring a *packet* (a `Cell`) from a *message* (an `ATMMessage`), the setup method of the packet is called with the argument pointing to the message from which the packet is extracted. With every cell acquisition, the sequence number of the message is incremented by one. Therefore, for every two consecutive cells derived from the same message, the serial number of the second cell is equal to the number of the first cell+1.

A cell arriving at a switch is buffered before retransmission. Although the complete structure of the buffer storage depends on the buffering policy, we can think of a generic cell buffer type, which can be defined as follows:

```
class CBuf {
  char CellHolder [sizeof (Cell)];
  void load (Cell *c) { *((Cell*) CellHolder) = *c; };
  Cell *cell () { return (Cell*) CellHolder; };
  virtual void free () { };
};
```

Attribute `CellHolder` is just an array of bytes capable of accommodating a cell. The first two methods are used to access this storage: `load` loads the buffer with the indicated cell and `cell` returns a pointer to the cell currently stored in the buffer. The last method should be called to deallocate the buffer: its contents depend on the organization of the buffer pool at the switch.

Type `CBuf` is generic and it must be extended to be useful. A complete buffer type will typically specify additional attributes, e.g., links needed to put the buffers into lists, sets, or more sophisticated hierarchies. These attributes will be referenced by the `dataCell` method of the switch and by the `free` method of the buffer.

10.4.3. A switch example

In this section we discuss fragments of a sample switch architecture with a specific buffering strategy: a FIFO pool of buffers associated with every output port. The strategy deals with two cell types* called "red" and "green." If there is no room to accommodate a new cell into a port queue, the switch will try to drop a red cell first. If no such cell is available, the switch will drop a green cell.

---

*Corresponding to the CLP (cell loss priority) flag in the cell header.

Below we list the type declaration of the cell buffer for our sample switch. This type is an extension of type CBuf discussed in section 10.4.2.

```
class FifoItem : public CBuf {
  friend class Fifo;
  FifoItem *prev, *next; Fifo *Pool;
  FifoItem (Cell *cl) {
    load (cl); prev = next = NULL; Pool = NULL;
  };
  void free () { Pool->Used--; delete this; };
};
```

The extension consists of three pointers; two of them (prev and next) provide bidirectional list links needed to implement the FIFO queue, and the third (Pool) points to the buffer pool (FIFO queue) to which the buffer is linked. The standard constructor builds a buffer from the specified cell and initializes the three pointers to NULL. The free method deallocates the memory assigned to the buffer structure and decrements the usage count of the buffer pool.

Class Fifo, mentioned as a "friend" of FifoItem in the above declaration, represents the actual storage associated with a given output port. Its complete structure is as follows:

```
class Fifo {
  FifoItem *Head, *Tail; int MaxSize, Used;
  void discard (FifoItem *f) {
    if (f->prev != NULL) f->prev->next = f->next;
    if (f->next != NULL) f->next->prev = f->prev;
    if (f == Tail) Tail = f->prev;
    if (f == Head) Head = f->next;
    f->free ();
  };
  Fifo (int s) {
    Head = Tail = NULL; MaxSize = s; Used = 0;
  };
  CBuf *head () {
    CBuf *h;
    if (Head) {
      h = Head;
      if ((Head = Head->next) != NULL) Head->prev = NULL;
      return h;
    } else return NULL;
  };
  void add (Cell *cl) {
```

```
        FifoItem *f;
        if (Used == MaxSize) {
          for (f = Tail; f != NULL; f = f->prev)
            if (flagSet (f->cell () . Attributes, RED) break;
          discard (f ? f : Tail);
        }
        f = new FifoItem (cl); f->Pool = this;
        if (Head) {
          Tail->next = f; f->prev = Tail; Tail = f;
        } else
          Tail = Head = f;
        Used++;
      };
    };
```

The two pointer attributes Head and Tail point to the first and the
last cell buffer in the queue. MaxSize (set by the constructor) gives
the maximum capacity of the buffer pool, and Used tells how many
cells are currently stored in the queue. Method head removes from the
queue the first cell buffer and returns a pointer to this buffer. Note
that the buffer is not deallocated until the output process responsible
for transmitting the cell has accomplished its task and executed free
for the cell buffer (see section 10.4.1).

A process willing to deposit a cell in the FIFO storage should call
add specifying the cell pointer as the argument. If the buffer pool
happens to be full (Used == MaxSize), the method will discard the
last-queued red cell, or simply the last cell if no red cell can be found.
Then, add creates a new FifoItem containing the cell, appends it at
the end of the FIFO list, and increments the used count by one.

Now we are ready to look at the declaration of the switch type.

```
    station ASwitch : Switch {
      ConnPool *Connections; Fifo **Buffers; TIME CTimeout;
      int *RouteSize, *Routes, *Allocated, *Bandwidth;
      void setup (int np) {
        Switch::setup (np);
        Connections = new ConnPool; Buffers = new Fifo* [np];
        RouteSize = new int [np]; Routes = new int [np];
        Allocated = new int [np]; Bandwidth = new int [np];
        for (int i = 0; i < np; i++) Allocated [i] = 0;
      };
      void callCell (Cell*, int);
      int admit (Cell*);
      void cancel (Cell*, int);
```

```
    void dataCell (Cell *cl, int BIndx) {
      Buffers [BIndx] -> add (cl);
      Arrivals [BIndx] -> put ();
    };
    CBuf *acquire (int BIndx) {
      return Buffers [BIndx] -> head ();
    };
};
```

The only unspecified type is ConnPool describing the set of connections currently processed by the switch. Besides Connections, the connection setup procedure (not discussed here) uses the four integer arrays, attribute CTimeout, and three methods: callCell, admit, and cancel.

Array Buffers represents the collections of FIFO buffers associated with individual output ports. Although this array is created by the setup method of ASwitch, the operation of filling it with buffer pools (as well as the other arrays unfilled by the setup method) will be carried out by the module responsible for building the network and assigning specific configuration parameters to the individual switches.

Type ASwitch redefines the virtual methods of Switch that describe its buffering strategy (dataCell and outCell) and the connection setup algorithm (callCell). The simple operation performed by dataCell is to add the new cell to the FIFO buffer associated with the port. Similarly, outCell extracts the first outgoing cell (the head) from the buffer corresponding to the indicated output port.

REFERENCES

1. S. BUDKOWSKI and P. DEMBINSKI, Computer Networks and ISDN Systems, **3**, 3–23, (1987).

2. T. BOLOGNESI and E. BRINKSMA, Computer Networks and ISDN Systems, **14**, 25–59, (1987).

3. L. LOGRIPPO et al., Software Practice and Experience, **18**, 557–563, (1988).

4. G. HOLZMANN, Design and Validation of Computer Protocols (Prentice-Hall, 1971).

5. R. MILLS and S. SKINNER, "COMNET III: The New Enterprise-wide Performance Analysis Tool," in Proceedings of MAS-COTS'93, (San Diego, CA, Jan. 1993), 349–350.

6. C. PALMER, M. NAGHSHINEH, and J. CHEN, "The GILDA LAN Design Tool," in Proceedings of MASCOTS'93, (San Diego, CA, Jan. 1993), 353–354.

7. J. JUMP and S. LAKSHMANAMURTHY, "NETSIM: A General-purpose Interconnection Network Simulator," in Proceedings of MASCOTS'93, (San Diego, CA, Jan. 1993), 121–125.

8. P. GBURZYNSKI and P. RUDNICKI, Software Practice and Experience, 21, 51–76, (1991).

9. B. R. BERTAN, IEEE Transactions on Consumer Electronics, 35, 557–563, (1989).

10. P. GBURZYNSKI and P. RUDNICKI, IEEE Journal on Selected Areas in Communications, 7, 424–427, (1989).

11. P. GBURZYNSKI and P. RUDNICKI, "On Executable Specifications, Validation, and Testing of MAC-level Protocols," in Proceedings of the 9th IFIP WG 6.1 Int. Symposium on Protocol Specification, Testing, and Verification, (North-Holland, The Netherlands, June 1989), 261–273.

12. P. GBURZYNSKI and G. SHANKAR, "A Layered Video Coding Algorithm for Multimedia Applications over ATM," in Proceedings of 33rd Annual Allerton Conference on Communication, Control, and Computing, (Urbana, IL, Oct. 1995), in press.

13. P. GBURZYNSKI and P. RUDNICKI, Infor, 27, 183–205, (1989).

14. P. GBURZYNSKI, Protocol Design for Local and Metropolitan Area Networks, (Prentice-Hall, 1996).

15. P. GBURZYNSKI and P. RUDNICKI, "On Formal Modelling of Communication Channels," in Proceedings of IEEE INFOCOM'89, (Ottawa, Canada, Apr. 1989), 143–151.

16. R. GROZ, "Unrestricted Verification of Protocol Properties in a Simulation Using an Observer Approach," in Proceedings of the IFIP WG 6.1 6th Workshop on Protocol Specification, Testing, and Verification, (North-Holland, The Netherlands, June 1986), 255–266.

17. R. ROOJOLAMINI, V. CHERKASSKY, and M. GARVER, IEEE Computer, 27, 17–28, (1994).

Chapter 11
NETWORK RELIABILITY EVALUATION

Gerardo RUBINO

11.1 INTRODUCTION

Network reliability concerns reliability metrics of large classes of multicomponent systems. In general, the structure of such a system is represented by a binary function of M binary variables where M is the number of components. Let us denote by Φ such a *structure function*. We adopt the usual convention where 1 represents the operational state (the device, component or system, is operational or *up*) and 0 the failed or *down* state. A *state vector* for such a system is a vector $\vec{x} = (x_1, \ldots, x_M)$ where x_i is a possible state, 0 or 1, of the ith component. With this notation,

$$\Phi : \{0,1\}^M \longrightarrow \{0,1\}$$
$$\vec{x} \mapsto \Phi(\vec{x}) = \begin{cases} 1 & \text{if the system is } up \text{ when the state vector is } \vec{x}, \\ 0 & \text{if the system is } down \text{ when the state vector is } \vec{x}. \end{cases}$$

The structure function Φ defines what is considered as an operational state for the whole system. Observe that this depends on the aspect that needs to be evaluated. It is frequent that several structure functions are associated with a single system in order to analyze different functionalities or to study it under different assumptions. Frequently, structure functions are assumed to be *coherent*, corresponding to systems verifying the following properties: (i) when all the components are down (resp. up), the system is down (resp. up); (ii) if the system is up (resp. down) and we change the state of a component from 0 to 1 (resp. from 1 to 0), the system remains up (resp. down); (iii) all the components are relevant. Formally, this can be written in the following way: let us denote by $\vec{0}$ (resp. by $\vec{1}$) a state vector having all its entries equal to 0 (resp. equal to 1), denote by $\vec{x} \leq \vec{y}$ the relation $x_i \leq y_i$ for all i, by $\vec{x} < \vec{y}$ the fact that $\vec{x} \leq \vec{y}$ with, for some j, $x_j < y_j$ and denote by $(\vec{x}, 0_i)$ (resp. by $(\vec{x}, 1_i)$) the state vector constructed from $\vec{x}$ by setting x_i to 0 (resp. to 1). Then, Φ is coherent iff (i) $\Phi(\vec{0}) = 0$, $\Phi(\vec{1}) = 1$; (ii) if $\vec{x} < \vec{y}$ then $\Phi(\vec{x}) \leq \Phi(\vec{y})$ and (iii) for each component i there exist some state vector $\vec{x}$ such that $\Phi(\vec{x}, 0_i) \neq \Phi(\vec{x}, 1_i)$ (and thus, due to (ii), $\Phi(\vec{x}, 0_i) = 0$ and

$\Phi(\vec{x}, 1_i) = 1)$. In the sequel, we will always assume that the considered systems are coherent.

After specifying the function Φ, a probabilistic structure is defined. The usual framework is to assume that the state of the ith component is a random binary (Bernoulli) variable (r.v.) X_i and that the M r.v. $X_1, \ldots, X_M$ are independent. The distribution of these r.v., that is in this case the numbers $r_i = \Pr(X_i = 1)$ (called the *elementary reliabilities*) are input data. The output parameter is the reliability R of the system, defined by

$$R = \Pr(\Phi(\vec{X}) = 1) = E(\Phi(\vec{X})) \qquad (1)$$

where $\vec{X} = (X_1, \ldots, X_M)$. Observe that this is a static problem, that is, time is not explicitly used in the analysis. When time relations are considered, the context changes and the general framework in which the analysis is usually done is the theory of stochastic processes and, in particular, of Markov processes. For an exposition concerning the general theory (including dynamic models) the reader can see Barlow et al.[8], Belyayev et al.[10] and Gertsbakh[21].

There are different ways of specifying a structure function. We are concerned here with the most widely known class of models, sometimes called *stochastic graphs* or simply *networks*. They are very useful, in particular, for communication network analysis. For instance, fault trees are another similar and widely used description tools. Stochastic graphs are graphs whose elements are weighted by probabilities. Their main application areas are in the analysis of communication networks and we will adopt it here as a reference system. The lines are modeled by the edges (or by the arcs in the directed case) and the vertices represent the nodes. The basic model in this class (and in the paper) is an undirected graph (lines are assumed to be bi-directional) with perfect nodes (corresponding to the situation where the reliability of a node is much higher than the reliability of a line). The graph is assumed to be connected and without loops. The state of line i at some instant is a binary r.v. X_i. The structure function Φ is then specified by means of some property of the graph. To be more specific, let us denote by $\mathcal{G} = (\mathcal{V}, \mathcal{E})$ the graph where $\mathcal{V}$ is the set of vertices and $\mathcal{E}$ is the set of edges (in some cases, we will explicitly consider *multigraphs* where there can be more than one edge between two vertices). The set $\mathcal{E}'$ of operational lines at the fixed considered instant defines a random subgraph $\mathcal{G}' = (\mathcal{V}, \mathcal{E}')$ of the previous one. The reliability of the system is then the probability that $\mathcal{G}'$ has some graph property. For instance, if we are interested in the fact that all the nodes can communicate with each other and we want to quantify the ability of the network to support this, the corresponding metric, R_V, called *all–terminal* reliability, is the probability that $\mathcal{G}'$ is connected. Another important case is when the user is interested only in the communications between two particular nodes, usually called *source* and *terminal*. Denoting these nodes by s and t, the associated metric is the so-called *2–terminal* or *source–to–terminal* reliability, $R_{s,t}$, defined as the probability that there exists in $\mathcal{G}'$ at least one path between s and t having all its lines operational. This last case of graphs having an "entry" point s and an "exit" point t (the terminology is used even if the graph is undirected), has a broad field of applications since it is a general tool describing the structure of a system, its *block diagram*, not only in the communications area. For instance, it is widely used in circuit analysis or more generally in the description of electrical systems. The previous considered metrics are particular cases of the $\mathcal{K}–terminal$ reliability in which a subset $\mathcal{K}$ of nodes is defined and the associated measure, $R_{\mathcal{K}}$, is the probability that all the nodes in $\mathcal{K}$ can communicate, that is, the probability that the nodes of $\mathcal{K}$ belong to the same connected component of $\mathcal{G}'$. By far, most of the research effort in the network reliability area has been done on the evaluation (exact or approximate) of this measure and the two particular cases described before (R_V and $R_{s,t}$).

These problems (and several other related reliability problems) have received considerable attention from the research community. Numerous published papers are devoted to their solution (see, for instance, Locks et al.[31], Colbourn[14], and Ball et al.[5] for references) mainly due to two reasons: the general use of these models, in particular in the communication network area, and the fact that in the general case the computation of these metrics are in the $\#P$–complete class (Valiant[51], Ball[4]), a family of NP–hard problems not known to be in NP. Recall that a $\#P$–complete problem is equivalent to counting the number of solutions to a NP–complete one. This implies that a $\#P$–complete problem is at least as hard as a NP–complete one. This last fact justifies the continuous effort to find faster solution methods. Even in very restricted (and important) families of graphs, the problems remain in the $\#P$–complete class. For instance, it is shown in Provan[41] that the computation of $R_{s,t}$ remains $\#P$–complete in the family of s, t–planar graphs (that is, planar graphs where nodes s and t are in the frontier) having vertex degree at most equal to three.

There is a wide field of applications of network reliability techniques.

We find these problems in evaluations of electrical power networks, transportation systems (specially urban transportation systems, see for instance Sanso et al.[46]), interconnection networks (that is, networks connecting processors, memories and other devices inside a multiprocessor computer), fault tolerant computer architectures, etc. As stated before, a central application area is in the evaluation of communication systems. The usefulness of "connectivity" measures such as the ones presented before is clear for instance in packet switching communication networks using dynamic routing which allows rerouting of data in case of the failure of a link. It must be said that many modern packet switching networks are rather dense and that the considered reliability measures tend to be close to one. This "high reliability" problem will appear again in the text, in Section 11.5 and in Section 11.7.

This paper intends to be an introduction to the area and to address the practical question of how to analyze a real size problem. We will discuss on some basic exact computing methods in Sections 11.2 and 11.4, and on techniques used to attempt a reduction in the size of the model in Section 11.3. It must be stated that all these techniques, in fact all known *exact* techniques, can not deal with a network having, say, one hundred elements (except, of course, in case of particular types of topologies). For instance, in the survey Hyang et al.[28] published in 1981, the authors define a *large* system (from the reliability evaluation point of view) as one having more than 10 components and they say that more than 20 components usually makes the reliability computation infeasible. In the more recent paper Provan[40], the threshold is placed around 50 components. Our own experience confirms this last figure. In the communication networks area, usual sizes are often larger. For instance, in Grotschel et al.[23] the authors report on computational results analyzing (in a deterministic context) the topology of real fiber optic telephone networks. They give the sizes of seven networks provided by Bell Communications Research, ranged from 36 nodes and 65 edges to 116 nodes and 173 edges. They also say that in this type of communication system, the number of nodes in practical implementations is not larger than, say, 200 nodes. In Grotschel et al.[24], the same authors report on a realistic model of the link connections in the global communication system of a ship, having 494 nodes and 1096 edges. Needless to say, exact methods are of no use in these cases. However, Monte Carlo algorithms appear to be an efficient way to obtain (probabilistic) answers to reliability questions even for networks having, for instance, more than one hundred components.

Section 11.5 is devoted to the introduction of these techniques. The Monte Carlo approach has its own drawbacks; some techniques used to deal with them are discussed here. In case of small models, say having less than 40 or 50 components, our experiences say that the most powerful technique is factoring (Section 11.4). Section 11.6 deals with bounds which may be an alternative in some cases, in particular when it is not possible to have exact results or to apply Monte Carlo methods. Conclusions are reported in Section 11.7.

11.2 DIRECT METHODS

The most direct brute force approach to compute R is simply to list the whole set of state vectors, checking for each one if the network is operational or not. We have

$$
\begin{aligned}
R &= \sum_{\vec{x}|\Phi(\vec{x})=1} \Pr(\vec{X} = \vec{x}) \\
&= \sum_{\vec{x}|\Phi(\vec{x})=1} \left(\prod_{i|x_i=1} r_i\right)\left(\prod_{j|x_j=0}(1 - r_j)\right).
\end{aligned}
$$

This formula is obviously valid for any structure function Φ. The problem is that it is quickly unusable due to the number of involved terms. For our reference model, an undirected graph with perfect nodes and M edges, we have 2^M state vectors.

A second brute force approach is to apply Poincare's formula working with *minpaths* or *mincuts*. Let us develop the minpaths version. A *path vector* is a state vector $\vec{x}$ such that $\Phi(\vec{x}) = 1$. A *path set*, or simply a *path*, is a set of components such that if they are up, then the system is up. If $\vec{x}$ is a path vector, then the set of edges $O(\vec{x}) = \{i|x_i = 1\}$ is a path; if π is a path, then any $\vec{x}$ such that $O(\vec{x}) = \pi$ is a path vector since Φ is coherent. A *minpath vector* is a path vector $\vec{x}$ such that for any $\vec{y} < \vec{x}$ we have $\Phi(\vec{y}) = 0$. In the same way, a *minpath set* (or simply a *minpath*) is a path π such that none of its proper subsets is a path. For instance, as regards the $R_{s,t}$ metric, a path corresponds to the standard concept of path in graph theory, between nodes s and t; a minpath corresponds to an *elementary* path between the source and the terminal (a path that does not visit a node more than once). If the all–terminal measure is considered, then paths are spanning subgraphs of $\mathcal{G}$ and minpaths are spanning trees of $\mathcal{G}$.

Let us denote by $\{\pi_1, \ldots, \pi_{MP}\}$ the list of minpaths in some order and by P_m the event: "every link in the mth minpath is working". Then,

$$\{\Phi(\vec{X}) = 1\} = \bigcup_{m=1}^{MP} P_m. \tag{2}$$

The problem is that these events are not disjoint. Applying Poincare's formula, we can write

$$R = \sum_{m=1}^{MP} (-1)^{m-1} \sum_{1 \le h_1 < h_2 < \cdots < h_m \le MP} \Pr\left(\bigcap_{j=1}^{m} P_{h_j}\right)$$

which can be made more explicit as

$$R = \sum_{m=1}^{MP} (-1)^{m-1} \sum_{1 \le h_1 < h_2 < \cdots < h_m \le MP} \prod_{i \in \bigcap_{j=1}^{m} \pi_{h_j}} r_i.$$

This is even worse than complete state enumeration (at least, in a naive implementation) since the previous formula contains $2^{MP} - 1$ terms and MP is usually exponential in the size of the network (in the number of edges, for instance). As an example, it is easy to show that the number of minpaths in the graph shown in Figure 11.1 corresponding to the source–to–terminal reliability between the marked nodes (that is, the number of elementary paths between those nodes in the graph) is $MP = (\sqrt[3]{2})^{M+1}$.

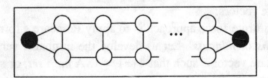

Figure 11.1: A "ladder" graph

However, Poincare's formula leads to many terms being canceled out and some research work has been done following this idea. For instance, in Satyarayana[48] and Satyarayana et al.[50], the authors give algorithms that generate only the resulting terms.

From (2), we can write

$$\{\Phi(\vec{X}) = 1\} = \bigcup_{m=1}^{MP} \left(P_m \bigcap_{j=1}^{m-1} \overline{P}_j \right)$$
$$= P_1 \cup \left(\overline{P}_1 \cap P_2 \right) \cup \left(\overline{P}_1 \cap \overline{P}_2 \cap P_3 \right) \cup \ldots$$

This is the starting point of the so-called *disjoint product sums* approach. The good point is that the events $(P_m \cap_{j=1}^{m-1} \overline{P}_j)$ are disjoint, so, we can simply add probabilities. The problem is now the construction of these events (and the computation of their probabilities). A few examples of this approach are Fratta et al.[20], Abraham[1], Ahmad[2], Ahmad et al.[3]. See also Locks[30], Niessen et al.[36] and other references in Colbourn[14]. These techniques need, in general, the preliminary generation of the whole list of minpaths. In Marie et al.[32], it is shown how to avoid this by an improvement of the method proposed in Ahmad[2] and Ahmad et al.[3]. Another interesting case is the work presented in Granov et al.[22]: instead of adding terms of the form $\prod_{i \in I} r_i$ or of the form $\prod_{i \in I} r_i \prod_{j \in J}(1 - r_j)$ where I and J are some disjoint sets of edges, the constructed terms are of the form

$$\prod_{i \in I} r_i \prod_{h=1}^{H} \left(1 - \prod_{j \in J_h} r_j\right),$$

J_1, J_2, ... being also disjoint sets of edges. It can be shown that this corresponds to the sum of many terms of the first form. The underlying key concept is multiple-variable inversion of cubes (see Miller[34]). See also Heidtmann[20] for a similar approach. A different algebraic presentation of the algorithm proposed in Granov et al.[22] and some extensions are published in Veeraraghavan et al.[52]. In Marie et al.[32], the same method is presented in a more compact and probabilistic form; moreover, the version in Marie et al.[32] allows a reduction in the computational cost with respect to the original one.

It must be observed here that a dual approach using mincuts can also be followed. A *cut vector* is a state vector $\vec{x}$ such that $\Phi(\vec{x}) = 0$. A *cut set*, or simply a *cut*, is a set of components such that if they are down, then the system is down. If $\vec{x}$ is a cut vector, then the set of edges $Z(\vec{x}) = \{i | x_i = 0\}$ is a cut; if γ is a cut, then any $\vec{x}$ such that $Z(\vec{x}) = \gamma$ is a cut vector (Φ is coherent). A *mincut vector* is a cut vector $\vec{x}$ such that for any $\vec{y} > \vec{x}$ we have $\Phi(\vec{y}) = 1$ and a *mincut* is a cut γ such that none of its proper subsets is a cut. In some cases, working with mincuts has advantages over the use of minpaths since it is usual that the number of mincuts in a graph is less than the number of minpaths. For instance, in the case of the "ladder" topology shown in Figure 11.1 and with respect to the $R_{s,t}$ measure, there are $(M+1)^2/9$ mincuts. An extremal situation is the case of a complete graph; if n is the number of nodes (so, there are $n(n-1)/2$ edges), considering the all–terminal metric leads to n^{n-2} minpaths (spanning trees) and $2^{n-1} - 1$ mincuts. We don't have space enough to detail the differences between the two approaches; the reader is suggested to consult Colbourn[14] and the references there.

There are many other papers giving algorithms that can be classified as "direct", with the meaning here that the topological structure of the system is not explicitly exploited. These approaches deal basically with Boolean algebra, intending to reduce the number of terms in the expansions and/or to compute the probability of disjoint products as efficiently as possible. Another point explored in these works is the fact that the computational effort is sensitive to the order of the minpaths (or mincuts) list and some heuristics have been proposed to choose it (see, for instance, Ball et al.[7]; see also the improvement made in Ahmad et al.[3] to the original algorithm published in Ahmad[2]).

As stated before, these exact methods fail in evaluating networks with, say, more than 50 components, because of their cost in computational time. In the next section, we review some techniques used to reduce the size of the models.

11.3   REDUCTION TECHNIQUES

The idea here is to develop low cost (actually polynomial cost) simplifications that can be applied as preprocessors, in order to reduce the size of the original problem. These methods are not necessarily effective, that is, the graphs can be irreducible with respect to them, but the overhead is negligible compared to the total time required to solve the initial models. In many cases, simplifications can be performed and the gain in the total solution time is significantly higher than the associated cost to apply them.

The most widely used reduction technique is to simplify series–parallel partial graphs of the original one. Consider the $\mathcal{K}$–terminal reliability. Two edges i and j are in $\mathcal{K}$–series if they are adjacent and if their only common vertex does not belong to $\mathcal{K}$. It is easy to check that replacing them by a single new edge and setting its elementary reliability to the product $r_i r_j$, leads to a new graph with the same reliability $R_{\mathcal{K}}$. The analogous operation can be done in case of parallel edges, that is, considering multigraphs (observe that after a series reduction, parallel edges may appear). The recursive application of these well known reductions is clearly polynomial in the size of the data. Extensions have also be found. For instance, see Satyanarayana et al.[47] for the so called *polygon–to–chain* technique which generalizes the series–parallel one. As an example, the family of graphs represented in Figure 11.1 which are series–parallel irreducible with respect to the pair of marked nodes, can be solved in time polynomial (actually linear) in the number of edges using the technique presented in Satyanarayana et al.[47].

Other approaches have been followed to deal with subclasses of the family of planar graphs. A survey can be found in Locks et al.[31]. Connectivity properties can also be used as a divide–and–conquer approach. For instance, assume that the considered metric is $R_{s,t}$, that the source and the terminal nodes belong to different *blocks* $\mathcal{G}_1$ and $\mathcal{G}_2$ and that there are exactly two blocks in $\mathcal{G}$. In other words, assume that $\mathcal{G}_1$ and $\mathcal{G}_2$ are partial graphs of the original one having only a vertex v in common, with $s \in \mathcal{G}_1$ and $t \in \mathcal{G}_2$, $v \neq s, t$. Then, it is clear that $R_{s,t} = R_{s,v} R_{v,t}$ where $R_{s,v}$ concerns $\mathcal{G}_1$ and $R_{v,t}$ concerns $\mathcal{G}_2$. This remark leads to the utilization of the decomposition in biconnected components and can be generalized to triconnected components (Hagstrom[25]).

Anyway, sometimes we have small models to be evaluated, perhaps representing a part of some larger system, and exact techniques can be considered. In the next section, we review a powerful family of exact methods which make explicit use of topological properties and which take particular advantage of reduction techniques as those presented before.

11.4 FACTORING

For any edge i of $\mathcal{G}$, its *contraction* consists of eliminating this line and "merging" its two extremities; the resulting graph, denoted by $\mathcal{G}_i^c$, has one less node and one less edge than $\mathcal{G}$. Just deleting line i leads to the graph $\mathcal{G}_i^d$ having the same node set as $\mathcal{G}$ and one less edge.

Consider the $R_{s,t}$ measure on an indirected graph $\mathcal{G}$. Factoring is a family of algorithms based on the following relation: for any edge $i \neq \{s, t\}$,

$$R_{s,t}(\mathcal{G}) = r_i R_{s,t}(\mathcal{G}_i^c) + (1 - r_i) R_{s,t}(\mathcal{G}_i^d). \tag{3}$$

This relation is made valid even if $i = \{s, t\}$ by defining $R_{x,x} = 1$. This can be generalized to the $R_{\mathcal{K}}$ measure:

$$R_{\mathcal{K}}(\mathcal{G}) = r_i R_{\mathcal{K}'}(\mathcal{G}_i^c) + (1 - r_i) R_{\mathcal{K}}(\mathcal{G}_i^d) \tag{4}$$

where $\mathcal{K}' = \mathcal{K}$ if at least one of the extremities of i is not in $\mathcal{K}$ and $\mathcal{K}' = (\mathcal{K} - \{x, y\}) \cup \{z\}$ if $i = \{x, y\}$ with $x, y \in \mathcal{K}$, node z being a new one representing the result of collapsing the extremities x and y of i. Relation (4) is simply obtained by conditioning with respect to the state of component i. It allows the reduction of the original problem to the computation of the reliabilities of two smaller graphs. Recalling that M is the number of edges of the graph, the recursive use of (4) leads to a binary tree with $2^M - 1$ nodes and 2^{M-1} leaves. To avoid this, reduction techniques are applied before each factoring step. The idea is that sooner or later simplifications will appear reducing the size of the constructed tree by eliminating many intermediate nodes.

Reported experiences say that in general this approach performs fast. Of course, in the worst case, reductions arrive late in the construction of the tree and the computational time is exponential in the size of the network. Another important property of factoring algorithms is that they need a storage in $O(M^2)$ since the stack used to implement the recursive procedure has, at most, the size $M - 1$. Recall that, in contrast, Boolean techniques usually need to start from the set of minpaths or mincuts whose cardinality is in general exponential in the number of elements of the graph.

Once the user has chosen the reduction techniques to apply, the key part of the algorithm is the choice of the edge to condition on (the *pivoting step* or *selection edge step*). A first observation is that different selection strategies lead to trees with different sizes. Considering the 2–terminal reliability measure, the general theory was developed in Satyarayana et al.[49] in the case of series–parallel reductions, leading to an optimal edge selection procedure. Optimal means that this procedure generates the minimum possible number of leaf nodes in the associated binary tree, that is, the size of the tree is the minimal possible one. See Wood[53] for similar results with the more general polygon–to–chain reductions.

Let us present here the basic principles of the optimal selection method when series–parallel reductions are applied. The metric is the source–to–terminal reliability. If x is a vertex of $\mathcal{G}$, we denote by $\mathcal{G} - x$ the subgraph of $\mathcal{G}$ obtained by deleting node x and its adjacent edges. Vertex x is a *cutvertex* of $\mathcal{G}$ if $\mathcal{G}$ has more than two vertices and $\mathcal{G} - x$ is not connected. Let u, v be two different vertices of $\mathcal{G}$. The graph $\mathcal{G}$ is u, v–*coherent* if any edge of $\mathcal{G}$ belongs to a minpath between u and v. Let $\mathcal{G}$ be a u, v–coherent graph. A family of minpaths $\mathcal{F} = \{\mu_1, \ldots, \mu_L\}$ between u and v is a u, v–*formation* of $\mathcal{G}$ if the union of all $\mu \in \mathcal{F}$ is $\mathcal{G}$. The *signed domination*

$d_{u,v}$ of $\mathcal{G}$ is the number of u, v–formations with an odd number of minpaths minus the number of u, v–formations with an even number of minpaths. The *domination* $D_{u,v}$ is the absolute value of $d_{u,v}$. These definitions are extended to any graph $\mathcal{G}$ by setting $d_{u,v} = 0$ and $D_{u,v} = 0$ if $\mathcal{G}$ is not u, v–coherent. It can be shown that if $\mathcal{G}$ is u, v–coherent, then $D_{u,v} > 0$. Also, $\mathcal{G}$ is completely reducible (to a single edge between u and v) by means of u, v–series–parallel reductions, iff $D_{u,v} = 1$. Domination has many interesting properties. Two fundamental ones are that for any edge e of $\mathcal{G}$,

$$D_{s,t}(\mathcal{G}) = D_{s,t}(\mathcal{G}_e^c) + D_{s,t}(\mathcal{G}_e^d) \tag{5}$$

and that domination is invariant under s, t–series–parallel reductions.

The main result in Satyarayana et al.[49] states that if $\mathcal{G}$ is not reduced to a single edge, if it is a s, t–coherent graph and if it is s, t–series–parallel irreducible, then there exists an edge e such that both graphs $\mathcal{G}_e^c$ and $\mathcal{G}_e^d$ are s, t–coherent. Moreover, if such an edge is chosen by the selection procedure, then the binary tree is optimal in size (and its number of leaves is exactly equal to $D_{s,t}(\mathcal{G})$, the domination of the original graph $\mathcal{G}$, assumed to be s, t–coherent). To prove this result, the key property is relation (5) (see Wood[54]). In Wood[53] an extension of these results is done for polygon–to–chain reductions; a different invariant called *minimal domination* is used but the principles are similar as those corresponding to series–parallel simplifications.

It remains the problem of implementing an effective optimal selection procedure. The main reference Satyarayana et al.[49] is not very explicit on this. Some details can be found in Wood[54]. The method needs to work with the triconnected components of the graph. In Hopcroft et al.[27], the authors give a $O(M)$ method to split a graph into its triconnected components. Let us say that the implementation of their algorithm is a hard task. For instance, in Resende[43] a different $O(M^2)$ choice procedure is proposed and in Page et al.[37] the authors propose to select randomly the next edge used to condition on and to backtrack if it is not a good one. In El Khadiri et al.[17], some numerical results of the implementation of the optimal strategy are reported. To illustrate the cost in time of the algorithm, let us consider the complete graph K_n with n nodes. Table 11.1 gives the execution times of the factoring algorithm as a function of n and the corresponding number of leaves in any optimal tree.

A more sparse topology used in our tests is shown in Figure 11.2. We denote this graph by s_5 according to the number of rows in the central rectan-

n	# edges	$L = D_{s,t}$	CPU time
8	28	720	3.5 sec
9	36	5040	25 sec
10	45	40320	3 min 20 sec
11	55	362880	30 min
12	66	3628800	4 hr 56 min

Table 11.1: The number L of leaves in the factorization binary tree and the executing time in seconds (Sun-4) of the factoring algorithm of Satyarayana et al.[49] as a function of the number of vertices of the complete graph K_n. The domination of K_n is $D_{s,t}(K_n) = (n-2)!$.

gle. The graph s_1 is a single edge between the source and the terminal; s_2 is the well known "bridge" topology. A nice property of this family of graphs is that if all the elementary reliabilities are equal to 1/2 then $R_{s,t} = 1/2$ (which follows from duality arguments). This allows the test of the algorithms with networks of arbitrary large size, known $R_{s,t}$ reliability and a not very high connectivity: in s_k there are $k^2 - k + 2$ nodes, $2k^2 - 2k + 1$ edges and the mean degree is $4 - 6/(k^2 - k + 2)$, whose value is between 3 and 4 for all $k > 2$. Compared with real communication network topologies, s_k has a rather high density of lines because of its regularity.

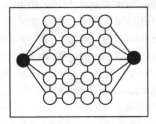

Figure 11.2: Regular topology s_5

For instance, the graph s_4 is evaluated in a few seconds by the factoring method and the graph s_5 is evaluated in about 15 min (on a Sun-4). The respective dominations are equal to 868 and 230274. None of our implementations of disjoint product algorithms takes less than 30 sec for s_4 and we stopped them after one day of calculations on s_5.

If we add a fifth row to s_5 constructing a "central square", i.e. a graph with 27 nodes instead of 22 and 50 edges instead of 41, the computing time of the factoring program increases from 15 min to about 4 hours. However, if we consider s_6, a network having 32 nodes and 61 edges, the factoring program was stopped after a week without finishing the computations. Observe that these execution times are independent on the effective values of the r_i's and of the output $R_{s,t}$. This is an advantage over the statistical methods presented in the next section which are sensitive to these values. However, if the reliability of the system is not too high, statistical methods allow the analysis of large topologies where exact methods fail. This is the topic of the next section.

11.5 MONTE CARLO

The estimation of the reliability R by the standard Monte Carlo method consists of generating independent samples $\vec{X}^{(1)}, \ldots, \vec{X}^{(N)}$ of $\vec{X}$ and estimating the unknown parameter R by the unbiased estimator

$$\widehat{R} = \frac{1}{N} \sum_{n=1}^{N} \Phi(\vec{X}^{(n)}).$$

The precision of an estimator is measured by its variance, "low" values meaning "good" estimations. We have $V(\widehat{R}) = R(1-R)/N$. This variance is estimated by its unbiased estimator $\widehat{V} = \widehat{R}(1-\widehat{R})/(N-1)$ which is used to construct a confidence interval for $\widehat{R}$, applying the Central Limit Theorem. For instance, with a confidence level of 95 % the confidence interval for R is $]\widehat{R} - 1.96\widehat{V}^{1/2}, \widehat{R} + 1.96\widehat{V}^{1/2}[$. To implement this experiment on a computer, pseudo-random versions $X_i^{(1)}, \ldots, X_i^{(N)}$ of each variable X_i are constructed and an appropriate procedure is used to check if $\Phi(\vec{X}^{(n)}) = 1$ for each n, where $\vec{X}^{(n)} = (X_1^{(n)}, \ldots X_M^{(n)})$. The number N of realizations needed to obtain a statistical error of ε is proportional to $R(1-R)/\varepsilon^2$; more specifically, to have for instance $\Pr(|\widehat{R} - R| \leq \varepsilon) \geq 0.95$, N must verify $N \geq (1.96)^2 R(1-R)/\varepsilon^2$. An important remark here is that the structure function Φ does not need to be coherent: all we need is a way of (efficiently) computing $\Phi(\vec{x})$ for any state vector $\vec{x}$. As we will see later, one of the interests of the Monte Carlo method is its ability of handle any computable structure function in quite general conditions.

Consider now the case of a very reliable network, which is the usual situation. For instance, let us consider the graph s_4 (see Section 11.4) having

14 nodes, 25 edges and mean degree equal to 3.57, and consider the source–to–terminal metric. If all the elementary reliabilities are equal to 0.99, we have $R_{s,t} \approx 0.9999999582$ (computed by the factorization algorithm). To have a couple of significant figures in the *unreliability* $1 - R_{s,t}$, say for $\varepsilon = 10^{-8}$, we need at least about 1.6×10^{11} realizations. An extrapolation from the execution time of up to 10^6 realizations of a direct implementation of the algorithm, gives that the crude Monte Carlo method needs more than three years on a Sun-4. Even for $\varepsilon = 10^{-7}$ we obtain a total execution time of about 12 days. In other words, the standard technique is of no use in the highly reliable case. Fortunately, powerful methods exist to avoid this drawback and networks much larger than s_4 can be efficiently evaluated. Let us point out that the "high reliable" case has become very important not only in the classical area of critical systems (those involving high risks for human life, as in nuclear reactor or aircraft control systems) but also in other fields like in banking systems or in modern high speed telecommunication networks.

From the user point of view, the quality of a Monte Carlo technique is measured by its *efficiency* defined as the product of the execution time T and the variance V of the used estimator. This means that two different Monte Carlo algorithms A_1 and A_2 must be compared with respect to their respective efficiencies $T_1 \times V_1$ and $T_2 \times V_2$, for a fixed number N of realizations (or by the *scaled efficiencies* $T_i \times V_i / N$). More known are the so-called *variance reduction* techniques where the mathematical effort is in designing new estimators having lower V values than previous ones. Some of them need supplementary informations to be applied, namely lists of minpaths or mincuts; the problem with them is that building those lists is a hard computational task. See Fishman[19] for a survey of several Monte Carlo techniques. See also Ross[45] where two other methods are compared on models having all their elementary reliabilities identical. Their efficiency is maximal when the list of mincuts is available. In Cancela et al.[13] this technique is improved and the same authors propose in Cancela et al.[12] another fast variance reduction algorithm which can be applied to networks where the components have different reliabilities.

As an example of a specialized Monte Carlo algorithm in the network reliability context, we present here a technique which works for graphs with identical elementary reliabilities and needs no mincuts list. It is particularly efficient in case of high reliability values. It uses the minimal size of a mincut, c, sometimes called the *breadth* of the graph, which can be computed by classical flow algorithms in polynomial time Colbourn[14]. The method is a variant of the one proposed in El Khadiri et al.[17]; it can also be seen as a specialization of the approach presented in Kumamoto et al.[29] with a more efficient sampling technique.

Let us denote by r the common elementary reliability of the lines and by $D = |Z(\vec{X})|$ the number of failed lines, a binomial r.v. with parameters M and r (recall that $Z(\vec{x})$ is the set of 0's entries in $\vec{x}$). Denote

$$R_c = \Pr(D < c) = \sum_{i=0}^{c-1} C_M^i r^{M-i}(1-r)^i.$$

By definition of mincut, if less than c lines are down, then the system is necessarily up and hence $R > R_c$. If we write $\mathrm{E}(\Phi(\vec{X}))$ by conditioning with respect to the event $\{D < c\}$, we obtain

$$R = \mathrm{E}(\Phi(\vec{X})) = \mathrm{E}(\Phi(\vec{X})|D < c)R_c + \mathrm{E}(\Phi(\vec{X})|D \geq c)(1 - R_c). \quad (6)$$

The first term in the r.h.s. is R_c since $\mathrm{E}(\Phi(\vec{X})|D < c) = 1$. Define a random vector $\vec{Y}$ with values in the set $\{\vec{x} \in \{0,1\}^M$ such that $|Z(\vec{x})| \geq c\}$ and distributed as follows: for any $\vec{x}$ in this set,

$$\Pr(\vec{Y} = \vec{x}) = \Pr(\vec{X} = \vec{x} \mid D \geq c) = \frac{r^{|O(\vec{x})|}(1 - r)^{|Z(\vec{x})|}}{1 - R_c}.$$

If we denote by R_0 the expectation $\mathrm{E}(\Phi(\vec{Y}))$, we have from (6),

$$R = R_c + (1 - R_c)R_0. \quad (7)$$

This leads to a new estimator $\tilde{R}$ of R defined by

$$\tilde{R} = R_c + (1 - R_c)\hat{R}_0$$

where

$$\hat{R}_0 = \frac{1}{N} \sum_{n=1}^{N} \Phi(\vec{Y}^{(n)})$$

and $\vec{Y}^{(1)}, \ldots, \vec{Y}^{(n)}$ is a sample of $\vec{Y}$. To construct it, the following method is used. Let us consider a r.v. D_0 with values in $\{c, c+1, \ldots, M\}$ and distribution

$$\Pr(D_0 = k) = \Pr(D = k|D \geq c) = \frac{\Pr(D = k)}{\Pr(D \geq c)} = \frac{C_M^k r^{M-k}(1 - r)^k}{\sum_{i=c}^{M} C_M^i r^{M-i}(1 - r)^i}.$$

Given D_0, the distribution of the subset of failed edges is uniform on the whole set of subsets having cardinality D_0. For instance, this means that the probability that a line is down given $\{D_0 = k\}$ is k/M. To sample according to $\vec{Y}$, we first sample from D_0 and then we choose D_0 edges uniformly to be set to state 0, the remaining $M - D_0$ lines being set to state 1.

The precision of the estimator is proportional to the square root of its variance. We have

$$V(\tilde{R}) = (1 - R_c)^2 V(\hat{R}_0)$$

and

$$V(\hat{R}_0) = \frac{R_0(1 - R_0)}{N} = \frac{(R - R_c)(1 - R)}{N(1 - R_c)^2}$$

leading to

$$V(\tilde{R}) = \frac{(R - R_c)(1 - R)}{N} = V(\hat{R}) - \frac{R_c(1 - R)}{N}.$$

Due to this last relation, the technique is a *variance reduction* method, even if, in fact, the effective variance reduction is small since R is usually close to 1; the gain here is in the execution time for a given precision. Let us denote by $E_1 = T_1 \times V_1/N$ the normalized efficiency of the standard Monte Carlo estimator as described before, and by $E_2 = T_2 \times V_2/N$ the normalized efficiency of the variance reduction technique. Basically, $T_1 = N(\tau_s + \tau_\Phi)$ where τ_s is the time necessary to sample the vector-state $\vec{X}$ and τ_Φ is the time necessary to check if $\Phi(\vec{X}) = 1$ (in general, a DFS algorithm). Since $V_1 = R(1 - R)/N$ we have $E_1 = (\tau_s + \tau_\Phi)R(1 - R)$. For the variance reduction technique, we have, for N realizations, an execution time equal to $T_2 = N(\tau_s' + \tau_g)$ where τ_s' is the new sampling execution time, $\tau_s' < \tau_s$ (there is no enough room to develop the analysis further). The variance V_2 is given by the expression of $V(\tilde{R})$, which leads to $E_2 = (\tau_s' + \tau_g)(R - R_c)(1 - R)$. Let us look at some numerical examples. For instance, let us come back to the s_4 graph having all the elementary reliabilities equal to 0.99 and system unreliability of about 4.18×10^{-6}. We have $c = 4$ and $1 - R_c = 1.06926534 \times 10^{-4}$. The variance reduction method gives a 95%-confidence interval for the unreliability equal to $]4.10 \times 10^{-6}, 4.34 \times 10^{-6}[$ in ≈ 11 min 30 sec. Recall that a direct implementation of the standard Monte Carlo approach leads to a computing time of about twelve days for a result with similar precision. If we set $r = 0.9999$, the factoring algorithm gives $1 - R = 5.55 \times 10^{-16}$ and the Monte Carlo technique gives, always with confidence level equal to 0.95, the interval $]5.06 \times 10^{-16}$, $5.83 \times 10^{-16}[$ in less than half an hour. Needless to say, for the same confidence interval, the crude Monte Carlo technique implemented as described before can certainly not finish the evaluation on the same computer (because there will be no more computer before the end of the calculations!) Let us point out the fact that the factoring algorithm solves this network in a few seconds, for any value of r, showing that in this range of models, it performs much better than statistical estimations. To illustrate the power and the drawbacks of Monte Carlo methods, let us consider the graph s_6 where factoring did not end after a week of computations. If the common elementary reliability is $r = 0.9$ we obtain an estimation of $1 - R \approx 1.33 \times 10^{-5}$ in the 95%–confidence interval $]1.14 \times 10^{-5}$, $1.52 \times 10^{-5}[$, in about half an hour (crude Monte Carlo needs about 5 hours to give a result with similar accuracy). However, increasing the value of r leads to much longer computer times. For $r = 0.99$, the variance reduction method takes too much time itself: to obtain two significant figures of the unreliability, our implementation needs about ten days of Sun-4 computer time (at a level of 95 %). If some other information on the graph is available, Monte Carlo techniques can be improved as shown in the given references (see Fishman[19] and Kumamoto et al.[29]). In case of the impossibility of performing a Monte Carlo estimation, a third possibility is to try bounds. This topic is briefly sketched in the next section.

Before leaving Monte Carlo methods, we must emphasize their flexibility in handling more general contexts. Graphs may be indirected, directed or mixed, nodes may be perfect or may fail, other reliability metrics may also be considered and the basic principles of these techniques remain valid. For instance, consider the random variable CC = "number of connected components of the graph" with values in the set $\{1, 2, \ldots, |\mathcal{V}|\}$. Observe that the all–terminal reliability is $R_{\mathcal{V}} = \Pr(CC = 1)$. A complementary information on the behavior of the network is thus given by the distribution of CC, or by its expectation. A more detailed information can be obtained from the random variable "number of communicating pairs of nodes" which we denote by NCP, having values in $\{0, 1, \ldots, |\mathcal{E}|(|\mathcal{E}| - 1)/2\}$. This metric is also called *resilience* in the literature. Its expectation is analyzed for instance in Mata-Montero[35]. From the relation $NCP = \sum_{s,t}[s$ and t connected$]$ where $[A]$ is the indicator function of the event A, we see that $E(NCP) = \sum_{s,t} R_{s,t}$. Observe also that $\Pr(CC = 1) = \Pr(NCP = |\mathcal{E}|(|\mathcal{E}| - 1)/2)$. The analysis of this random variable can give more insight into the modeled system than a measure such that the all–terminal reliability. In Mata-Montero[35] it is observed that two graphs may have the same all–terminal reliability while different resiliences. The modification of the previous Monte Carlo methods to estimate these metrics can be done in a straightforward manner. Observe that when less than c edges are down, we have $CC = 1$ and $NCP = |\mathcal{E}|(|\mathcal{E}| - 1)/2$, so that the previous technique with variance reduction can be followed in order to improve a crude approach. As an example, consider the graph in Figure 11.3 which is a version of the well known Arpanet network. We set all the elementary reliabilities to $r = 0.9$ to avoid

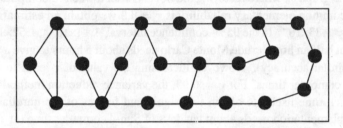

Figure 11.3: A version of the Arpanet communication network

long computing times and to allow the use of the standard Monte Carlo technique that the reader can easily implement. The all–terminal reliability is ≈ 0.752. As there are 21 nodes, the maximal number of communicating pairs is $21 \times 20/2 = 210$. A Monte Carlo estimation gives $\mathrm{E}(CC) \approx 1.31$ and $\mathrm{E}(NCP) \approx 197$.

As another example of the flexibility of Monte Carlo methods, let us consider the metric "mean number of communications pairs given that the failures have disconnected the graph into two components". It obviously gives supplementary insight into the ability of the network to support many potential communications. As said in the Introduction, modern packet switching networks are often quite dense. This implies that it is in general difficult to compare two different topologies relying the same set of nodes on the basis of classical measures because their values are too close of each other. Conditional measures such as $\mathrm{E}(NCP|CC = 2)$ can be useful in this context. After modifying the previous algorithm to estimate this conditional expectation, we get for the Arpanet model, $\mathrm{E}(NCP|CC = 2) \approx 167$. For instance, we find that setting $r = 0.95$ increases the all–terminal reliability to ≈ 0.933 and decreases $\mathrm{E}(CC)$ to ≈ 1.07 but the number of communicating pairs does not change very much: we obtain $\mathrm{E}(NCP) \approx 207$ and $\mathrm{E}(NCP|CC = 2) \approx 171$.

11.6 BOUNDS

Bounding methods can be, in some cases, a good tradeoff between cost and accuracy. For instance, working from Poincare's formula or from disjoint product sums, many ways of bounding different reliability metrics have been published. The results are irregular, depending strongly on the different metrics ($R_{s,t}$, $R_{\mathcal{K}}$, all–terminal reliability), the irregularity being both on the cost and on the accuracy of the methods. Among many other papers, the reader can see for instance the recent works Brecht et al.[11], Beichelt et al.[9], Prekopa et al.[39]. The subject is extensively discussed in the monograph Colbourn[14]. See also Roberts et al.[44]. In the case of components having the same elementary reliability r and considering the reliability as a polynomial in r, interesting results have been obtained by bounding its coefficients (see for instance Provan[40]).

In this paper, we want just to underline the good results obtained in the case of highly reliable systems when the list of mincuts of minimal size is available (see Colbourn[14] and the references there for the construction of such a list). We follow the presentation made in Gertsbakh[21]. With the notation given in Section 11.2, we can write for a general coherent structure function Φ,

$$1 - R = \sum_{\vec{x}|\Phi(\vec{x})=0} \Pr(\vec{X} = \vec{x}).$$

Ordering the terms according to the number of failed lines and denoting by c the *breadth* of the model, that is, the minimal size of a mincut, we obtain

$$1 - R = \sum_{l=c}^{M} \sum_{\substack{\vec{x}|\Phi(\vec{x})=0, \\ |Z(\vec{x})|=l}} \Pr(\vec{X} = \vec{x}).$$

Let us write $r_i = 1 - \varepsilon\theta_i$ with, for instance, $\varepsilon = 1 - \max_i\{r_i\}$ or $\varepsilon = 1 - \min_i\{r_i\}$ (assume that, for all i, $0 < r_i < 1$). If for all i, $r_i \approx 1$, we have $\varepsilon \approx 0$. Writing the unreliability $1 - R$ as a function of ε and considering its Taylor expansion in 0, we get

$$1 - R = f(\vec{\theta})\varepsilon^c + O(\varepsilon^{c+1})$$

where $\vec{\theta} = (\theta_1, \ldots, \theta_M)$ and

$$f(\vec{\theta}) = \sum_{\substack{\vec{x}|\Phi(\vec{x})=0, \\ |Z(\vec{x})|=c}} \prod_{i \in Z(x)} \theta_i.$$

294 G. RUBINO

In case of identical elementary reliabilities, this expression simplifies in

$$1 - R = MC_c\varepsilon^c + O(\varepsilon^{c+1})$$

where MC_c is the number of mincuts of (minimal) size c. For instance, consider again the model s_4 with $r = 0.99$. The unreliability is $1 - R = 4.18\times10^{-8}$. We have $c = MC_c = 4$, $\varepsilon = 0.01$ and $MC_c\varepsilon^c = 4\times10^{-8}$ which is quite good. If $r = 0.9999$, the factoring algorithm gives $1 - R = 5.55\times10^{-16}$ and the approximation $MC_c\varepsilon^c$ gives 4×10^{-16}. Observe that even if constructing the list of mincuts of minimal size is considerably less expensive that constructing the whole mincuts list, computing just the number MC_c is very expensive if the network is large (indeed, this computation is itself a NP–hard problem).

11.7 CONCLUSIONS

The first important point concerning network reliability evaluation is its cost: the exact computation of these metrics is highly expensive; almost all the related problems are NP–hard and typically only graphs having a few dozens of elements can be evaluated exactly.

A second important point to be noted is that many different metrics have been considered in the literature: $R_\mathcal{K}$, distributions or moments of r.v. such as NCP, corresponding metrics in directed (or mixed) graphs, or in graphs having nodes subject to failures, ... For some of them there are many evaluation techniques available, while for other measures very little is known. It is important to verify if the model belongs to some particular class (for instance, if it is series–parallel or if it belongs to some families of planar graphs); in such a case, depending on the type of topology and on the considered measure, simplifications or specific algorithms can be applied.

A third important point is that there is no general and widely used software package to put this technology into industry. There are code developments specific to some companies and several university computer programs but there is no general tool in the network reliability area having a large distribution.

Concerning the evaluation techniques, if exact results are needed (and if the size of the network allows that), factoring algorithms, when available, appear to be the fastest. The drawbacks here are the following:

- Factoring algorithms are complex and difficult to implement.

- Theoretical results are available only in a few cases (basically, for undirected graphs and the R_K measure).

As far as exact analysis is concerned, observe that Boolean techniques are very general. For instance, for any structure function Φ and any considered metric, if the user can generate the minpaths (or the mincuts) list, approaches such as disjoint product sums can be applied.

The second alternative discussed in this paper is the Monte Carlo approach. Its main characteristics are the following:

- Monte Carlo techniques allow, in many cases of practical interest, the evaluation of large networks. This is very important in particular in the communications area; this evaluation is not possible with exact techniques.

- Their efficiency is sensitive to the numerical values of the elementary reliabilities (the reliabilities of the components). From one side, this is a bad point since the computational cost of crude Monte Carlo increases when these data values approach 1; from the other side, this fact can be exploited to design estimation techniques performing better than in the case of crude methods.

- Monte Carlo is very general and can be easily adapted to the evaluation of many metrics. Analytical techniques often behave exactly in the opposite way and changing the metrics usually leads to new classes of problems. The phenomenon is, in some sense, proportional to the efficiency of the exact method: the most powerful it is (see factoring, for instance), the most difficult is its adaptation (or modification) to a new reliability measure or to a new type of model.

Last, bounding techniques are also available and sometimes they lead to fast evaluations. This particularly happens if the user has some additional information about its model, such as the breadth of the graph or the number of mincuts with minimal size, or the list of these mincuts, etc. It can also be noted that there are algorithms that compute exact values efficiently (in the complexity theory meaning) when such an additional information is available. For instance, in Ball et al.[6] the authors present a method to compute the all–terminal reliability in time polynomial in the number of minpaths and in Provan et al.[42] an algorithm to compute the source–to–terminal reliability is proposed, with time complexity polynomial in the number of mincuts.

Interesting research problems are opened in all these areas. Given the cost of exact techniques, further improvements of existing algorithms or new ideas are needed, as it is the case with almost all NP–hard problems. Particularly interesting is, in our opinion, the work on the powerful family of factoring methods. The problems are typically in combinatorics, graph theory and algorithmic methodology. For the same complexity reasons, bounding techniques are also a very promising research area. The work on Monte Carlo methods adapted to network reliability problems has just begun. Only a few algorithms have been proposed. The related research problems combine the previous points with statistical issues. As stated before, some metrics have not been extensively analyzed yet and there are other proposals in several papers (as it is done here in Section 11.5). Other interesting topics are the problem of dealing with dependent components and the extension of the framework to multistate systems (for instance, see respectively Ebrahimi[15] and El Neweihi et al.[18]).

A domain not mentioned before in the paper and where research efforts are also needed is in parallelization. New architectures are now available offering much more computational power than before. However, in most cases the algorithms discussed before need to be seriously modified to run efficiently on these computers. For instance, see El Khadiri et al.[16] for some reported results concerning Monte Carlo evaluations on a multiprocessor machine with distributed memory.

Last, let us say a few words about *performability*. This concept introduced first in Meyer[33], intends to integrate in a single measure both the aspects reliability (or more generally, dependability) and performance. When we want to take into account other factors than just the topology of a network and the reliability of its components (for instance, if we want to integrate in the model the capacity of the lines or the traffic in the system), performability techniques may be used. This leads in general to multistate systems (not just binary systems as in this paper) and, in principle, the models are more informative. On the opposite side, the technology is just at the beginning. We refer to Ball et al.[5] for a good discussion on this topic.

Commented main bibliography

Let us outline here some main references of the bibliography. They are particularly important texts (books or papers) to begin in this application area.

Ball et al.[5] *A recent survey. An excellent text, that can be seen as complementary to this chapter. It has a long bibliography. The reader can find information on topics not discussed here (complexity issues, performability models).*

Barlow et al.[8], **Belyayev et al.**[10] *Two basic references in general reliability theory. They are mathematically oriented texts and they cover most of the background in reliability, not only for static models as in this chapter but also for dynamic ones (stochastic processes).*

Colbourn[14] *This book is completly dedied to the network reliability area. It is rather algebraically oriented with, for instance, many details on the particular case of identical components. There is also a detailed presentation of bounding techniques.*

Gertsbakh[21] *A reference book, with many recent developments not found in the two first references of this list.*

Locks et al.[31] *A special issue of the IEEE Transactions on Reliability, containing good survey papers in the most important subtopics of reliability evaluation using stochastic graphs.*

Roberts et al.[44] *This is based on a workshop entirely dedied to the area, at Rutgers University, USA. It has 16 papers covering many topics in network reliability and related areas.*

References

1 ABRAHAM, J. A. – An improved algorithm for network reliability. *IEEE Transactions on Reliability*, vol. R-28 (1), April 1979, pp. 58–61.

2 AHMAD, S. – A simple technique for computing network reliability. *IEEE Transactions on Reliability*, vol. R-31 (1), Apr. 1982.

3 AHMAD, S. AND JAMIL, A. T. M. – A modified technique for computing network reliability. *IEEE Transactions on Reliability*, vol. R-36 (5),
Dec. 1987.

4 BALL, M. O. – Computational complexity of network reliability analysis: An overview. *IEEE Transactions on Reliability*, vol. R-35 (3), 1986.

5 BALL, M. O., COLBOURN, C. J. AND PROVAN, J. S. – *Network reliability*. – Technical Report TR 92–74, Harvard University, 1992.

6 BALL, M. O. AND NEMHAUSER, G.L. – Matroids and a reliability
analysis problem. *Mathematics of Operations Research*, vol. 4, 1979, pp.
132–143.

7 BALL, M. O. AND PROVAN, J. S. – Disjoint products and efficient
computation of reliability. *Op. Res.*, vol. 36, 1988, pp. 703–716.

8 BARLOW, E. E. AND PROSCHAN, F. – *Statistical Theory of Reliability
and Life Testing*. – New York, Holt, Rinehart & Winston, 1975.

9 BEICHELT, F. AND SPROSS, L. – Bounds on the reliability of binary coherent structures. *IEEE Transactions on Reliability*, vol. R-38 (4), 1989.

10 BELYAYEV, Y. K., GNEDENKO, B. V. AND SOLOVYEV, A. D. – *Mathematical Methods of Reliability Theory*. – Academic Press, New York,
1969.

11 BRECHT, T. B. AND COLBOURN, C. J. – Lower bounds on two–
terminal network reliability. *Discrete Applied Mathematics*, vol. 21,
1988, pp. 185–198.

12 CANCELA, H. AND KHADIRI, M. EL. – An improvement to the total
hazard method for system reliability evaluation. *Probability in the Engineering and Informational Sciences*, 1995. – à paraître.

13 CANCELA, H. AND KHADIRI, M. EL. – A recursive variance reduction
method for estimating communication network reliability. IEEE *Transactions on Reliability*, 1995. – à paraître.

14 COLBOURN, C. J. – *The Combinatorics of Network Reliability*. – New
York, Oxford University Press, 1987.

15 EBRAHIMI, N. – Binary structure functions with dependent components. *J. of Appl. Prob.*, vol. 22, 1990, pp. 627–640.

16 EL KHADIRI, M., MARIE, R. AND RUBINO, G. – Parallel estimation of 2-terminal network reliability by a crude monte carlo technique. *In: The Sixth International Symposium on Computer and Information Sciences, Baray, M. and Ozgüç, B., editors*, pp. 559–570. – 1991.

17 EL KHADIRI, M. AND RUBINO, G. – Reliability evaluation of communication networks. *In: Safety of Computer Control Systems 1992 (SAFECOMP'92), IFAC Symposium, edited by Frey, H.* – 1992.

18 EL NEWEIHI, E. AND PROSCHAN, F. – Degradable systems: a survey of multistate system theory. *Comm. Stat. Theor. Meth.*, vol. 13 (4), 1984, pp. 405–432.

19 FISHMAN, G. S. – A comparison of four Monte Carlo methods for estimating the probability of s-t conectedness. *IEEE Trans. Reliab.*, vol. R-35 (2), June 1986.

20 FRATTA, L. AND MONTANARI, U. G. – A boolean algebra method for computing the terminal reliability in a communication network. *IEEE Transactions on Circuit Theory*, vol. CT-20, 1973, pp. 203–211.

21 GERTSBAKH, I. B. – *Statistical Reliability Theory.* – Marcel Dekker, Inc., New York and Bassel, 1989.

22 GRANOV, A., KLEINROCK, L. AND GERLA, M. – A new algorithm for symbolic reliability analysis of computer communications networks. *In: Proc. Pacific Telecom. Conf.* – January 1970.

23 GRÖTSCHEL, M., MONMA, C. L. AND STOER, M. – *Computational results with a cutting plane algorithm for designing communication networks with low-connectivity constraints.* – Technical Report 188, Universität Augsburg, Allemagne, Institüt fur Mathematik, 1989.

24 GRÖTSCHEL, M., MONMA, C. L. AND STOER, M. – *Polyhedral approaches for network survivability.* – Technical Report 189, Universität Augsburg, Allemagne, Institüt fur Mathematik, 1990.

25 HAGSTROM, J. N. – Using the decomposition tree of a network in reliability computation. *IEEE Trans. on Reliab.*, vol. R-32, 1983, pp. 71–78.

26 HEIDTMANN, K. D. – Smaller sums of disjoints products by subproduct inversion. *IEEE Trans. on Reliab.*, vol. R-38 (3), 1989.

27 HOPCROFT, J. E. AND TARJAN, R. E. – Dividing a graph into triconnected components. *SIAM J. on Comput.*, vol. 2, Sept. 1973.

28 HYANG, C. L., TILLMAN, F. A. AND LEE, M. H. – System–reliability evaluation techniques for complex/large systems. *IEEE Trans. on Reliab.*, vol. R-30 (5), 1981.

29 KUMAMOTO, H., TANAKA, K. AND INOUE, K. – Efficient evaluation of system reliability by monte carlo method. *IEEE Trans. on Reliab.*, vol. R-26 (5), Dec. 1977.

30 LOCKS, M. O. – Recursive disjoint products: a review of three algorithms. *IEEE Transactions on Reliability*, vol. R-31, 1982.

31 Locks, M. O. and Satyarayana, A., editors. – *Network Reliability – The State of the Art*. IEEE Transactions on Reliability. – 1986.

32 MARIE, R. AND RUBINO, G. – Direct approaches to the 2-terminal reliabiity problem. *In: The Third International Symposium on Computer and Information Sciences*, éd. par E.Gelembe, E.Orhun and E.Başar. Ege University, pp. 740–747. – Çeşme, Izmir, Turkey, 1988.

33 MEYER, J. F. – On evaluating the performability of degradable computing systems. *IEEE Tran. on Comp.*, vol. C-29, 1980, pp. 720–731.

34 MILLER, R. – *Switching theory. Volume 1: combinatorial circuits.* – John Wiley & Sons, 1965.

35 MATA-MONTERO, E. – Resilience of partial k-tree networks with edge and node failures. *Networks*, vol. 21, 1991, pp. 321–344.

36 NIESSEN, U. AND SCHNEEWEISS, W. – A practical comparison of several algorithms for reliability calculations. *Reliability Engineering and System Safety*, vol. 31, 1991, pp. 309–319.

37 PAGE, L. B. AND PERRY, JO ELLEN. – A practical implementation of the factoring theorem for network reliability. *IEEE Transactions on Reliability*, vol. R-37 (3), 1988.

38 PAGE, L. B. AND PERRY, JO ELLEN. – Reliability of directed networks using the factoring theorem. *IEEE Transactions on Reliability*, vol. R-38 (5), 1989.

39 PRÉKOPA, A., BOROS, E. AND LIH, KEH-WEI. – The use of binomial–moments for bounding network reliability. *DIMACS Series in Discrete Mathematics and Theoretical Computer Science*, vol. 5, 1991.

40 PROVAN, J. S. – "bounds on the reliability of networks. *IEEE Transactions on Reliability*, vol. R-35 (3), 1986.

41 PROVAN, J. S. – The complexity of reliability computations in planar and acyclic graphs. *SIAM Journal of Computing*, vol. 15 (3), Aug. 1986.

42 PROVAN, J. S. AND BALL, M. O. – Computing network reliability in time polynomial in the number of cuts. *Operations Research*, vol. 32, 1984, pp. 516–526.

43 RESENDE, L. – Implementation of a factoring algorithm for reliability evaluation of undirected networks. *IEEE Transactions on Reliability*, vol. R-37 (5), 1988.

44 ROBERTS, F., HWANG, F. AND MONNA, C. – Reliability of computer and communication networks. – DIMACS Series in Discrete Mathematics and Theoretical Computer Science, Vol. 5, 1989.

45 ROSS, S. – System reliability evaluation by simulation: random hazards versus importance sampling. *Probability in the Engineering and Informational Sciences*, vol. 6, 1992, pp. 119–126.

46 SANSO, B. AND SOUMIS, F. – Communication and transportation networks reliability using routing models. *IEEE Trans. on Reliab.*, vol. R-30 (5), 1981.

47 SATYANARAYANA, A. AND WOOD, K. – A linear-time algorithm for computing k-terminal in series-parallel networks. *SIAM Journal of Computing*, vol. 14 (4), Nov. 1985.

48 SATYARAYANA, A. – A unified formula for the analysis of some network reliability problems. *IEEE Transactions on Reliability*, vol. R-31, 1982, pp. 23–32.

49 SATYARAYANA, A. AND CHANG, M. K. – Network reliability and the factoring theorem. *Networks*, vol. 13, 1983.

50 SATYARAYANA, A. AND PRABHAKAR, A. – New topological formula and rapid algorithm for reliability analysis of comples networks. *IEEE Transactions on Reliability*, vol. R-27, 1978, pp. 82–100.

51 VALIANT, L. G. – The complexity of enumeration and reliability problems. *SIAM Journal of Computing*, vol. 8, 1979, pp. 410–421.

52 VEERARAGHAVAN, M. AND TRIVEDI, K. – An improved algorithm for symbolic reliability analysis. *IEEE Transactions on Reliability*, vol. R-40 (3), 1991.

53 WOOD, K. – A factoring algorithm using polygon-to-chain reductions for computing k-terminal network reliability. *Networks*, vol. 15, 1985, pp. 173–190.

54 WOOD, K. – Factoring algorithms for computing k-terminal network reliability. *IEEE Transactions on Reliability*, vol. R-35 (3), 1986.

Notes on the Contributors

IAN F. AKYILDIZ received his BS, MS, and PhD
degrees in Computer Engineering from the University of Erlangen-
Nuernberg, Germany, in 1978, 1981 and 1984, respectively.
Currently, he is a **Full Professor** with the School of Electrical and
Computer Engineering, Georgia Institute of Technology. He has held
visiting professorships at the Universidad Tecnica Federico Santa Maria,
Chile, Universite Pierre et Marie Curie (Paris VI) and Ecole Nationale
Superieure Telecommunications in Paris, France. He has published over
hundred technical papers in journals and conference proceedings. He is a
co-author of a textbook entitled *Analysis of Computer Systems*
published by Teubner Verlag in Germany in 1982. He is an editor for
Computer Networks and ISDN Systems Journal, for *IEEE Transactions
on Computers,* for *ACM-Baltzer Journal of Wireless Networks,*
and for *ACM-Springer Journal of Multimedia Systems.*

He guest-edited several special issues, such as on *Parallel and Distributed
Simulation Performance* for *ACM Transactions on Modeling and
Simulation;* and on *Networks in the Metropolitan Area*
for *IEEE Journal of Selected Areas in Communications.*

Dr. Akyildiz is an IEEE FELLOW, a member of ACM (SIGCOMM)
and is a National Lecturer for ACM since 1989. He received the "Don
Federico Santa Maria Medal" for his services to the Universidad of
Federico Santa Maria in Chile. Dr. Akyildiz is listed on "Who's Who in the
World (Platinum Edition)". He received the ACM Outstanding
Distinguished Lecturer Award for 1994.

His current research interests are in ATM and Wireless Networks.

KALLOL BAGCHI received his MSc in Mathematics from Calcutta
University and Ph.D. in Computer Science in 1988 from Jadavpur
University, Calcutta, India. He has worked in industry in India and in
Finland. He taught a course at the University of Oulu, Finland in 1986. He
worked as an **Assistant** and **Associate Professor** in Computer Science and
Engineering at Aalborg University, Denmark from 1987-1992. In 1993, he
visited Stanford University, CA. He also completed a certificate in

Computer Networking from Columbia University, NY. His interests are in performance modeling and simulation, parallel systems. He has authored or co-authored over 40 international papers in these areas. He has been an associate editor or member of the editorial board of the International Journal in Computer Simulation for the last few years and have guest-edited several issues of the journal. He was a member of the board of directors of SCS in 1993. He has been cited in World Who's who and in Who's who in Science and Engineering. He is a member of the ACM and IEEECS. He has been associated with the MASCOTS workshop, since its inception. At present, he is **pursuing a second Ph.D. degree** in business (DIS) at Florida Atlantic University.

ONNO J. BOXMA received the PhD degree in mathematics from the University of Utrecht. During 1978-1979, he was an IBM Postdoctoral Fellow in Yorktown Heights, NY. Since August 1985 he has been with CWI; since 1989, he is **Head of the Department of Operations Research**, Statistics and System Theory. He also holds a **Professorship** in Operations Research at Tilburg University. Onno Boxma is member of IFIP WG 7.3 and is associate editor of the journals *Markov Processes and Related Fields, Mathematics of Operations Research, Performance Evaluation* and *Queueing Systems*.

ATIKA COHEN was born in Morocco. She is an engineer in Data processing. In 1990, she received PhD degree in Computer Sciences from the University of Brussels, Belgium, where she is **Associate Professor** since 1986. Her current research interests are in modeling and simulation networks.

MARCO B. COMBÉ received the M.Sc. degree in mathematics from Leiden University, The Netherlands, in 1990. Subsequently he was a PhD student at the research institute CWI (Centre for Mathematics and Computer Science) in Amsterdam; he defended his PhD thesis in 1995 at Tilburg University, The Netherlands. Since 1995 he is **employed** by the **N.V. Bank Nederlandse Gemeenten** in The Hague.

MARCO CONTI received the Laurea degree in Computer Science at the University of Pisa, Italy, in 1987. In the same year he joined the **Networks and Distributed Systems department at CNUCE**, an institute of the Italian National Research Council (CNR) , where he is a **Research Scientist**. From 1989 to 1993 he was involved in a five-year national project "Progetto Finalizzato Telecomunicationi" aimed at designing and tuning the Italian broadband network infrastructure. He has worked on modeling and performance evaluation of Metropolitan Area Network MAC protocols. He has written over 50 research papers in the areas of design, modeling and performance evaluation of computer communication systems. His current research interest includes design, modeling and performance evaluation of ATM and Wireless Networks.

WLODEK DOBOSIEWICZ received the M.Sc. and Ph.D. degrees in computer science from the University of Warsaw, Warsaw, Poland. He has been an **Associate Professor** at Monmouth University since 1994. He is currently working on MAC-layer protocols for high-speed computer networks. He has also published on sorting.

SUSANNA DONATELLI received her doctor degree in Computer Science from the University of Torino, Italy, in 1984, her M.S. in Electrical an Computer Engeneering from the University of Massachusetts at Amherst in 1988 and her Ph.D. in Computer Science at the University of Torino in 1990. Since November 1990, she is a **Researcher** at the Computer Science Department of the University of Torino, Italy. Dr. Donatelli is co-author of a number of papers on Petri Nets (theory and application) and on performance modelling and evaluation of communication networks and parallel computer architectures. She has recently co-authored the book *Modelling with Generalized Stochastic Petri Nets*, for the John Wiley Series in Parallel Computing. Her most recent work has been on the use of Generalized Stochastic Petri Nets for the qualitative and quantitative analysis of distributed software, that led to the development of the tool EPOCA.

GIULIANA FRANCESCHINIS is a **Researcher** at the Computer Science Department of the University of Torino, Italy. She holds a ``Laurea" degree in Computer Science from the University of Torino (1986) and a Doctoral degree in Computer Science from the same University (1992). Since 1987 she co-authored more than 20 published papers in refereed journals and conferences. She has been appointed in the scientific program committee of an international simulation conference and of two international Petri net conferences. Her research interests are in the fields of Petri nets theory and applications, performance evaluation, parallel discrete-event simulation, parallel architectures.

PAWEL GBURZYNSKI received his MSc and PhD in computer ccience from the University of Warsaw, Poland in 1976 and 1982, respectively. Before coming to Canada in 1984, he had been a research associate, systems programmer, and consultant in the Department of Mathematics, Informatics and Mechanics at the University of Warsaw. Since 1985 he has been with the Department of Computing Science, University of Alberta where he is a **Professor**. Dr. Gburzynski's research interests are in Communication Networks, Operating Systems, Simulation, and Performance Evaluation.

YEN-WEN LU is a PhD candidate and **Research Assistant** in the Department of Electrical Engineering, Stanford University. His current research interests include parallel data routing, parallel signal/image processing, and low power VLSI design. He received his BS from National Taiwan University in 1991 and his MS in Electrical Engineering from Stanford University in 1993.

MARCO AJMONE MARSAN is a **Full Professor** at the Electronics Department of Politecnico di Torino, in Italy. He holds a Dr. Ing. degree in Electronic Engineering from Politecnico di Torino, and a Master of Science from the University of California, Los Angeles. Since november 1975 to october 1987 he was at the Electronics Department of Politecnico di Torino, first as a Researcher, then as an Associate Professor. Since November 1987 to October 1990 he was a Full Professor at the Computer Science Department of the University of Milan, in Italy. He has coauthored over 150 journal and conference papers in the areas of Communications and Computer Science, as well as the two books *Performance Models of Multiprocessor Systems* published by the MIT Press, and *Modelling with Generalized Stochastic Petri Nets* published by John Wiley. His current interests are in the fields of performance evaluation of data communication and computer systems, communication networks and queueing theory.

RAFFAELA MIRANDOLA received the Laurea degree in Computer Science from the University of Pisa, Pisa, Italy, in 1989 and the Ph.D. degree in Computer Science from the University of Rome-TorVergata, Rome, Italy, in 1994. She presently holds **Research Associate** positions with the Laboratory of Computer Science, the University of Rome-TorVergata. Her main research interests are in the areas of methodology and tools for the performance and dependability analysis of software and computer/communication systems.

RADUANE MRABET was born in Morocco. His degrees are in Computer Science. In 1995, he received PhD degree in the same field from the University of Brussels, Belgium. Currently, he is **Associate Professor** in Morocco.

FABIO NERI is currently an **Associate Professor** in the Electronics Department at Politecnico di Torino, Turin, Italy. He received his Dr. Ing. degree and Ph.D. in Electrical Engineering from Politecnico di Torino in 1981 and 1987, respectively.From 1982 to 1983 he was a visiting scholar at George Washington University in Washington, DC. From 1991 to 1992 he was with the Information Engineering Department at University of Parma, Parma, Italy, as an Associate Professor. His research interests are in the fields of discrete event simulation, queuing theory, and performance evaluation of communication networks.

IOANIS NIKOLAIDIS is a **Research Scientist** with the Europen Computer Industry Research Center in Munich, Germany. He was born in 1967 in Serres, Greece. He received his B.S. in Computer Engineering and Informatics in 1989 from the University of Patras, Greece and his M.S. and Ph.D. in Computer Science from the College of Computing of the Georgia Institute of Technology in 1991 and 1994 respectively. He worked as a coop for IBM, Research Triangle Park, North Carolina in the summer of 1991. His research interest include performance and modeling of computer and communication systems, parallel simulation techniques, high--speed network protocols and multimedia computing. He is a member of IEEE and ACM.

GERARDO RUBINO has a **Professor** position at the ENST-B engineering school, Rennes, France. He also belongs to the IRISA research laboratory in computer science at control, also at Rennes. He holds a Ph.D in Computer Science from the University of Rennes (1984). His main research interests are in the modelling area, specifically in reliability theory, performance evaluation and performability analysis, both from the analytical point of view and for simulation purposes. In particular, he has research activities in network reliability, partially supported by industrial partners. He is an associate editor of the *Naval Research Logistics Journal*.

DOUGLAS SCHMIDT is an **Assistant Professor** of Computer Science at Washington University in St. Louis, Missouri, USA. His research focuses on design patterns, implementation, and experimental analysis of object-oriented techniques for developing high-performance distributed communication systems on parallel processing platforms that run over high-speed networks. Dr. Schmidt has published widely in IEEE, IFIP, ACM, and USENIX technical conferences and journals on communication software systems, parallel processing for high-performance networking protocols, distributed object computing, and object-oriented design patterns and programming. He is the program chair for the 1996 USENIX Conference on Object-Oriented Technologies and Systems (COOTS) and the 1996 Pattern Languages of Programming conference and has recently co-edited a book entitled *Pattern Languages of Program Design* with Jim Coplien of AT&T Bell Labs.

SRIDHAR SESHADRI received the degree of Bachelor of Technology from the Indian Institute of Technology, Madras, India, in 1978, the Post Graduate Diploma in Management from the Indian Institute of Management, Ahmedabad, India, in 1980 and the Ph.D. degree in Management Science from the University of California at Berkeley in 1993. His research interests are in the area of stochastic modeling and optimization, with applications to manufacturing, distribution, telecommunications, database design and finance. He is with Stern School of Business, New York University, where he is an **Assistant Professor.**

VIJAY SRINIVASAN received a B.S. degree in computer science from North Carolina State University in 1992, and a Ph.D. degree in computer science from Duke University in 1995. Since May 1995, he is a **Researcher** in IBM's Networking Architecture group in the Research Triangle Park of North Carolina. His research interests include development of algorithms for the control and management of network services, evaluation of these algorithms using analytical, numerical and simulation techniques, and in intelligent networking. His current work involves issues related to multiprotocol routing, and support for integrated services over different subnetwork technologies.

TATSUYA SUDA received the B.E., M.E., and Dr.E. degrees in applied mathematics and physics from Kyoto University, Kyoto, Japan, in 1977,

1979, and 1982, respectively. From 1982 to 1984, he was with the Department of Computer Science, Columbia University, New York, as a Postdoctoral Research Associate. Since 1984, he has been with the Department of Information and Computer Science, University of California, Irvine, where he is currently a **Professor**. He received an IBM postdoctoral fellowship in 1983. He was the Conference Coordinator from 1989 to 1991, the Secretary and Treasurer from 1991 to 1993, the Vice Chairman from 1993 to 1995, and is currently the Chairman of the IEEE Technical Committee on Computer Communications. He serves as an Editor of the IEEE Transaction on Communications and as an Area Editor of the International Journal of Computer and Software Engineering. He is a member of the Editorial Board of the Encyclopedia of Electrical and Electronics Engineering, Wiley and Sons. He was the Chair of the 8th IEEE Workshop on Computer Communications and is the TPC co-chair of the IEEE Infocom 97.

He has been engaged in research in the fields of computer communications, high speed networks, multimedia systems, distributed systems, object oriented communication systems and performance modeling and evaluation. Dr. Suda is a member of IEEE and ACM.

JEAN WALRAND is a **Professor** of Electrical Engineering and Computer Sciences at the University of California at Berkeley, a department he joined in 1981 after being assistant professor at Cornell University since 1979. His research interests are in the performance evaluation of communication networks and in stochastic models.

He is the author of "An Introduction to Queueing Networks" (Prentice-Hall, 1988) and of "Communication Networks: A First Course" (IRWIN/AKSEN, 1991), and a co-author of "High Performance Communication Networks" (Morgan Kaufmann, October 1996).

Professor Walrand received his Ph.D. from UC Berkeley. He is a Fellow of the IEEE and a recipient of the Lanchester Prize from the Operations Research Society of America.

For more details, please consult http://www.eecs.berkeley.edu/~wlr

CAREY WILLIAMSON is an **Associate Professor** in the Department of Computer Science at the University of Saskatchewan in Saskatoon, Canada, and an **Adjunct Professor** at Telecommunications Research

Laboratories (TRLabs) in Saskatoon. A Ph.D. graduate of Stanford University in 1992, Dr. Williamson's research interests are in high speed networks, network traffic measurement, workload characterization, network traffic modeling, network simulation, computer systems performance evaluation, and ATM (Asynchronous Transfer Mode). He is currently supervising six graduate students working in these areas. Dr. Williamson is a member of ACM, IEEE, CMG (Computer Measurement Group), and SCS (Society for Computer Simulation).

GEORGE W. ZOBRIST received his BS and PhD in Electrical Engineering from the University of Missouri-Columbia in 1958 and 1965, respectively and his MSEE from the University of Wichita in 1961.

He has been employed by industry, government laboratories and various Universities during his career. He is presently **Chairman/Professor** of Computer Science at the University of Missouri-Rolla.

His current research interests include: Simulation, Computer Aided Analysis and Design, Software Engineering and Local Area Network Design. He is presently Editor of IEEE Potentials Magazine, VLSI Design and International Journal in Computer Simulation.

Author Index

311

Subject Index